Built Up in the Faith

366 Daily Devotions

for New Christians

Donald Root

"As ye have therefore received Christ Jesus the Lord, so walk ye in him: Rooted and built up in him, and stablished in the faith, as ye have been taught, abounding therein with thanksgiving." Colossians 2:6-7

BUILT UP IN THE FAITH

March 2002 (first printing)
September 2016 (second printing & revisions)

©2002 by Donald Root
United States Copyright Number
Library of Congress: TX 5-676-816

ISBN: 978-0-9968079-5-1

All rights reserved. No portion of this book may be reproduced in any form without the written permission of the author.

Thanks to:

Pastor Ronald J. Tobin, Tomah Baptist Church –
encouragement, advice, review of content

Kara Baldwin – advice
Debbi Rippentrop – cover design, co-editing

Published by The Old Paths Publications, Inc.,
Cleveland, GA, 30528.
www.theoldpathspublications.com
TOP@theoldpathspublications.com

TOMAH BAPTIST CHURCH
1701 Hollister Avenue
Tomah, WI 54660
(608) 372-2071

HOW TO USE THIS BOOK

This devotional book has been written as a tool to help introduce new Christians to the Bible and its teachings. It has <u>366 daily devotional lessons</u>, enough to last for one year. In that year you will be guided through the entire historical story of the Bible, meeting all of the key <u>Bible characters</u> and visiting all the key <u>Bible stories</u>. Along the way you will be taught the most important <u>Bible truths</u> – the ones that are the foundation of the Christian faith. You will also be given <u>practical Biblical advice</u> for how to live in a manner that is pleasing to God! By the time you finish you will have read at least one verse from <u>all 66 books</u> of the Bible.

So, how do I use this book? First, set aside a <u>specific time</u> each day to spend alone with God. The daily lessons in this book have been written so you won't need to set aside a large amount of time, unless you want to. Then, <u>pray</u>, asking for God to help you understand what you read. Beginning with "Day 1", write in the <u>date</u>. Since you supply the date, you can begin at any time. Notice the <u>title</u>, and read the <u>text verse</u>. Each devotion has a short <u>lesson</u>. I recommend reading it before looking up the scripture passage. Many times it will provide helpful information about the scripture to be read. Many lessons refer back to previous lessons. This is done to reinforce the truths being taught. Next, find the <u>scripture passage</u> in your Bible and read it. Most of them are quite short. They have been selected to complement each day's lesson. Finally, read the <u>question</u> at the bottom and spend some time "pondering" the answer. The questions have been designed to cause you to think further about the lesson, draw a logical conclusion, or make a personal application. Some of the questions are drawn from the lesson in this book, and some are written to draw your attention to the scripture passage you have read. <u>Meditate</u> on the lesson and the question during the day. No answers are given to the questions because most of them need to come from within yourself.

The book is divided into twelve <u>Units</u>. Each unit will take about one month to complete, except the first one, which is longer. At the end of each unit is a <u>review page</u>. The Unit Review's are very simple. My intent is to simply cause you to stop and reflect on what you have learned over the previous month.

Don't become discouraged if you miss a day. Pick up where you left off and try again. If you stay consistent for all 366 lessons you will have formed a daily habit of spending time in God's Word! If you add this to what you learn in church you will be surprised how much you have learned about God's Word in a year's time.

May God help you and bless you!
Donald Root

TABLE OF CONTENTS

	Page
HOW TO USE THIS BOOK (*Bible History / Bible Truths*)	3
TABLE OF CONTENTS	4
Unit One: Lessons 1 to 39 *Adam & Eve, Cain & Abel, Noah / Creation, Faith, The Bible, God, Sin, The Plan of Salvation*	5
Unit Two: Lessons 40 to 60 *Job, Abraham, Isaac / Assurance of Salvation, Living by Faith*	46
BOOKS OF THE BIBLE	69
Unit Three: Lessons 61 to 88 *Esau & Jacob, Israel / The Bible, Repentance, The Attributes of God*	70
BOOKS OF THE BIBLE BY GROUP	100
Unit Four: Lessons 89 to 121 *Joseph, Captivity in Egypt, Moses / God the Father, God the Son*	101
Unit Five: Lessons 122 to 155 *The Exodus, The Wilderness Wandering / God the Spirit, The Law*	136
Unit Six: Lessons 156 to 183 *Joshua & Caleb, The Judges, Ruth / Sin, Angels, Satan*	172
Unit Seven: Lessons 184 to 213 *Samuel, Saul, David / Hell, Government, Heaven*	202
Unit Eight: Lessons 214 to 244 *David, Solomon / Home, Principles from Proverbs*	234
SUMMARY OF THE STORY OF THE BIBLE	267
Unit Nine: Lessons 245 to 274 *Judah & Israel, The Kings, The Prophets / The Judgments, Rewards*	268
THE KINGS OF ISRAEL	300
Unit Ten: Lessons 275 to 305 *The Captivity, Daniel, Ezra & Nehemiah / Future Things*	301
Unit Eleven: Lessons 306 to 336 *The Life of Christ / Christian Living, Prayer*	334
SOME OLD TESTAMENT PROPHECIES FULFILLED BY JESUS CHRIST	367
Unit Twelve: Lessons 337 to 366 *The Acts of the Apostles, The Epistles / Discernment, The Local Church, Christian Living*	368
WHERE DO I GO FROM HERE?	400
SUBJECT INDEX	401

Unit One

Lessons 1 to 39

Bible History

Adam & Eve
Cain & Abel
Noah

Bible Truths

Creation
Faith
The Bible
God
Sin
The Plan of Salvation

Day 1   Date: _____
In the Beginning

"In the beginning God created the heaven and the earth." (Genesis 1:1)

What better place to <u>begin</u> than at the <u>beginning</u>! This is the very first verse in the Bible. It is found in the book of *Genesis*, the "book of beginnings". It records the beginning of heaven and earth (our text verse), of plant, animal, and human life, and of all human institutions and relationships.

But notice that God was <u>already</u> present *"in the beginning"*. Everything that exists had a beginning, a moment of creation, <u>except</u> the Creator Himself! Also notice that this verse does not defend the pre-existence of God, it simply and eloquently states it as FACT!

Scripture to read: Genesis 1:1-25

Question to ponder: *According to verses 3, 6, 9, 11, 14, 20, and 24, did God use any existing materials to create the things He made?*

Day 2   Date: _____

Understood by Faith

"Through faith we understand that the worlds were framed by the word of God, so that things which are seen were not made of things which do appear." (Hebrews 11:3)

The eleventh chapter of the book of Hebrews is commonly called "the <u>faith</u> chapter". In the first verse we are given a definition of faith: *"the substance of things hoped for, the evidence of things not seen"*. In other words, believing (having hope and confidence) in something for which the evidence is not available to be seen.

Our text verse explains that creation must be believed *"through faith"*, because we were not there to witness the actual event. Notice that the things we see in creation were <u>spoken</u> (*"by the Word of God"*) into existence by God.

Scripture to read: Genesis 2:1-6

Question to ponder: *Can any of the false explanations for the beginning of the world and man ("big bang", Darwinism, etc.) be believed in any way other than by faith?*

Day 3   Date: _____
By the Word of God

"So then faith cometh by hearing, and hearing by the word of God." (Romans 10:17)

Faith must have an <u>object</u>; it must be focused upon something or someone. In a letter written to believers of the church at Rome (the book of the Bible entitled *"Romans"*), the author, the apostle Paul, explained that the Christian faith must first be <u>heard</u> to be believed. The message that our faith is based upon is found in the Word of God, the <u>Bible</u>.

We believe (through faith) that God created the world, because He tells us so in the <u>Bible</u>. We believe in His Son, Jesus Christ, because the message of salvation is given to us in the <u>Bible</u>.

Scripture to read: Romans 10:13-17

Question to ponder: *How important is it to know that our faith is based upon a reliable source?*

Day 4   Date: _____

Inspired by God

"All scripture is given by inspiration of God, and is profitable for doctrine, for reproof, for correction, for instruction in righteousness" (II Timothy 3:16)

It is important to understand that the Bible, the Word of God, is a supernatural book. This verse, taken from a letter by Paul to a young preacher by the name of Timothy, explains that the Bible (*scripture*) is inspired by God. It literally means "God-breathed", that each and every word of scripture came to us directly from God Himself! This is called verbal inspiration. God said exactly what He wanted to say, using exactly the words He wanted to use. The Bible does not just contain the word of God; it IS the Word of God!

Notice that since it is the inspired Word of God, it is profitable to teach us what is right (*doctrine*) and what is wrong (*reproof*), to teach us how to get it right (*correction*) and how to keep it right (*instruction in righteousness*)!

Scripture to read: II Timothy 3:10-17

Question to ponder: *According to verse 15, what is the chief benefit we receive from the scriptures?*

Day 5   Date: _____

The Authority of the Word of God

"But he answered and said, It is written, Man shall not live by bread alone, but by every word that proceedeth out of the mouth of God."
(Matthew 4:4)

The Lord Jesus was being tempted by the devil shortly after beginning his public ministry. After the first of three specific attempts by the devil to get him to sin, Jesus answered with the words of our text verse.

Since the Bible is the inspired ("God-breathed") Word of God (the Creator), it is our absolute and final <u>authority</u> for <u>faith</u> (what we believe) and <u>practice</u> (how we live). God has given us this book, the Bible, to inform us of all that we <u>need</u> to know. The Bible is totally <u>sufficient</u> to meet our every need. If it is in the Bible, we need to heed it and obey it. If it is not in the Bible, we need to measure it against the Bible to see if it is true.

Scripture to read: Psalms 19:7-11

Question to ponder: *If the Lord Jesus Christ believed God's Word to be more necessary than bread (daily food), how necessary is it for us?*

Day 6   Date: _____
God

"Holy, holy, holy, is the LORD of hosts: the whole earth is full of his glory." (Isaiah 6:3b)

Isaiah was a prophet of God who was given a remarkable privilege at the beginning of his ministry. Through a vision, he was allowed to see into the throne room of God in Heaven. He saw a glimpse of the glory of God. The seraphims spoken of are angels which inhabit Heaven and praise God for His holiness.

At the very core of God's essence is His holiness. It refers to His sinless perfection. To be holy means to be "set apart", to be in a different category. God is so holy as to be truly unique. There is no being anywhere like God. When Isaiah saw God as He really is, his immediate response was "*Woe is me! for I am undone...*"

Scripture to read: Isaiah 6:1-5

Question to ponder: *Why do you suppose that Isaiah's vision of God caused him to notice his own sin?*

Day 7 Date: _____
Man

"So God created man in his own image, in the image of God created he him; male and female created he them." (Genesis 1:27)

On the sixth and final day of creation, God created mankind in his own image. That means that we are a reflection of what God is like in many ways, without actually being gods ourselves. There are things we can learn about God by examining the way we are made, just like there are things you can learn about yourself by examining the image in the mirror. Notice that the water, land, sea, vegetation, celestial bodies, and animal life are not said to be in God's image. Among created beings, only mankind is a moral being (able to tell right from wrong) made in God's image.

Verses 26 and 27 of *Genesis*, chapter one, record a summary statement of the creation of man. Verses 28 to 31 record God's blessing and instructions to man. Chapter two, verses 7 to 25, records a more detailed account of the events of day six. Adam was created first, named the animals, then was presented with his wife, Eve.

Scripture to read: Genesis 1:26-31; 2:7-25

Question to ponder: *What greater responsibilities does man have because he is in God's image?*

Day 8   Date: _____
Why Am I Here?

"Thou art worthy, O Lord, to receive glory and honour and power: for thou hast created all things, and for thy pleasure they are and were created." (Revelation 4:11)

The apostle John was another man (see Lesson 6) who was privileged to see a vision of the throne room of God. His vision is recorded in the last book of the Bible, Revelation. In his vision, twenty four elders worship God and are quoted by our text verse. These elders represent believers who have trusted in Jesus Christ as Savior.

In their words of praise they answer the age-old question asked by man, "Why am I here"? We have been created for God's pleasure and that we should, by our lives, give glory, honor, and power to God!

Scripture to read: Revelation 4:1-11

Question to ponder: *Am I living my life for God's glory, or for mine? For God's pleasure, or for mine?*

Day 9   Date: _____
Creation's Message

"The heavens declare the glory of God; and the firmament sheweth his handywork." (Psalms 19:1)

The book of *Psalms* is an inspired ("God-breathed") book of songs: the hymn and praise book of Israel. It is located in the center of the Bible.

The nineteenth psalm begins with praise to God for His creation. It declares that creation itself has a message about the glory of God. Beginning in the seventh verse, the psalm switches to praise to God for the Word of God. It declares the perfection of scripture and its effectiveness in our lives. The psalm closes with a prayer, asking God for assistance in living a life that is pleasing to Him.

Scripture to read: Psalms 19:1-14

Question to ponder: *Are the words of my mouth, and the meditation of my heart, acceptable to God?*

Day 10   Date: _____

The Fall of Man

"And when the woman saw that the tree was good for food, and that it was pleasant to the eyes, and a tree to be desired to make one wise, she took of the fruit thereof, and did eat, and gave also unto her husband with her; and he did eat." (Genesis 3:6)

God had given to Adam and Eve the fruit of every tree in the Garden of Eden to eat (*Genesis 2:16*). But, He had prohibited them from eating of the fruit of one tree only – the tree of the knowledge of good and evil. By this, their obedience to His word would be tested.

Satan, the devil, disguised as a serpent, caught Eve alone and deceived her into disobeying God. Adam followed by knowingly joining Eve in her sin. Thus, sin (disobedience to God) was introduced into the new world. The consequences would be far reaching. Notice the manner in which both Adam and Eve acted when confronted by God.

Scripture to read: Genesis 3:1-13

Question to ponder: *In what ways did Adam and Eve respond differently to God after their sin than they had before?*

Day 11   Date: _____

The Woman's Seed

"And I will put enmity between thee and the woman, and between thy seed and her seed; it shall bruise thy head, and thou shalt bruise his heel." (Genesis 3:15)

God pronounced judgment upon the serpent (Satan) for leading Adam and Eve into sin. In our text verse we see mention of two seeds: the seed of the serpent and of the woman. God foretells that the seed of the serpent would one day bruise the <u>heel</u> of the seed of the woman, but the seed of the woman would one day bruise the <u>head</u> of the seed of the serpent.

Only one person in history has been born of the seed of the woman (without the seed of the man) – Jesus Christ! To bruise the heel is a painful injury, but not fatal. Satan inflicted a <u>temporary</u> bruise to Christ when He was crucified. To bruise the head refers to a fatal injury. Jesus Christ inflicted a <u>permanent</u>, victorious, bruise to Satan when He rose again from the dead three days later! Here in the third chapter of the Bible we find the first reference to God's plan of salvation for mankind!

Scripture to read: Genesis 3:14-24

Question to ponder: *What comfort do you think that this promise gave to Adam and Eve?*

Day 12   Date: _____

All Have Sinned!

"As it is written, There is none righteous, no, not one" (Romans 3:10)

"For all have sinned, and come short of the glory of God" (Romans 3:23)

These verses, along with the entire scripture reading for today, clearly state that <u>every</u> person ever born has sinned. We are "not righteous" (that is, "right before God") as a condition of birth and we add to that by committing sin by <u>choice</u>. We are no different than our original parents, Adam and Eve. They, upon sinning, received a <u>sin nature</u> (a natural bent, or attraction, toward sinning) and passed it on to their children – and on to us - through birth.

This is the first fact one must know, and acknowledge, in order to find a personal remedy for sin.

Scripture to read: Romans 3:10-23

Question to ponder: *Am I willing to admit that I am a sinner?*

Day 13   Date: _____

The Ten Commandments (1-4)

"Thou shalt have no other gods before me." (Exodus 20:3)

In the Garden of Eden sin was defined by the tree of the knowledge of good and evil. After Eden, man's <u>conscience</u> guided him in the understanding of sin. Of course, God gave verbal guidelines as He communicated with various men in those days. About 2,500 years after Eden, God gave to a man named <u>Moses</u> two tables of stone with ten commandments written on them. Here we find the foundation of moral living before God. But, more to the point, here we find the *"knowledge of sin"* that proves us all *"guilty before God"* (*Romans 3:19-20* from yesterday's scripture reading). These first four commandments address our relationship to God.

1. "Thou shalt have no other gods before me."
2. "Thou shalt not make unto thee any graven image."
3. "Thou shalt not take the name of the LORD thy God in vain."
4. "Remember the Sabbath day, to keep it holy."

Scripture to read: Exodus 20:1-17

Question to ponder: *Have I kept these first four commandments perfectly?*

Day 14   Date: _____

The Ten Commandments (5-10)

"Ye have heard that it was said by them of old time, Thou shalt not kill; and whosoever shall kill shall be in danger of the judgment: But I say unto you, That whosoever is angry with his brother without a cause shall be in danger of the judgment"
(Matthew 5:21-22a)

The Lord Jesus Christ, in his "Sermon on the Mount", interpreted several of the Ten Commandments in a much more stringent manner than previously taught. As if it isn't hard enough to keep them by our actions, He explained that even our <u>motives</u> are taken into account by God! Truly, by this standard, we are <u>all</u> guilty before God! The last six commandments address our relationships with other people.

5. *"Honour thy father and thy mother."*
6. *"Thou shalt not kill."*
7. *"Thou shalt not commit adultery."*
8. *"Thou shalt not steal."*
9. *"Thou shalt not bear false witness against thy neighbor."*
10. *"Thou shalt not covet."*

Scripture to read: Matthew 5:17-30

Question to ponder: *Have I kept these six commandments perfectly?*

Day 15   Date: _____

Guilty of All

"For whosoever shall keep the whole law, and yet offend in one point, he is guilty of all."
(James 2:10)

The problem with attempting to keep the Law (of which the Ten Commandments are the foundation) is that it only takes one offence to become a "law-breaker". It (the Law) is an absolute standard. You may "*keep the whole law*", and then slip one time ("*offend in one point*"), and you have become as guilty as if you had continuously broken all the commandments.

James, the writer of this letter, gives an example of breaking the law by showing favoritism to a rich man while despising another man who is poor. He goes on to explain that the Law has one Author. Therefore, any single transgression (breaking) of the Law is against God and renders the offender guilty of all ("a transgressor") before God.

Scripture to read: James 2:1-13

Question to ponder: *In light of this teaching, is there any person, anywhere, who could possibly stand guiltless before God?*

Day 16   Date: _____

The Deceitful Heart

"The heart is deceitful above all things, and desperately wicked: who can know it?"
(Jeremiah 17:9)

<u>Jeremiah</u> was a prophet of God who lived about 600 years before the birth of Jesus Christ. In the book of the Bible called by his name, he writes of the complete wickedness (depravity) of man. The heart (mind) of man is so wicked that a man even deceives himself into thinking thoughts opposed to God. The deceitful and wicked <u>thoughts</u> of the heart produce <u>actions</u> of sinful rebellion against God (see Lesson 12, scripture reading: *Romans 3:10-23*).

Jeremiah asks the question, *"who can know it?"* The answers come immediately from God himself: *"I the LORD search the heart…"*

Scripture to read: Jeremiah 17:5-14

Question to ponder: *If God knows even the thoughts of my heart, how could I possibly conceal <u>any</u> sin from Him?*

Day 17   Date: _____

The First Murder

"And he <God> said, What hast thou done? the voice of thy brother's blood crieth unto me from the ground." (Genesis 4:10)

God had warned Adam concerning the forbidden fruit, *"in the day that thou eatest thereof thou shalt surely die" (Genesis 2:17)*. Adam (and Eve) did not die <u>physically</u> right away, but did experience <u>spiritual</u> death – separation from fellowship with God – immediately. Because of their sin, they had to be expelled from the Garden of Eden.

It would get worse! Eve bore two sons, <u>Cain</u> and <u>Abel</u>. One day each brought an offering to God. Apparently God had given instructions concerning what was acceptable to Him. Abel's offering, which included the shedding of an animal's blood, was accepted. When Cain saw that his own offering wasn't, he responded by killing his brother. Adam and Eve had hoped their salvation would come through these boys. Instead, they saw the awful consequence of death, just as God had warned!

Scripture to read: Genesis 3:23 – 4:15

Question to ponder: *How do I respond when I learn that I have fallen short of God's expectations?*

Day 18   Date: _____

Death by Sin

"Wherefore, as by one man sin entered into the world, and death by sin; and so death passed upon all men, for that all have sinned" (Romans 5:12)

The sin of Adam and Eve not only caused <u>sin</u> to gain an entrance into the world, but also <u>death</u>. Had they not sinned, the world would know nothing of death.

Because of their sin, we, their offspring, are born with a <u>sin nature</u>. That sin nature condemns us to death as well. In *James 1:15*, the Bible tells us *"sin, when it is finished, bringeth forth death"*. The sin nature also causes us to sin, thereby confirming the verdict of death by our <u>actions</u>. All men have sinned. Therefore all men are condemned to die!

Scripture to read: Romans 5:12-19

Question to ponder: *In how many different ways do I see evidence of death in the world around me on a regular basis?*

Day 19   Date: _____

The Process of Sin

"But every man is tempted, when he is drawn away of his own lust, and enticed. Then when lust hath conceived, it bringeth forth sin: and sin, when it is finished, bringeth forth death." (James 1:14-15)

Sin does not come upon us from <u>without</u>. The Bible clearly states in our text verses that the sins we commit find their source <u>within</u> us. Our own <u>lust</u> (attraction to evil) causes us to respond to the lure of evil and to move toward it. Our own lust conceives the sin and "gives birth" to it. Notice that the temptation (invitation to sin) is powerless to influence us except for the lust within us.

Also notice that the sin which at first appears so attractive to us ultimately "gives birth" to death.

Scripture to read: James 1:13-21

Question to ponder: *In what ways do we ignore the real nature of sin when we are in the middle of "the process"?*

Day 20   Date: _____

The Wages of Sin

"For the wages of sin is death; but the gift of God is eternal life through Jesus Christ our Lord." (Romans 6:23)

When we work for an employer we are entitled to receive <u>wages</u> in compensation for our labor. They are <u>earned</u> and are <u>due</u> to us. Any person off the street could not walk into the office of our employer and demand a paycheck. They would be denied because they had not labored, and therefore had not earned a paycheck.

We have earned an <u>eternal</u> paycheck for our labors in this life. Because of our sin, that paycheck is <u>death</u>. It is earned, and therefore due to us.

Notice, on the other hand, that eternal life is a <u>gift</u>. It cannot be earned through any labors of man.

Scripture to read: Romans 7:7-14

Question to ponder: *In light of this verse, would you want to stand before God and ask Him to just give you what you deserve?*

Day 21   Date: _____

Noah and the Flood

"And, behold, I, even I, do bring a flood of waters upon the earth, to destroy all flesh, wherein is the breath of life, from under heaven; and every thing that is in the earth shall die." (Genesis 6:17)

After Cain and Abel, God gave Adam and Eve a third son, named <u>Seth</u>. Seth's family line is traced in the fifth chapter of Genesis. Mankind did not learn from the sin in the Garden, or from the tragedy of Cain's murder of Abel. Genesis 6:5 records that *"the wickedness of man was great in the earth, and that every imagination of the thoughts of his heart was only evil continually."* Finally, after over 1,500 years, God pronounced a horrible judgment upon His creation. He would destroy man, and much of created animal life, from off the face of the earth.

But, in the midst of all this evil, God had reserved one man, a descendent of Seth, to Himself through whom He would work to preserve human life on earth and ultimately bring salvation to all mankind. *"But Noah found grace in the eyes of the LORD" (Genesis 6:8).*

Scripture to read: Genesis 6:5-22

Question to ponder: *Is God afraid to execute judgment upon sin?*

Day 22   Date: _____

God's Pure Eyes

"Thou art of purer eyes than to behold evil, and canst not look on iniquity: wherefore lookest thou upon them that deal treacherously, and holdest thy tongue when the wicked devoureth the man that is more righteous than he?" (Habakkuk 1:13)

One of the perplexing questions of life for God's faithful to deal with is the continual presence of evil in the world and the seeming delays in God's judgment upon that evil. <u>Habakkuk</u> was a prophet of God who struggled with this issue. He saw the holiness of God very clearly and also saw sin for what it truly is – <u>an offence against God</u>!

In this short book of the Bible, God answers His distressed prophet by revealing His future plans of judgment upon the evildoers of that day. The prophet closes his writing with increased praise to God for His glory!

Scripture to read: Habakkuk 1:1-4; 3:1-6

Question to ponder: *Do I see <u>my</u> sin as an offence against God?*

Day 23   Date: _____

Condemned Already

"He that believeth on him is not condemned: but he that believeth not is condemned already, because he hath not believed in the name of the only begotten Son of God." (John 3:18)

As we have previously read (Lessons 18-20), our sin nature condemns us to death. It needs to be understood that this is a condition into which we are <u>born</u>. The death sentence is not passed upon us in a moment in which we reject the Savior – it is ours already <u>from the moment of birth</u> because we were born as unbelievers!

The Bible does indicate that God will not hold a person accountable for sin who has not reached an age of <u>understanding</u> of sin, and therefore <u>accountability</u> for sin. But we dare not pass over our predicament lightly, because we who can read this are most certainly capable of understanding, and therefore <u>condemned already</u>! Notice, however, that this condemnation is escaped through belief!

Scripture to read: John 3:18-21

Question to ponder: *Is it fair for God to condemn us to die even from the moment of birth?*

Day 24   Date: _____

Without Excuse

"For the invisible things of him from the creation of the world are clearly seen, being understood by the things that are made, even his eternal power and Godhead; so that they are without excuse" (Romans 1:20)

One common objection against Biblical Christianity is that there are people who have never heard the gospel message of salvation. No one has ever opened the Bible to them and explained the way of salvation. Are those people accountable to God for their sin? Is it fair that they are *"condemned already"*?

God answers, yes! He has given them a testimony in creation that clearly shows them what they need to know about Him. *Romans, chapter 2, verse 14*, also explains that when these people *"which have not the law <Bible>, do by nature the things contained in the law <Bible>, these, having not the law, are a law unto themselves"*. Even though they do not have the Bible, they know by their conscience that certain things are innately wrong.

Scripture to read: Romans 1:16-20; 2:12-16

Question to ponder: Do *I* have any excuse for rejecting *God*?

Day 25   Date: _____

Appointment with Death

"And as it is appointed unto men once to die, but after this the judgment" (Hebrews 9:27)

Because of our sin, we all face an inevitable <u>appointment</u> with death. No one knows the time of their appointment, but all know that the appointment is <u>certain</u>.

Death is not the end of our conscience existence, however. Just as <u>spiritual</u> death is separation from fellowship with God (see Lesson 17), so <u>physical</u> death is separation – of our body from our soul. We face an appointment <u>after</u> death as well, that of the judgment. *Romans, chapter 14, verse 12*, tells us *"So then every one of us shall give account of himself to God"*. That appointment is just as certain as our appointment with death.

Scripture to read: Psalms 90:1-17

Question to ponder: *Am I ready to face God if my "appointment" were to happen today?*

Day 26   Date: _____

The Second Death

"And death and hell were cast into the lake of fire. This is the second death. And whosoever was not found written in the book of life was cast into the lake of fire." (Revelation 20:14-15)

The book of *Revelation*, in the verses assigned for reading today, describes the judgment of all those who die without salvation. This judgment is called the "Great White Throne Judgment" because of the throne God executes judgment from. It is at this judgment that the final sentence of an eternity spent separated from God is issued.

Unbelievers ("the dead") will there be condemned to an eternity of indescribable punishment in Hell (the Lake of Fire). They <u>will</u> have conscious existence. Eternal <u>death</u>, not <u>life</u>, will be their fate.

Scripture to read: Revelation 20:11-15

Question to ponder: *Is <u>my</u> name written in the book of life?*

Day 27   Date: _____

The Ark

"And the LORD said unto Noah, Come thou and all thy house into the ark; for thee have I seen righteous before me in this generation."
(Genesis 7:1)

When God informed <u>Noah</u> of His plan to destroy all flesh from off the earth in a universal flood, he also instructed Noah to build an ark. Noah, who had never seen a flood, or even rain, built the ark <u>by</u> <u>faith</u> according to the instructions given by God. Noah and his family entered the ark, along with two of every sort of living flesh, and waited for God's judgment to fall upon the earth. It rained 40 days and 40 nights until the waters of the flood covered the whole earth and every living creature, including man, that lived upon the face of the earth had died.

But Noah and his family were safe inside the ark. Just as Noah found salvation from the flood inside the ark, today God has provided a way of escape from the judgment of His wrath against sin. Jesus Christ is God's provision for our salvation.

Scripture to read: Genesis 7:1-24

Question to ponder: *Was there any way for the people outside the ark to escape from the flood?*

Day 28   Date: _____

Christ Died for Us

"But God commendeth his love toward us, in that, while we were yet sinners, Christ died for us." (Romans 5:8)

The Bible declares that *"the wages of sin is death"*. Because of our sin, there is nothing we can do to save ourselves. We need intervention from a source outside ourselves. The marvelous truth of God's Plan of Salvation is that He has taken it upon <u>Himself</u> to make a provision for our salvation.

God's Plan of Salvation reveals (commendeth) His great love to us. The amazing thing about it is that we are totally unlovable. We, who because of our sin are <u>enemies</u> of God, are the objects of His great love! This kind of love is totally foreign to the way we are by nature, but is totally consistent with the nature of God.

Scripture to read: Romans 5:6-11

Question to ponder: *Would I be willing to die for someone who was my enemy?*

Day 29   Date: _____

Made Sin for Us

"For he hath made him to be sin for us, who knew no sin; that we might be made the righteousness of God in him." (II Corinthians 5:21)

The apostle Paul wrote two letters to a church he started in the city of Corinth, Greece. Our text verse is taken from the second of these letters.

When Jesus Christ hung on the cross He took the punishment for our sin. He died in our place. He took the death that we deserved. Because He was sinlessly perfect, He did not need to die for any sin of His own. Jesus Christ offered up His own body as a substitute for each of us! Because He willingly did so, we have the opportunity to be made righteous in God's eyes! Today's scripture reading is taken from a letter written by the apostle Paul to the churches he started in the eastern European region of Galatia. In today's reading, Paul refers to Christ taking sin's curse (death) for us.

Scripture to read: Galatians 3:10-13

Question to ponder: *If I had to die for my own sin, could I ever pay my debt in full?*

Day 30   Date: _____

God So Loved the World

"For God so loved the world, that he gave his only begotten Son, that whosoever believeth in him should not perish, but have everlasting life." (John 3:16)

The most familiar and best-loved verse in the entire Bible is our verse for today. It was written by the man who became known as "the Apostle of Love", John. He was the youngest of the twelve men (apostles) Jesus chose for specialized training while He was on earth.

This verse shows us that God's kind of love <u>gives</u> sacrificially. It also reveals Jesus Christ as the *"only begotten Son of God"*. To the Jew this term meant "of the same nature", thereby declaring Jesus Christ to be <u>equal</u> with God. Some modern Bible versions read *"one and only Son"*. This is inaccurate, and loses the special meaning of "only begotten". This verse also tells us that salvation comes through <u>belief</u> in Jesus Christ.

Scripture to read: John 3:13-17

Question to ponder: *How is God's love different than the "love" that is portrayed by the world today?*

Day 31   Date: _____

The Gift of God

"For by grace are ye saved through faith; and that not of yourselves: it is the gift of God: Not of works, lest any man should boast." (Ephesians 2:8-9)

Some things are so valuable that a price cannot be assigned to them, even if someone wanted to purchase them with money. So it is with salvation. The price that God paid for our salvation was so unspeakably great it can only be obtained as a gift.

A gift cannot be paid for by the recipient. If so, it ceases to be a gift. Likewise, you cannot work for a gift. It then becomes owed to you. Salvation comes by God's grace – His favor toward us – and through the vehicle of our faith – belief in His Son, Jesus Christ.

Notice what our text verses say would happen if we could work our way to Heaven. We would brag about how we got there. Receiving salvation as a gift leaves us with only one person to praise – the Savior!

Scripture to read: Ephesians 2:1-9

Question to ponder: *What are some ways people try to work their way to Heaven?*

Day 32   Date: _____

The Only Way

"Jesus saith unto him, I am the way, the truth, and the life: no man cometh unto the Father, but by me." (John 14:6)

In the evening before His crucifixion, Jesus took some time to speak words of comfort to His disciples. He explained the necessity of His leaving them, but also His plan to prepare a place (Heaven) for them (and us) to dwell with Him forever.

In response to a question from one of the twelve disciples (apostles, see Lesson 30), Jesus explained that He is the <u>way</u> to Heaven. He further emphasized that there is no other acceptable way to the Father, and Heaven, but Him.

This means that any person attempting to gain entrance into Heaven through any other means than the way provided by Jesus Christ will find that God the Father will not accept their alternative "way". As Jesus said, <u>No man</u> can come to the Father any other way!

Scripture to read: John 14:1-6

Question to ponder: *Can I approach God in my own name?*

Day 33   Date: _____

None Other Name

"Neither is there salvation in any other: for there is none other name under heaven given among men, whereby we must be saved." (Acts 4:12)

The book of Acts (short for "*The Acts of the Apostles*") is an historical account of the spread of the gospel message of salvation after the departure of Jesus from earth. This message was carried on by the apostles, the twelve men personally trained by Jesus (see Lessons 30 and 32).

As they began to spread the good news of salvation they were confronted by many of the same religious leaders who had crucified Jesus Christ. In today's scripture two of the apostles, Peter and John, were asked by what authority they preached and performed miracles. They responded, "*by the name of Jesus Christ*".

Only Jesus Christ has died to pay the debt of our sins. Salvation is in His name alone!

Scripture to read: Acts 4:1-12

Question to ponder: *Who are some men in history who have falsely proclaimed "salvation" through their own name?*

Day 34   Date: _____

Whosoever Shall Call

"For whosoever shall call upon the name of the Lord shall be saved." (Romans 10:13)

How does one become saved? Our scripture reading for today explains that you must <u>believe</u> in your heart and <u>confess</u> with your mouth. What must you believe? That you are a sinner, that you deserve to be punished eternally for your sin (death), that Jesus Christ died in your place and rose again from the dead, and that He is the <u>only</u> way of salvation. If you believe these things in your <u>heart</u>, then you must confess them to God with your <u>mouth</u>. This means to <u>admit</u> your lost condition and <u>ask</u> Him to save you.

Salvation is a <u>one-time</u> transaction that takes place between God and you. When you do the above, God saves you, and the transaction is complete!

Notice that God places no restrictions on who may call upon Him for salvation. *"Whosoever"* means <u>anybody</u> and <u>everybody</u> is welcome!

Scripture to read: Romans 10:8-13

Question to ponder: *Has there been a specific time and place when I have called upon the name of the Lord for my salvation?*

Day 35   Date: _____

What Must I Do to Be Saved?

"And brought them out, and said, Sirs, what must I do to be saved? And they said, believe on the Lord Jesus Christ, and thou shalt be saved, and thy house." (Acts 16:30-31)

The apostle Paul made three missionary journeys for the purpose of spreading the gospel message. On his second journey, he took the gospel into Europe for the first time. While in the city of Philippi, he was thrown in jail after casting a demon out of a young girl who was being used for financial gain by her masters. Instead of complaining, Paul and his companion, Silas, sang praises to God while imprisoned. An earthquake interrupted their singing, but instead of seeking to escape, Paul and Silas remained in the prison. The prison keeper, after being saved from committing suicide, responded to these remarkable events with the question posed in our text verse.

Notice again that belief on the Lord Jesus Christ is the sole prerequisite for salvation.

Scripture to read: Acts 16:12-34

Question to ponder: *Was the answer to the question any different for the members of the jailor's household?*

Day 36   Date: _____

God Be Merciful to Me!

"And the publican, standing afar off, would not lift up so much as his eyes unto heaven, but smote upon his breast, saying, God be merciful to me a sinner." (Luke 18:13)

The life and earthly ministry of Jesus Christ is recorded in four *"gospels", Matthew, Mark, Luke, and John.* Each of these four men recorded a different perspective on the Lord's ministry.

Jesus often taught using "parables". A parable is a story that relates a heavenly truth using common everyday situations. In this parable, the Lord contrasted a religious man (a Pharisee) who did not see his own sinful condition before God with a despised tax collector (a publican) who freely acknowledged his need of a savior. The Pharisee thought he was good (righteous) enough on his own. The publican simply cried out to God for mercy. This was his "call" (see Lesson 34) upon the Lord for salvation. Jesus explained that of the two men, only the publican would see Heaven.

Scripture to read: Luke 18:9-14

Question to ponder: *What was the Pharisee trusting in to earn his own salvation?*

Day 37   Date: _____

Repentance

"When Jesus heard it, he saith unto them, They that are whole have no need of the physician, but they that are sick: I came not to call the righteous, but sinners to repentance." (Mark 2:17)

In the gospel written by <u>Mark</u> (a travelling companion of the apostle Paul), he records an incident that happened shortly after Jesus called the writer of the first gospel to follow him. <u>Matthew</u>, also called Levi, had been a tax collector (publican). Publicans were looked down upon by the religious leaders (see Lesson 36) because they worked for the Roman government, and because most of them were dishonest.

In this account, Jesus was being criticized for associating with a publican. The Lord's reply revealed that He could help no one who did not see his or her own need. He also equated salvation with <u>repentance</u>. Repentance involves a <u>change</u> of mind and a corresponding <u>change</u> in behavior. It is not enough to be sorry for our sin; we must seek to turn away from it.

Scripture to read: Mark 2:13-17

Question to ponder: *If someone does not show a changed life after salvation, did they truly repent?*

Day 38   Date: _____

Born of God

"But as many as received him, to them gave he power to become the sons of God, even to them that believe on his name: Which were born, not of blood, or of the will of the flesh, nor of the will of man, but of God." (John 1:12-13)

These verses explain that any person who receives Jesus Christ as their savior, i.e. calls upon the name of the Lord, is born into the family of God! The authority (power) to claim this family as your own comes from God Himself.

Notice that this "birth" does not come through an earthly family relationship (*"of blood"*) or through the efforts of our own will (*"of the will of the flesh"*). Nor does it come through the efforts or desire of another person (*"of the will of man"*). This birth, authorized by God Himself, comes *"of God"*. He does all the *"work"*. Our part is to *"believe on his name"* and *"receive him"*.

Scripture to read: John 1:6-13

Question to ponder: *Once you are born into an earthly family, can anything change that as a matter of fact? Can that event be undone?*

Day 39   Date: _____

Born Again

"Jesus answered and said unto him, Verily, verily, I say unto thee, Except a man be born again, he cannot see the kingdom of God." (John 3:3)

Early in his earthly ministry, Jesus received a visit from a religious leader named <u>Nicodemus</u>. While Nicodemus was working up to the questions that were on his mind, Jesus responded with the above answer that cut right to the need of Nicodemus.

Jesus explained that in order to have eternal life (enter the kingdom of God) a person needs to experience a <u>spiritual</u> birth just as they need to experience a <u>physical</u> birth (of the flesh) in order to experience physical life. This spiritual birth Jesus called being "*born again*". This spiritual birth cannot be seen with the eye, just as we cannot see the wind. We only see the evidence of the wind; so we only see the resulting evidence of spiritual birth in a person.

Scripture to read: John 3:1-12

Question to ponder: *Into what kind of a family would a <u>spiritual</u> birth cause you to be born?*

Unit One Review
Lessons 1 to 39

List the key historical events found in these lessons:

Lesson 1: _____

Lesson 7: _____

Lesson 10: _____

Lesson 17: _____

Lessons 21 & 27: _____

Define these terms in your own words, with help from the lessons noted in parenthesis:

Faith (2) _____
_____

Inspiration (4) _____
_____

Holiness (6) _____
_____

Sin nature (12) _____
_____

Sin (10, 22) _____
_____

Death (25, 26) _____
_____

Born again (39) _____
_____

Unit Two

Lessons 40 to 60

Bible History

Job
Abraham
Isaac

<u>Bible Truths</u>

Assurance of Salvation
Living by Faith

Day 40   Date: _____
Everlasting Life

"He that believeth on the Son hath everlasting life: and he that believeth not the Son shall not see life; but the wrath of God abideth on him." (John 3:36)

One of the hardest things sometimes for a new believer to fully comprehend is that the salvation that God gives when a person "calls upon the name of the Lord" is eternally secure. Once a person is admitted into the family of God through the new birth, he is a child of God forever! We do not work to receive our salvation; therefore we cannot work to keep our salvation.

Please notice in our text verse that *"he that believeth on the Son hath everlasting life"*. If you have believed, then everlasting life is a possession. You have it! Now! It is not something that will be given to you in the future. It is yours now, and forever!

Scripture to read: John 3:31-36

Question to ponder: *Can God be trusted to keep a promise such as this one?*

Day 41   Date: _____

No Condemnation

"There is therefore now no condemnation to them which are in Christ Jesus, who walk not after the flesh, but after the Spirit." (Romans 8:1)

When Jesus was talking with Nicodemus (see Lesson 39), He told him "That which is born of the flesh is flesh; and that which is born of the Spirit is spirit". *In verse 9 of today's scripture we read* "But ye are not in the flesh, but in the Spirit, if so be that the Spirit of God dwell in you".

We were born with a sin nature that condemned us to die from the moment of birth (see Lesson 23). Upon receiving Jesus Christ as Savior, we are "born again" spiritually and are now "<u>in</u> Christ Jesus, and <u>in</u> the Spirit". Today's text verse declares that, on the basis of this, we no longer face condemnation. The verse uses two very strong words to emphasize the certainty of this blessing, "is" and "now". We have been made free from sin and from its penalty, death, <u>forever</u>!

Scripture to read: Romans 8:1-13

Question to ponder: *What would you be willing to do for someone who had rescued you from certain death?*

Day 42   Date: _____

Knowing It

"These things have I written unto you that believe on the name of the Son of God; that ye may know that ye have eternal life, and that ye may believe on the name of the Son of God." (I John 5:13)

The apostle John, in addition to the gospel by his name, also wrote three letters that appear near the very back of the Bible. Each of these bear his name and are labeled *First, Second* and *Third John*.

In our text verse, John adamantly explains that it is possible to <u>know</u> that you have eternal life. This assurance of eternal life is based upon your belief in Jesus Christ, the Son of God. This is something that John wanted us to know that we can have <u>now,</u> in this life. In the previous verse, John put it very simply: if you have the Son you <u>have</u> (eternal) life; if you do not have the Son you <u>do not have</u> (eternal) life.

Scripture to read: I John 5:9-15

Question to ponder: *Do I <u>have</u> the Son?*

Day 43   Date: _____

Human Government

"Whoso sheddeth man's blood, by man shall his blood be shed: for in the image of God made he man." (Genesis 9:6)

After the floodwaters dried up from the face of the earth, and Noah and his family were able to leave the ark, God blessed them and gave them instructions for replenishing the human family upon the earth. Here, for the first time, man was given a non-vegetarian diet. Here also, God implemented a new program for checking the sinful nature of man.

In *Genesis, chapter 4*, after Cain had murdered Abel, God had to intervene to protect Cain from the vengeance of others. Now, God instructed Noah that He was giving authority to man to execute justice through the means of capital punishment for anyone who committed murder. For the first time, man would be accountable to man in a system of organized government. More instructions would be added later, but this scripture passage forms the charter statement for the institution of government.

Scripture to read: Genesis 8:14 – 9:19

Question to ponder: *According to our text verse, why does the murder of a human being require a special penalty?*

Day 44 Date: _____
The Tower of Babel

"Therefore is the name of it called Babel; because the LORD did there confound the language of all the earth: and from thence did the LORD scatter them abroad upon the face of all the earth." (Genesis 11:9)

God had told Noah and his family to *"Be fruitful, and multiply, and replenish the earth"* (Genesis 9:1). Now, approximately 100 years later, the people were making plans to *"build us a city and a tower…lest we be scattered abroad upon the face of the whole earth"* (Genesis 11:4). The people were making plans to rebel against the clear instructions of God. Once again, God would intervene with a judgment upon the rebellion of mankind.

Until this time there had only been one spoken language upon the earth. God caused the people to speak in differing languages. Since they could no longer communicate with each other, they unwillingly separated and began to scatter across the face of the earth.

Scripture to read: Genesis 11:1-9

Question to ponder: *Compare verse 6 with Genesis 6:5. What would be the ultimate result if the people were allowed to continue with their plans?*

Day 45   Date: _____

Job

"There was a man in the land of Uz, whose name was Job; and that man was perfect and upright, and one that feared God, and eschewed evil." (Job 1:1)

Sometime after the flood, a man lived by the name of Job (pronounced "jobe"). Although he is referred to in other books of the Bible, we are not told exactly when he lived and his story does not connect with any other Bible character.

The story of Job is that of a man who trusted God with his whole heart, lived his life in a manner pleasing to God, yet suffered almost unbearable trials. The *book of Job* tells of his loss and suffering, the cruelty of his "friends", and of the ultimate restoration of Job's health and prosperity. Although Job had some very dark days, yet he did not falter in his faith toward God. In *Job 42:12* we read, *"So the LORD blessed the latter end of Job more than his beginning"*.

Scripture to read: Job 1:1-22

Question to ponder: *How much difficulty in life would it take for me to complain against God?*

Day 46   Date: _____

The Promise to Abraham

"And I will bless them that bless thee, and curse him that curseth thee: and in thee shall all families of the earth be blessed." (Genesis 12:3)

Today's scripture is one of the key passages in the whole Bible. The first three verses record a three-fold promise given by God to a man named <u>Abram</u> (Abraham). Abraham was told by God to leave his (paternal) family, travel to a land he knew nothing about (the "Promised Land"), and believe God that He would keep His promise. This continues God's practice of working through a select few.

The promise, called the "Abrahamic Covenant", gave to Abraham a place to live (land), an innumerable posterity (a great nation – Israel), and a special blessing upon his family. He was also promised that all families of the earth would be blessed through his family. This continues the promise given to Adam and Eve in the Garden of Eden (see Lesson 11) of a coming Savior!

Scripture to read: Genesis 12:1-9

Question to ponder: *Would I be willing to take such a step of faith if God asked me?*

| **Day 47** | **Date:** _____ |

From Adam to Abraham

"Now these are the generations of the sons of Noah, Shem, Ham, and Japheth: and unto them were sons born after the flood." (Genesis 10:1)

The story of the human family from Adam to Abraham covers about 2,000 years of history. The one thing that stands out in reviewing these years is the total inability of man to live a righteous life on his own. In the first 2,000 years of history only a few men lived lives pleasing to God.

In the Garden, Adam and Eve lived in <u>innocence</u> (no experiential knowledge of sin), in a perfect environment, and still fell into sin. Expelled from Eden, mankind lived by the knowledge of good and evil he now had, and made decisions based upon his <u>conscience</u>. This led to such great wickedness that a second major judgment followed – the Flood. Following the Flood, man became accountable to man under a system of <u>human government</u>. Again, failure resulted in a judgment – at Babel. Now, a <u>promise</u> was given to the family of Abraham. Would they do any better than their ancestors?

Scripture to read: Genesis 11:10-26

Question to ponder: *How does a list of names such as this show God's interest in each person?*

Day 48   Date: _____

The Faith of Abraham

"And he believed in the LORD; and he counted it to him for righteousness."
(Genesis 15:6)

Abraham had separated from his family as God had asked. He had received the wonderful promise given in *Genesis, chapter twelve* (see Lesson 46). After some time, God spoke to him again. This time, Abraham had a question for God. He was being promised great things, but was an old man and still had no children. God directed his attention to the stars of the heaven and told him his offspring would be as bountiful as they are.

Our text verse for today records Abraham's response. Against all evidence, he took God at His word and believed Him. The Bible says God counted that act of faith as Abraham's moment of salvation. *Romans, chapter four*, points to this incident as an illustration of salvation by grace through faith, and not by works.

Scripture to read: Genesis 15:1-6

Question to ponder: *Because of the special promise already given to Abraham, in what way was his faith here also faith in Jesus Christ?*

Day 49   Date: _____

The Just Shall Live by Faith

"But without faith it is impossible to please him: for he that cometh to God must believe that he is, and that he is a rewarder of them that diligently seek him." (Hebrews 11:6)

A person is saved through the act of exercising faith in the person and work of the Lord Jesus Christ. Once saved, faith is all the more important for it is only through faith that we can please God. In *Hebrews 10:38* we read *"Now the just <saved> shall live by faith…"*. Then, in chapter eleven, faith is defined for us (see Lesson 2) and illustrated by citing the examples of people such as Abraham.

Faith is simply taking God at His Word and acting upon it. Or, in other words, using the Word of God (the Bible) as our guide for everyday life as we seek to please the One who gave us our salvation. Living by faith should be an everyday way of life!

Scripture to read: Hebrews 11:1-10

Question to ponder: *How can I be sure to live each day by faith?*

Day 50   Date: _____

Created Unto Good Works

"For we are his workmanship, created in Christ Jesus unto good works, which God hath before ordained that we should walk in them."
(Ephesians 2:10)

Salvation cannot be earned through good works, lest we ruin Heaven by boasting about ourselves! On the other hand, God hasn't saved us just to let us go back to our sin either. Today's verse informs us that God has a plan for those who He saves – that they should "walk in good works". As a matter of fact, if someone is not doing good works it may be evidence that they are not truly saved!

James, an early church leader, wrote that it is our works (after salvation) that give life to our faith. He said, *"faith without works is dead"*. Again, Abraham's faith is cited, being proved by the deeds that he did demonstrating his faith. Read today's scripture and see how practical James is in explaining the importance of good works.

Scripture to read: James 2:14-26

Question to ponder: *Do the works in my life give evidence that my faith is real?*

Day 51   Date: _____

A New Creature

"Therefore if any man be in Christ, he is a new creature: old things are passed away; behold, all things are become new." (II Corinthians 5:17)

Today's verse teaches us the comprehensive nature of the salvation that God has given to us. Not only has our eternal destiny been changed, but our whole life! We who are *"in Christ"* are a totally new creation. The *"old things"* have to do with our former life before Christ.

Our scripture reading for today discusses the "old man" and the "new man". Notice that the *"old man"* is corrupt; subject to fleshly lusts, which deceive us into sin. The *"new man"* is *"created in righteousness and true holiness"*. What else would you expect of someone *"born again"* into God's family? We take on the nature of our new family!

Scripture to read: Ephesians 4:17-32

Question to ponder: *Since your salvation has anyone commented that you seem to be a "new person"?*

Day 52   Date: _____

All to the Glory of God

"Whether therefore ye eat, or drink, or whatsoever ye do, do all to the glory of God." (I Corinthians 10:31)

Today's verse is taken from the first letter of the apostle Paul to the church at Corinth. The believers in that city were faced with a question. In purchasing meat from the meat market (the "shambles") they could possibly be purchasing meat which had been previously offered in sacrifice to false gods (idols). There was a dispute whether this was appropriate for a believer in Jesus Christ to do. Paul wrote to explain that it didn't matter unless, in doing so, another believer who opposed using that meat would be offended.

In making everyday choices, Paul explained that we are to live for God's glory, not our own. In so doing, we fulfill the purpose for which we were originally created (see Lesson 8). This kind of selfless living can be used to lead other people to salvation (verse 33).

Scripture to read: I Corinthians 10:23-33

Question to ponder: *Do I live my life to please God, or myself?*

Day 53 Date: _____
Not Conformed to this World

"And be not conformed to this world: but be ye transformed by the renewing of your mind, that ye may prove what is that good, and acceptable, and perfect, will of God." (Romans 12:2)

When the Bible speaks of "the world" it often is referring to the general lifestyle and thought patterns of the people in the world who are not believers. Because of their sin nature, their general pattern of life is in <u>opposition</u> to the things of God. A believer is not to be influenced by, or conformed to, the world in this way. Today's verse instructs believers to resist the influence of this world system.

We are to "renew our minds" by thinking as God thinks rather than as the world thinks. Of course, God's kind of thinking is found in the pages of the Bible. In so doing, our lives will be dramatically changed (transformed) and we will demonstrate to the world around us that God's will is "*good, and acceptable, and perfect*".

Scripture to read: Romans 12:9-21

Question to ponder: *What are some kinds of activity, dress, entertainment, music, and speech, etc., which are identified with the world?*

Day 54   Date: _____

Choices

"And Lot lifted up his eyes, and beheld all the plain of Jordan, that it was well watered every where, before the LORD destroyed Sodom and Gomorrah, ... Then Lot chose him all the plain of Jordan; and Lot journeyed east: and they separated themselves the one from the other." (Genesis 13:10-11)

Life can be summarized by the choices we make, either good ones or bad ones. When Abraham journeyed to the Promised Land, he took his nephew Lot with him. In time their wealth became such that the land could not support both their livestock and they decided to separate. Abraham gave Lot the first choice and Lot made a choice based upon greed. Furthermore, he *"pitched his tent toward Sodom"*, a very wicked city.

The 18th and 19th chapters of Genesis record the judgment of God upon Sodom and Gomorrah for the wickedness of their sin. Sadly, by this time Lot and his family were under their evil influence. Only Lot and two of his daughters ultimately escaped the awful judgment upon these cities.

Scripture to read: Genesis 19:1-29

Question to ponder: *Do I make choices based upon selfish motives, like greed?*

Day 55   Date: _____

Fellowship with Him

"If we confess our sins, he is faithful and just to forgive us our sins, and to cleanse us from all unrighteousness." (I John 1:9)

Once we are "born again" into the family of God our <u>relationship</u> with God is eternally secure. We have been saved from the penalty of sin and are freed from condemnation (see Lesson 41). However, until we get to Heaven, we still have the problem of daily sin in our lives. As taught in today's scripture reading, this sin affects our <u>fellowship</u> with God.

Continual fellowship can be maintained with God by confessing (admitting) sin, as we become aware of it. Our text verse for today records the promise of God that such a prayer of confession will never go unanswered. God eagerly desires to forgive us our sin and cleanse us from it. This cleansing is done by the blood which Jesus Christ shed when he died for our sins.

Scripture to read: I John 1:3-10

Question to ponder: *Do I let sin go unconfessed in my life?*

Day 56   Date: _____

Circumcision

"This is my covenant, which ye shall keep, between me and you and thy seed after thee; Every man child among you shall be circumcised."
(Genesis 17:10)

When Abraham was 99 years old, God appeared to him to reaffirm the "Abrahamic Covenant" given years earlier (see Lesson 46). This time God gave to Abraham a sign by which he and his offspring after him would demonstrate their faith in God and identification with this covenant.

This sign was the circumcision of every male child born into this family, to be performed on the child's eighth day. So important was circumcision that even slaves brought into a household of Abraham's family were to be circumcised as well.

It was in this meeting that God changed his name from Abram to Abraham and his wife's name from Sarai to Sarah. The name Abraham means "father of many nations".

Scripture to read: Genesis 17:1-16

Question to ponder: *In what way would circumcision demonstrate faith in God?*

Day 57　　Date: _____

The Son of Promise

"And God said, Sarah thy wife shall bear thee a son indeed; and thou shalt call his name Isaac: and I will establish my covenant with him for an everlasting covenant, and with his seed after him." (Genesis 17:19)

When time passed and Abraham and Sarah still had no children, they became impatient and formed a "solution" of their own. Abraham had a son by Hagar, Sarah's handmaid. This son, Ishmael, became the father of many of the Arab nations. God appeared to Abraham again to reaffirm the promise of a son to he and Sarah.

Finally, a son was born to Abraham and Sarah. Remarkably, this occurred when Abraham was 100 years old and Sarah was 90 years old. Isaac was the son who had been promised years earlier by God, and the son to whom the original promises of God to Abraham would pass on to. Through his miraculous birth, fulfilling a long-awaited promise, we see a picture of a future Son who would be born miraculously in answer to a promise originally given to mankind in the Garden of Eden.

Scripture to read: Genesis 21:1-13

Question to ponder: *Which Son did Isaac picture?*

Day 58   Date: _____
His Only Begotten Son

"By faith Abraham, when he was tried, offered up Isaac: and he that had received the promises offered up his only begotten son. Of whom it was said, That in Isaac shall thy seed be called: Accounting that God was able to raise him up, even from the dead; from whence also he received him in a figure." (Hebrews 11:17-19)

One day, when Isaac was still a lad, God tested the strength of Abraham's faith in Him. He instructed Abraham to take the son he had waited so long for, Isaac, and offer him as a burnt-offering to God. Incredibly, Abraham rose up early the very next day and immediately set out to obey God. How could he do such a thing without questioning God? Was not this the very son through whom the promises of God to him were to be fulfilled?

The "faith chapter" of *Hebrews* gives us insight into Abraham's thoughts. He reasoned that if God was able to give a son to a couple their age (dead as far as childbearing was concerned), He was well able to raise him up, even from the dead if necessary, to keep His promises!

Scripture to read: Genesis 22:1-6

Question to ponder: Is *my faith in God that strong?*

Day 59   Date: _____

God Will Provide

"And Abraham said, My son, God will provide himself a lamb for a burnt-offering: so they went both of them together." (Genesis 22:8)

As Abraham and Isaac went to the place God had told Abraham, Isaac noticed that they had everything necessary for a burnt-offering but the lamb. Upon questioning his father, Abraham answered as noted in our text verse. The Bible records that Abraham obediently prepared the altar and Isaac obediently submitted to his father. Abraham had knife in hand, ready to slay his beloved son, when *"the angel of the LORD"* called out from heaven for him to stop. Then, God provided a ram for the sacrifice.

This passage is rich in meaning. It pictures God not sparing His only begotten Son so that we might have a sacrifice for our sin. Less than 2,000 years later, Jesus Christ – a direct descendent of Abraham and Isaac – would be offered for us on this same mountain!

Scripture to read: Genesis 22:7-14

Question to ponder: *What do you think this incident did for the faith of Isaac?*

Day 60   Date: _____

A Bride for Isaac

"And they blessed Rebekah, and said unto her, Thou art our sister, be thou the mother of thousands of millions, and let thy seed possess the gate of those which hate them." (Genesis 24:60)

Before his death, Abraham wanted to provide a proper bride for his son Isaac. He sent his trusted servant to his homeland to find a wife for Isaac from among his kindred. *Genesis, chapter 24*, tells the beautiful story of how God directed the servant's steps to Rebekah, the granddaughter of Abraham's brother, Nahor. Rebekah's father and brother recognized the providence of God in the servant's mission and consented to let her go with him to become Isaac's wife.

The home was instituted by God in the Garden of Eden when He created Eve and presented her to Adam (*Genesis 2:21-25*). In this story we see the importance Abraham placed upon finding the wife of God's choosing for his son.

Scripture to read: Genesis 24:1-67

Question to ponder: *How were the words of blessing spoken to Rebekah by her family fulfilled?*

Unit Two Review
Lessons 40 to 60

List the key historical people found in these lessons:

Lesson 43: _____

Lesson 45: _____

Lesson 46: _____

Lesson 57: _____

Lesson 60: _____

List the exciting truths about eternal life found in each of these lessons:

Lesson 40: _____

Lesson 41: _____

Lesson 42: _____

Lesson 51: _____

List the responsibilities we have as believers found in these lessons:

Lesson 50: _____

Lesson 52: _____

Lesson 53: _____

Lesson 55: _____

BOOKS OF THE BIBLE

BOOKS OF THE OLD TESTAMENT

Genesis	II Chronicles	Daniel
Exodus	Ezra	Hosea
Leviticus	Nehemiah	Joel
Numbers	Esther	Amos
Deuteronomy	Job	Obadiah
Joshua	Psalms	Jonah
Judges	Proverbs	Micah
Ruth	Ecclesiastes	Nahum
I Samuel	Song of Solomon	Habakkuk
II Samuel	Isaiah	Zephaniah
I Kings	Jeremiah	Haggai
II Kings	Lamentations	Zechariah
I Chronicles	Ezekiel	Malachi

BOOKS OF THE NEW TESTAMENT

Matthew	Ephesians	Hebrews
Mark	Philippians	James
Luke	Colossians	I Peter
John	I Thessalonians	II Peter
Acts	II Thessalonians	I John
Romans	I Timothy	II John
I Corinthians	II Timothy	III John
II Corinthians	Titus	Jude
Galatians	Philemon	Revelation

Unit Three

Lessons 61 to 88

Bible History

Esau & Jacob
Israel

Bible Truths

The Bible
Repentance
The Attributes of God

Day 61   Date: _____

Moved by the Holy Ghost

"For the prophecy came not in old time by the will of man: but holy men of God spake as they were moved by the Holy Ghost." (II Peter 1:21)

The apostle <u>Peter</u>, as he was nearing death, wrote this letter (his second) in which he urged the believers to continue to be faithful to the Lord Jesus Christ after his death. In today's scripture reading he stresses the validity of the gospel message and the scriptures. He relates an experience he had in which he personally saw the glory and majesty of Jesus Christ and heard the Father's voice from heaven. Yet he asserts that the scriptures which we have today are <u>a more sure witness</u> than even that incredible experience.

The Bible was written by over forty authors from different walks of life, living over a period of about 1,600 years. Peter calls them *"holy men of God"*. That means they were "set apart" for the job. Every word they wrote was *"moved"* (borne along) by the Holy Ghost so that the result is the "Word of God".

Scripture to read: II Peter 1:15-21

Question to ponder: *Does an eyewitness always get a totally accurate picture of an incident?*

Day 62   Date: _____

Quick and Powerful

"For the word of God is quick, and powerful, and sharper than any twoedged sword, piercing even to the dividing asunder of soul and spirit, and of the joints and marrow, and is a discerner of the thoughts and intents of the heart." (Hebrews 4:12)

Because the Bible is the Word of God, it has many of the attributes of God Himself. In today's verse, we read of the special power that it has to work in our lives.

The word "*quick*" as used here means "alive". The Bible is a living book. It not only has the power to give spiritual life, but its words are life themselves. Notice the special power it has to analyze our lives. This verse refers to the fact that we are made in God's image: body ("*joints and marrow*"), soul and spirit. James, in today's scripture reading, likens the Word of God to looking in a mirror (a glass). It reveals our spiritual condition as a mirror reveals our physical condition. James encourages us to act upon what we see of ourselves in the Word of God.

Scripture to read: James 1:22-25

Question to ponder: *If I saw something about myself in the mirror that I didn't like, would I continue on my way without making any changes?*

Day 63   Date: _____

God's Word – Forever!

"The grass withereth, the flower fadeth: but the word of our God shall stand for ever."
(Isaiah 40:8)

Just as God is <u>eternal</u> and has no beginning or ending, so His Word is <u>eternal</u>. Although it was given to men over about 1,600 years it had been in Heaven for eternity past! Jesus said, *"Heaven and earth shall pass away, but my words shall not pass away"* (Matthew 24:35).

Since God has promised to keep His Word forever, we can be sure we have it today! It has been translated into many languages, and has come through many centuries, but God has superintended over the preservation of His Word just as He supernaturally inspired the original writing of it through the *"holy men of God"*. It was without error (inerrant) in those original writings and has been providentially <u>preserved</u> and is still <u>infallible</u> (perfect) today!

Scripture to read: Psalms 119:89-104

Question to ponder: *Do you think God's Word has been preserved for us today through the intelligence of men, or the providential power of God?*

Day 64   Date: _____

God's Word – Effective!

"So shall my word be that goeth forth out of my mouth: it shall not return unto me void, but it shall accomplish that which I please, and it shall prosper in the thing whereto I sent it." (Isaiah 55:11)

God has given us a wonderful promise that His Word will accomplish His purpose when it is used. Just as the rain and the snow water the earth and cause the earth's vegetation to grow, so God's Word will likewise prosper. You don't need to defend God's Word, just use it! It is alive and powerful (see Lesson 62) and will always produce results.

Today's scripture reading contains some wonderful truths about the nature and character of God. He is waiting for the sinner's call of repentance, eager to show mercy, and ready to pardon sin! We might entertain thoughts of unrighteousness, but God warns that His thoughts are infinitely higher than ours are, and His Word will effectively reach us!

Scripture to read: Isaiah 55:1-13

Question to ponder: *If you held a sharp two-edged sword in your hand would it be more effective to warn your enemy how dangerous it is, or simply use it to defend yourself?*

Day 65   Date: _____

Spiritually Discerned

"But the natural man receiveth not the things of the Spirit of God: for they are foolishness unto him: neither can he know them, because they are spiritually discerned." (I Corinthians 2:14)

The Bible uses the term "natural man" to describe an unsaved person. In other words, a man in the condition into which he was born – possessing a sin nature. The things of the Spirit of God are the things contained in the Bible, which was inspired by the Spirit of God. In our "natural" condition we are <u>unable</u> to receive and understand the truths of scripture. Only when we are "born again" spiritually are our eyes (minds) <u>opened</u> to the truths of God's Word – because the Spirit of God helps us understand (discern) them. This supernatural process is called "illumination".

As our scripture reading for today explains, the preaching of the cross (of Jesus Christ) is foolishness to unsaved people. To us who know Him, however, it is *"the power of God"*.

Scripture to read: I Corinthians 1:18-25

Question to ponder: *Since it is the Spirit of God who helps us understand the Bible, what should we do before each time we read the Bible?*

Day 66   Date: _____

Addition and Subtraction

"For I testify unto every man that heareth the words of the prophecy of this book, If any man shall add unto these things, God shall add unto him the plagues that are written in this book: And if any man shall take away from the words of the book of this prophecy, God shall take away his part out of the book of life, and out of the holy city, and from the things which are written in this book." (Revelation 22:18-19)

These two verses at the very end of the Bible form a very solemn warning to any man who would dare to alter the Word of God. This includes <u>adding</u> things not contained in the inspired scriptures. It also includes <u>removing</u> words, phrases, or teachings from the inspired text that God intended to be there. Remember, our thoughts are not to be compared with God's (see Lesson 64). We dare not try to interpret what (we think) God meant to say and put it into our own words when translating scripture. Yet, that is what many modern versions attempt to do. Others remove key passages claiming so-called "better manuscripts" do not include them. Careful!

Scripture to read: Psalms 119:33-40

Question to ponder: *Do I want to use a Bible version that adds to or subtracts from God's Word?*

Day 67   Date: _____

Sale of the Birthright

"Then Jacob gave Esau bread and pottage of lentiles; and he did eat and drink, and rose up, and went his way: thus Esau despised his birthright." (Genesis 25:34)

Today's scripture reading tells of the twin sons born to Isaac and Rebekah. It also tells of the incident in which the elder son, Esau, sold his birthright to the younger son, Jacob.

The birthright was the right of the eldest son in a family to a double portion of the family inheritance. In this family, that of Abraham and Isaac, it also carried with it the special promise of God given to Abraham – the Abrahamic Covenant (see Lesson 46). What Esau sold was a place in the lineage (family tree) of the promised Savior! It meant so little to Esau that he sold it for a bowl of soup (pottage) to meet a temporary physical need!

Scripture to read: Genesis 25:19-34

Question to ponder: *Can you think of some ways in which people put temporary physical "needs" ahead of spiritual things today?*

Day 68   Date: _____

The Stolen Blessing

"And he said, Is not he rightly named Jacob? for he hath supplanted me these two times: he took away my birthright; and, behold, now he hath taken away my blessing. And he said, hast thou not reserved a blessing for me?" (Genesis 27:36)

When Isaac was old, he determined to bless his oldest son, Esau, with the blessing normally reserved for the oldest son. This would normally have been appropriate, except that God had told his wife that Esau, the elder son, would serve Jacob, the younger. He made plans with Esau to bless him, asking him to prepare some venison, a favorite of his. Rebekah overheard, and decided to take matters into her own hands. Together with Jacob, she successfully deceived Isaac into giving the blessing of the older son to Jacob. The words of today's verse are Esau's words of remorse when he and Isaac realized what had happened.

Notice that Esau blamed Jacob for "taking away my birthright". This, of course, is a selfish twisting of the truth; he had knowingly and foolishly <u>sold</u> it.

Scripture to read: Genesis 27:1-36

Question to ponder: *Why do we shift the blame for our misdeeds to others?*

Day 69   Date: _____

No Place of Repentance

"Lest there be any fornicator, or profane person, as Esau, who for one morsel of meat sold his birthright. For ye know how that afterward, when he would have inherited the blessing, he was rejected: for he found no place of repentance, though he sought it carefully with tears."
(Hebrews 12:16-17)

Genuine repentance (see Lesson 37) involves a change in <u>direction</u>. It is not merely being sorry for our sins, or being sorry we were caught! When Esau discovered that he had not only lost the birthright, but now the blessing also, he cried bitter tears. But, as our verse for today indicates, his tears could not undo what was already done. Some of sin's consequences cannot be undone in this life. Esau found no place of repentance – no way to change the direction of events that would unfold.

Unfortunately, he compounded his sin by hating his twin brother and plotting to kill him. Jacob also reaped the consequences of his deceit. He would be forced to flee for his life.

Scripture to read: Genesis 27:37-46

Question to ponder: *Was Esau really repentant?*

Day 70   Date: _____

Godly Sorrow

"For godly sorrow worketh repentance to salvation not to be repented of: but the sorrow of the world worketh death." (II Corinthians 7:10)

The apostle Paul, in his second letter to the church at Corinth, expressed joy that the people of that church had responded positively to his first letter. In that letter he rebuked them for several problems in their church. The letter made them sorry, but then they set about to make the <u>corrections</u> Paul had called for. They demonstrated true repentance: not simply <u>sorrow</u> over sin, but a <u>change of direction</u> in a positive manner.

Esau was sorry for what he had foolishly lost, and for what was taken from him by deceit, but he did not demonstrate godly repentance. His bitterness and plot to kill his brother proved that his sorrow had not changed him.

Scripture to read: II Corinthians 7:8-13

Question to ponder: *Are there areas of my life where I have not demonstrated godly repentance?*

| Day 71 | Date: _____ |

Only One God

"I am the LORD, and there is none else, there is no God beside me: I girded thee, though thou hast not known me: That they may know from the rising of the sun, and from the west, that there is none beside me. I am the LORD, and there is none else." (Isaiah 45:5-6)

The first of the Ten Commandments states *"Thou shalt have no other gods before me"* (see Lesson 13). Because man is created for fellowship with God, only a fool would say, *"There is no God"* (Psalms 14:1 and 53:1). Man naturally seeks a god to worship, and indeed every civilization throughout history has worshipped a god, or many gods. However, because of his sin nature, man usually chooses to worship a <u>false</u> god he has created in his own mind or with his own hands.

Today's scripture reading describes the folly of worshipping false gods. Our God is a <u>living</u> God. The false gods of unbelievers have no life, and those that worship them have no spiritual life (verse 8).

Scripture to read: Psalms 115:1-8

Question to ponder: *Am I unknowingly worshipping any false gods, which I may have put ahead of God?*

Day 72   Date: _____

The Trinity

"For there are three that bear record in heaven, the Father, the Word, and the Holy Ghost: and these three are one." (I John 5:7)

The doctrine of the Trinity – that God is three distinct persons in one God – is one of the hardest for our minds to comprehend. Indeed, it is beyond our understanding. Today's text verse is one of the plainest statements on the Trinity in the Bible. No doubt this is why most modern Bible versions leave it out, falsely claiming that it lacks the authority to be included with scripture (see Lesson 66).

When God created man He said, "*Let us make man in our image*" (Genesis 1:26). The Hebrew word used for "God" in Genesis, chapter one, is "Elohim". It is a "uni-plural" noun indicating plurality within unity. Man, created in God's image, has a body, soul, and spirit (see Lesson 62).

Today's scripture reading is the account of the baptism of Jesus at the beginning of His earthly ministry. Here we see the Father (from Heaven), the Son (Jesus), and the Spirit all present at once.

Scripture to read: Matthew 3:13-17

Question to ponder: *Should we be able to fully comprehend our God?*

Day 73   Date: _____

Everlasting to Everlasting

"Before the mountains were brought forth, or ever thou hadst formed the earth and the world, even from everlasting to everlasting, thou art God." (Psalms 90:2)

On the first day of creation *"God divided the light from the darkness. And God called the light Day, and the darkness he called Night. And the evening and the morning were the first day."* This was the beginning of time as recorded in Genesis 1:4-5. Time was created for man. God exists <u>outside</u> of the limitations of time, in <u>eternity</u>. He sees *"the end from the beginning"* (*Isaiah 46:10*). God has never had a beginning and will never end. Truly, He is *"from everlasting to everlasting"*.

In today's scripture reading, God's <u>eternality</u> is contrasted with the fleeting nature of our lives. In light of the fact that God lives forever, and our lives on earth are so short, we are admonished *"So teach us to number our days, that we may apply our hearts unto wisdom."*

Scripture to read: Psalms 90:1-17

Question to ponder: *Since our lives on this earth are so short, what should be our highest priority?*

Day 74   Date: _____

God Almighty

"And God Almighty bless thee, and make thee fruitful, and multiply thee, that thou mayest be a multitude of people." (Genesis 28:3)

Esau hated his younger twin brother and planned to kill him as soon as their father, Isaac, died. Rebekah heard of his plans and arranged with Isaac for Jacob to flee to her brother, Laban. As he said farewell to his son, Isaac blessed him as recorded in today's verse, and furthermore acknowledged that the promise made originally to Abraham was now Jacob's.

In so doing, Isaac referred to God as *"God Almighty"*. This refers to the omnipotence of God, meaning that His power is infinite. There are no limits to God's power. This is clearly seen in creation. What greater display of power could there be than to speak and call this vast world into existence "out of nothing"?

Scripture to read: Genesis 28:1-5

Question to ponder: *Is there any reason for God to fear being "overthrown" by a superior power?*

Day 75   Date: _____

Omniscient and Omnipresent

"Whither shall I go from thy spirit? or whither shall I flee from thy presence?" (Psalms 139:7)

The first six verses of this psalm describe in very personal language the depth of the knowledge of God. Not only is His knowledge of everything and anything without limit, but that infinite knowledge includes my very thoughts! David, the author of this (and most) psalms, exclaims, *"Such knowledge is too wonderful for me; it is high, I cannot attain unto it."*

The next verses describe a fruitless "effort" to escape the presence of God. We cannot, for God is "everywhere present", or "omnipresent". No matter where we flee to, we find God present there. These two truths, the omniscience ("omni" = all; "science" = knowledge) and omnipresence of God are both alarming and comforting. Alarming if we seek to rebel against God; comforting if we seek His fellowship.

The psalm concludes with a prayer to use these attributes of God for a holy purpose.

Scripture to read: Psalms 139:1-24

Question to ponder: *If I need help, will I ever be away from the awareness or assistance of God?*

Day 76   Date: _____

The Wisdom of God

"O the depths of the riches both of the wisdom and knowledge of God! how unsearchable are his judgments, and his ways past finding out!" (Romans 11:33)

Wisdom and knowledge are two different things. Knowledge refers to an accumulation and retention of information. Wisdom is, among other things, the proper <u>application</u> of knowledge. God's wisdom, like His other attributes, is <u>infinite</u>. There is no end to the wisdom of God.

We refer to an older person as wise when we see that they are able to avoid mistakes that other people make. We seek their "wisdom" to help us avoid mistakes that could be costly to us. God does all things <u>perfectly</u> and makes no mistakes. When we see something that would cause us to question if God has erred, it means only that <u>we</u> lack the knowledge and understanding of God. God not only does everything in the best possible way, but a better way could not possibly be imagined!

Scripture to read: Romans 11:33-36

Question to ponder: *Should I question "why?" or should I ask God to help me see as He sees?*

Day 77   Date: _____

No Shadow of Turning

"Every good gift and every perfect gift is from above, and cometh down from the Father of lights, with whom is no variableness, neither shadow of turning." (James 1:17)

One of the things we must learn to live with in this world is change. It is often said that the one thing that never changes in this world is change. How wonderful to know that our God is immutable, He never changes!

If God were to change, how would He? He could not change for the better, for He is perfect as He is. He could not change for the worse, for then He would cease to be God. Whenever we come to God we find Him the same as always – ready to receive us and to meet our deepest needs! In this world of constant change, we have a God who we can depend upon.

Scripture to read: Psalms 102:25-28

Question to ponder: *In what ways does God's immutability guarantee my salvation?*

Day 78   Date: _____

I Will Not Leave Thee

"And, behold, I am with thee, and will keep thee in all places whither thou goest, and will bring thee again into this land; for I will not leave thee, until I have done that which I have spoken to thee of." (Genesis 28:15)

As Jacob left his home to flee to his Uncle Laban no doubt his heart was filled with fear over the future. How would he be received by Laban? Would he ever see his parents or his homeland again? Would he be a fugitive from Esau for the rest of his life?

One night, while using stones for pillows as he slept, God appeared to Jacob in a dream. Jacob saw a ladder stretched from earth to heaven, with the angels of God ascending and descending on it and God Himself standing above it. Here, God confirmed that the promise originally given to Abraham (see Lesson 46) would pass on through Jacob's line. His promise also included a reminder of the eternal faithfulness of God, another of the wonderful attributes of our infinite God.

Scripture to read: Genesis 28:10-22

Question to ponder: *In what ways is God's faithfulness a comfort to me?*

Day 79   Date: _____

The Righteous Judge

"All the ways of a man are clean in his own eyes; but the LORD weigheth the spirits." (Proverbs 16:2)

We all have our own ideas about what is just and fair. We usually find a way to justify ourselves, however. Our concept of justice is very self-centered. The Proverbs is a book of wise sayings, given to man from God. Our text verse for today reminds us that there is <u>one</u> objective Judge over all, Who renders impartial justice over His creation.

It is not enough to say that God is <u>just</u>, or <u>fair</u>. That would imply that God is obligated to perform to a standard outside of Himself. Rather, <u>God Himself</u> – His ways and His being – is the standard that defines justice. If God does it, it <u>is</u> just and equitable, simply because that is the way He is!

In our scripture reading for today, David appeals to God for justice in a situation where he had been falsely accused. Notice God's attitude toward sin in verse 11. Remember that we are all born into sin.

Scripture to read: Psalms 7:1-17

Question to ponder: *If God is angry with the wicked every day, what hope did I have prior to salvation?*

Day 80   Date: _____

His Mercy Endureth Forever

"O give thanks unto the LORD; for he is good: for his mercy endureth for ever." (Psalms 136:1)

People often say they only want what they deserve. If we received from God's hand what we <u>deserved</u> we would all plunge immediately into eternal judgment! <u>Mercy</u> is defined as withholding judgment that is due. God's mercy is His infinite compassion and goodness in action, withholding from us the judgment that we deserve. How comforting to know that God's mercy never ends! Today's scripture is a song of praise for God's mercy, especially as it had been revealed in the history of the nation Israel.

A contradiction exists between the infinite <u>justice</u> of God, demanding punishment for sin, and the infinite <u>mercy</u> of God, demanding compassion and forgiveness to the sinner. These two are reconciled in the work of the Savior. God's justice was satisfied by the death of Christ so His mercy could be extended to all who receive the gift of salvation.

Scripture to read: Psalms 136:1-26

Question to ponder: *If God's mercy endures for ever, can I ever lose my salvation?*

Day 81   Date: _____

Grace that Gives

"But grow in grace, and in the knowledge of our Lord and Saviour Jesus Christ. To him be glory both now and for ever. Amen." (II Peter 3:18)

<u>Grace</u> is defined as unmerited favor. All that we receive from God is of grace, because we are not deserving of anything good. We are saved by grace. But God doesn't stop there! After giving us salvation He continues to bless our lives with numberless blessings. All this at no cost to us! But it cost Him <u>everything</u>! He gave His only begotten Son. God's grace has been defined by the acrostic: **G**od's **R**iches **A**t **C**hrist's **E**xpense.

In our scripture reading for today, the apostle Peter describes some of the riches we have because of God's grace. The text verse above is the closing benediction in this letter of Peter's.

Scripture to read: II Peter 1:1-11

Question to ponder: *How is it possible for God's grace to be multiplied (increased) in my life according to today's scripture?*

Day 82   Date: _____

Rachel and Leah

"And Jacob served seven years for Rachel; and they seemed unto him but a few days, for the love he had to her." (Genesis 29:20)

When Jacob found his Uncle Laban's family they were glad to receive him and hear news of Rebekah. After a month Laban proposed that Jacob be paid for his service to him. Laban had two daughters, Leah and Rachel. Jacob offered to serve seven years if Laban would give the younger, Rachel, to him as his wife. Laban agreed and as today's verse indicates, Jacob served the seven years.

Now, Jacob was about to meet his match in trickery. The wedding feast was called and Jacob was given his wife. In the morning Jacob discovered that the girl behind the veil was not Rachel, but Leah. He was forced to work another seven years for Rachel.

Although multiple wives were common among Old Testament men, God does not condone the practice. The correct pattern for marriage is given in the story of Adam and Eve in *Genesis 2:21-24*.

Scripture to read: Genesis 29:14-28

Question to ponder: *According to Genesis, chapter 2, how many wives should a man have?*

Day 83   Date: _____

Israel

"And he said, Thy name shall be called no more Jacob, but Israel: for as a prince hast thou power with God and with men, and hast prevailed." (Genesis 32:28)

Jacob stayed with Laban twenty years in total. During this time he had eleven sons by his two wives and their two handmaids. God blessed Jacob, and in spite of Laban's repeated efforts to cheat him his household and flocks increased exceedingly.

Jacob watched as his uncle and father-in-law increased in his jealousy over his prosperity. Finally, in a dream, God told Jacob to leave Laban and return to his homeland. Jacob left without telling Laban, was pursued and overcome by Laban, and finally made a covenant of peace with Laban.

As he was about to meet his brother Esau again, Jacob spent a sleepless night wrestling with an unnamed man. After wrestling to a draw, Jacob demanded a blessing of the man. The man responded as shown in today's text verse above.

Scripture to read: Genesis 32:22-32

Question to ponder: *The name Israel means "a prince of God". Was Jacob deserving of this name?*

Day 84   Date: _____

Twelve Sons

"And he lifted up his eyes, and saw the women and the children; and said, Who are those with thee? And he said, The children which God hath graciously given thy servant." (Genesis 33:5)

Jacob was greatly afraid to meet his brother Esau, especially when it was reported to him that Esau was coming to meet him with four hundred men! Jacob divided his company and sent presents ahead in an effort to appease Esau. When they finally met, however, Esau ran to him, embraced him, and wept for joy. God had also prospered him greatly and he had no desire for revenge.

Today's verse records Esau's question and Jacob's response regarding Jacob's family. Another son was born later to Jacob, at which time Rachel died in childbirth. The twelve sons of Jacob (Israel) are listed in *Genesis 35:23-26*. These sons became the fathers of the twelve tribes of the nation Israel.

Scripture to read: Genesis 33:1-17

Question to ponder: *Why do you suppose that it took until Jacob for the promise made to his grandfather (Abraham) and father (Isaac) to begin to take shape in the form of a large family?*

Day 85   Date: _____

God is Light

"This then is the message which we have heard of him, and declare unto you, that God is light, and in him is no darkness at all." (I John 1:5)

The Bible gives us many statements about God in an effort to help us understand Him. One such statement is *"God is light"*. We understand the difference between light and darkness in everyday life. In the Bible, light speaks of God and truth. Darkness speaks of sin, because those who are lost in sin cannot see. Today's scripture reading tells how Satan, the "god of this world", uses the darkness of sin to keep people from the gospel.

On the first day of creation, God said, *"Let there be light" (Genesis 1:3)*. The words used in the original language of the Old Testament (Hebrew) do not indicate a creative act, but rather that the light was caused to appear (into the newly created heavens and earth). Light had already existed (from eternity past) because *"God is light"*.

Scripture to read: II Corinthians 4:1-6

Question to ponder: *What does it mean, "in him is no darkness at all"?*

Day 86   Date: _____

God is Love

"He that loveth not knoweth not God; for God is love." (I John 4:8)

In the writing of the New Testament, God used two Greek words for "love". One refers to "brotherly love", and the other to the highest kind of love, the kind of love God shows to us. It is a love that gives sacrificially. This love was demonstrated by God <u>giving</u> His Son for us. In verse 10 of today's scripture reading, the word "propitiation" means that the penalty for our sins was <u>satisfied completely</u> by Jesus' death on the cross.

But, love is not merely something God <u>does</u>. Love is what God <u>is</u>! We learn what love is, and how it acts, by observing God. His character and actions <u>define</u> love. If God does it, it <u>is</u> loving! Often, God is accused of being unloving. This is not true. Rather, we have an inaccurate understanding of love and seek to hold God accountable to our definition of love. We need to learn to define love by what God says love is and does.

Scripture to read: I John 4:7-21

Question to ponder: *Is love merely a sentimental feeling, or is it something beyond that?*

Day 87   Date: _____

God Exalted High Above All

"For thou, LORD, art high above all the earth: thou art exalted far above all gods." (Psalms 97:9)

When the above verse speaks of God as being *"high above all the earth"* it is not speaking of altitude. God certainly dwells in Heaven as a place of residence, but His omnipresence means He is to be found throughout His creation. Instead, this verse is speaking of God being exalted in the quality of His being. God is far above all else in that He is the Creator, without beginning or end, and all else is created.

In fact, there is an infinite distance between God and all else. We may be higher in order and quality of being than a plant or an insect, but God is infinitely higher than we are. There is an immeasurable distance between God and the highest of His creation. In *Isaiah 40:18*, Isaiah asks, *"To whom then will ye liken God? or what likeness will ye compare unto him?"* The answer of course, is that God cannot be compared legitimately to anything.

Scripture to read: Psalms 8:1-9

Question to ponder: *Does God care for us because of something about us, or something about Him?*

Day 88   Date: _____

Things Too Wonderful for Me

"Who is he that hideth counsel without knowledge? therefore have I uttered that I understood not; things too wonderful for me, which I knew not." (Job 42:3)

God encourages us to learn about Him, for He teaches us that *"He is a rewarder of them that diligently seek him" (Hebrews 11:6).* Yet, in actuality, we are ill equipped to understand God. When Job was in the midst of his trials (see Lesson 45), he cried out to God for answers. God responded, not with the answers Job sought, but with a rapid-fire sequence of over seventy questions (chapters 38-41). In the end Job had to surrender to God's infinitely superior knowledge and wisdom.

We know of God what God has chosen to reveal about Himself. This revelation is found in creation and the Bible. There are things that are *"too wonderful"* for us to understand. If we could, we would be greater than God for we would be able to contain His sum total within our minds. Praise God that He is higher than we are!

Scripture to read: Ezekiel 1:25-28

Question to ponder: *In today's scripture reading, why do you suppose the prophet Ezekiel uses such vague language to describe his vision of God?*

Unit Three Review
Lessons 61 to 88

List the key people in Jacob's family tree found in the lessons noted in parenthesis:

Grandfather (67): _____

Parents (67): _____ _____

Brother (67): _____

Wives (82): _____ _____

Sons (84): _____ _____ _____
_____ _____ _____
_____ _____ _____
_____ _____ _____

List something you learned about the Bible from each of these lessons:

Lesson 61: _____

Lesson 62: _____

Lesson 63: _____

Lesson 64: _____

Lesson 65: _____

Lesson 66: _____

From lessons 71 to 88, list some attributes of God:

_____ _____ _____ _____

_____ _____ _____ _____

_____ _____ _____ _____

_____ _____ _____ _____

BOOKS OF THE BIBLE BY GROUP

The Old Testament

The Books of the Law: *Genesis, Exodus, Leviticus, Numbers, Deuteronomy*

The Books of History: *Joshua, Judges, Ruth, I Samuel, II Samuel, I Kings, II Kings, I Chronicles, II Chronicles, Ezra, Nehemiah, Esther*

The Books of Poetry: *Job, Psalms, Proverbs, Ecclesiastes, Song of Solomon*

The Major Prophets: *Isaiah, Jeremiah, Lamentations, Ezekiel, Daniel*

The Minor Prophets: *Hosea, Joel, Amos, Obadiah, Jonah, Micah, Nahum, Habakkuk, Zephaniah, Haggai, Zechariah, Malachi*

The New Testament

The Gospels and Acts: *Matthew, Mark Luke, John, Acts*

The Epistles: *Romans, I Corinthians, II Corinthians, Galatians, Ephesians, Philippians, Colossians, I Thessalonians, II Thessalonians, I Timothy, II Timothy, Titus, Philemon, Hebrews, James, I Peter, II Peter, I John, II John, III John, Jude*

Prophecy: *Revelation*

Unit Four

Lessons 89 to 121

Bible History

Joseph
Captivity in Egypt
Moses

Bible Truths

God the Father
God the Son

Day 89   Date: _____

The First Person of the Trinity

"Ye have heard how I said unto you, I go away, and come again unto you. If ye loved me, ye would rejoice, because I said, I go unto the Father: for my Father is greater than I." (John 14:28)

The three persons of the Trinity (Father, Son, and Spirit) are co-equals with each other (see Lesson 72). They work together in unity and perfect harmony. God, however, is a God of order. Accordingly, there exists an order within the Trinity. The Father is the "first person" of the Trinity.

In today's verse, Jesus refers to the Father as *"greater than I"*. This does not refer to an inequality within the Trinity, but an arrangement of order. Jesus, as the "second person" of the Trinity, deferred to the Father. He often spoke of "doing the Father's will". Just as our body does the will of our mind, acting at its direction, so the Son performs the Father's will. It is the Father that is the initiator within the Trinity. Notice in today's scripture reading that it is the Father that sent both the Son and the Spirit (Holy Ghost).

Scripture to read: John 14:23-31

Question to ponder: *What happens in any organization that does not have a clearly defined head?*

Day 90   Date: _____

Our Heavenly Father

"If ye then, being evil, know how to give good gifts unto your children, how much more shall your Father which is in heaven give good things to them that ask him?" (Matthew 7:11)

The Bible not only teaches that the Father is the Son's Father, but ours as well! When we receive the Son as our Savior, we become "the sons of God" (see Lesson 38). This is accomplished by God Himself – He makes us His sons!

Our fathers on earth are imperfect and often fail us. Our Heavenly Father loves us with a perfect love and never fails to do what is best for us. He is eager to give us good things when we ask, as today's verse encourages us. He also corrects us when we need correction, but always in a manner that seeks to strengthen and improve us.

Scripture to read: Matthew 7:7-11

Question to ponder: *Do earthly fathers give their sons everything they ask for, especially if they know it is not good for them?*

Day 91 Date: _____

Father and Son

"And now, O Father, glorify thou me with thine own self with the glory which I had with thee before the world was." (John 17:5)

In today's scripture we listen in as the Son prays to the Father only hours before going to the cross to bear the penalty for our sin. Here we find intimate conversation revealing the heart of our God in fellowship within the Trinity.

The terms "Father" and "Son" are used to convey to us a closeness of relationship between the first two persons of the Trinity. In no way does the use of these terms indicate that the Father existed before the Son, as is the case in earthly father-son relationships. This Father-Son relationship has existed for all eternity!

Scripture to read: John 17:1-11

Question to ponder: *What does verse 5 teach us about the Father and the Son?*

Day 92 Date: _____
Beloved of His Father

"Now Israel loved Joseph more than all his children, because he was the son of his old age: and he made him a coat of many colours."
(Genesis 37:3)

Favoritism had wrought much damage in the household of Isaac and Rebekah. Now, Israel (Jacob) continued this fault in the rearing of his children. Of his twelve sons, <u>Joseph</u> was his favorite. Joseph was the oldest son of his favorite wife, <u>Rachel</u>. Israel made a special coat for Joseph, clearly indicating his intent to grant Joseph the position of eldest son (see Lesson 67). His ten older (half) brothers hated him for this. The problem was compounded by dreams Joseph had which seemed to indicate he would rule over his brothers, and even his parents.

Just as much of his grandfather Isaac's life pictured that of Jesus Christ (see Lessons 57-60), so Joseph's life points to the Savior. Just as the Son is specially beloved of the Father, so Joseph was by Israel.

Scripture to read: Genesis 37:1-11

Question to ponder: *Does God treat His children equally?*

Day 93   Date: _____

Sold into Egypt

"Then there passed by Midianites merchantmen; and they drew and lifted up Joseph out of the pit, and sold Joseph to the Ishmeelites for twenty pieces of silver: and they brought Joseph into Egypt." (Genesis 37:28)

One day his brothers saw an opportunity to rid themselves of Joseph. Having been sent by his father to check on the state of his flocks, Joseph was taken by his brothers and sold into slavery. The brothers then devised a scheme whereby their father was led to believe that Joseph was dead. The brothers watched their father grieve bitterly, but allowed him to believe the lie anyway.

Approximately 1,700 years later, the Heavenly Father sent His beloved Son to His brethren, the Israelite people. They rejected Him and crucified Him. Interestingly, the price received to betray the Lord Jesus Christ was thirty pieces of silver (*Matthew 26:14-16*). The price the brothers received for Joseph was twenty pieces of silver.

Scripture to read: Genesis 37:12-36

Question to ponder: *When people are blinded by their sin, who do they often hurt by their actions?*

Day 94   Date: _____

Fleeing Temptation

"There is none greater in this house than I; neither hath he kept back any thing from me but thee, because thou art his wife: how then can I do this great wickedness, and sin against God?"
(Genesis 39:9)

Upon arriving in Egypt, Joseph was sold into the household of Potiphar, the captain of the Egyptian guard. God allowed Joseph to find favor (grace) in Potiphar's eyes and soon he was made manager of all Potiphar's house. Potiphar's wife began to seduce Joseph, seeking to lure him into adultery. Joseph refused continually, and one day when Potiphar was away had to flee from the house in order to resist her advances. She lied to her husband and Joseph was thrown into prison.

Joseph was a man of godly character. He resisted a sin many would have given in to. Notice that he saw the sin in question not only as a sin against his master, but as <u>against God</u>. Joseph understood the true nature of sin. All sin is against God. Also notice how Joseph handled temptation. He <u>fled</u>!

Scripture to read: Genesis 39:1-23

Question to ponder: *What would happen in my life if I saw each sin as being against God?*

Day 95   Date: _____

From Everlasting

"But thou, Bethlehem Ephratah, though thou be little among the thousands of Judah, yet out of thee shall he come forth unto me that is to be ruler in Israel; whose goings forth have been from of old, from everlasting."
(Micah 5:2)

<u>Micah</u> was a prophet who lived about 700 years before Christ was born. Here, at God's inspiration, he predicts that the promised Savior, who would be a king, would be born in the insignificant town of Bethlehem. Notice that this promised One is described as being <u>eternal</u>.

In today's scripture reading Paul, the author of *Romans*, calls this promised One, Jesus Christ, the *"Son of God"*. Micah was only one of several prophets who foretold His birth. Notice that verse three says that Jesus *"was made of the seed of David according to the flesh"*. Jesus was born into the lineage of King David of Israel. But, he existed prior to that *"from everlasting"* as the second person of the Trinity.

Scripture to read: Romans 1:1-8

Question to ponder: *How could Micah accurately predict the birthplace of the Savior 700 years in advance?*

Day 96   Date: _____

In the Beginning was the Word

"In the beginning was the Word, and the Word was with God, and the Word was God." (John 1:1)

Today's scripture is a key passage teaching us much about Jesus Christ. He is called the "Word" because He <u>communicates</u> to us what we need to know about God. Notice the similarity of our text verse with the very first verse of the Bible, *"In the beginning God created the heaven and the earth"* (*Genesis 1:1*). Jesus Christ, the Word of God, was with God "in the beginning". That means He is eternal God, as the verse says. Modern cults claim this verse means Jesus Christ is "a god", but that is an inaccurate interpretation. The original Greek wording very specifically says the Word was "<u>the</u> God".

Notice verses three and ten. Jesus Christ, the second person of the Trinity, is as much the Creator as God the Father! He is the source of <u>life</u> (verse four). He is also called by another of His titles, "the Light".

Scripture to read: John 1:1-10

Question to ponder: *What does it mean he "lighteth every man that cometh into the world"?*

Day 97   Date: _____

All the Fulness of the Godhead Bodily

"For in him dwelleth all the fulness of the Godhead bodily."
(Colossians 2:9)

The apostle Paul wrote this letter to a church in the eastern European city of Colosse. In it, he addresses those who taught that Jesus Christ was not God. Notice verse fifteen from today's scripture reading. God the Father is invisible, but we see His image in His Son, Jesus Christ. Today's text verse refers to His having a body, yet being fully God. Chapter one, verse nineteen, also expresses that Jesus Christ is not limited in His deity.

In today's scripture we also see again that Jesus Christ is presented as the Creator. As the *"firstborn of every creature"* He has an exalted position over all created beings. Verse seventeen teaches that He not only created everything, but He is actively overseeing His creation and keeping it together (*"by him all things consist"*). Jesus Christ is to have preeminence (first place) over all things!

Scripture to read: Colossians 1:12-19

Question to ponder: *Why would anyone seek to undermine the truth about who Jesus Christ is?*

Day 98   Date: _____

The Word was made Flesh

"And the Word was made flesh, and dwelt among us, (and we beheld his glory, the glory as of the only begotten of the Father,) full of grace and truth." (John 1:14)

The first verse of the gospel of *John* declares that the Word was in the beginning with God, and was God (see Lesson 96). Today's verse adds that the Word, having existed from everlasting (see Lesson 95), became <u>flesh</u> (a man) and lived on earth with man. This is speaking, of course, of Jesus Christ.

When we speak of God becoming man, in the person of Jesus Christ, we are speaking of His "incarnation". In the first of three letters written later in his life (see Lesson 42), John is very careful to specify that he, and the rest of the apostles, were eye witnesses of the life of the Word. In today's scripture notice how carefully John testifies of what he witnessed. In today's text verse, notice that John was certain not only of the humanity of Christ, but also of His deity.

Scripture to read: I John 1:1-4

Question to ponder: *How many proofs does John give in I John 1:1 of his testimony?*

Day 99   Date: _____

He Hath Declared Him

"Jesus saith unto him, Have I been so long time with you, and yet hast thou not known me, Philip? he that hath seen me hath seen the Father; and how sayest thou then, Shew us the Father?" (John 14:9)

In today's verse Jesus is responding to a question from one of his disciples, Philip. Philip had asked Jesus to show (shew) the Father to the disciples. His answer declares the truth that the three persons of the Trinity (Father, Son, and Holy Spirit) are one (*I John 5:7*, see Lesson 72).

The eighteenth verse from today's scripture reading explains further. God the Father is invisible (see Lesson 97, *Colossians 1:15*). It is the second person of the Trinity, the Son, who is visible. He is the One who communicates God to us in a form in which we can see.

(The John of verses six and fifteen of chapter one is John the Baptist, not the author of this gospel.)

Scripture to read: John 1:14-18

Question to ponder: *Which of our three "parts" communicates ourselves visibly to others (body, soul, or spirit)?*

Day 100   Date: _____

The Likeness of Men

"But made himself of no reputation, and took upon him the form of a servant, and was made in the likeness of men" (Philippians 2:7)

Jesus Christ is our great example for living. In today's scripture, we read of the tremendous <u>humility</u> that He demonstrated in leaving the glory that He had in Heaven with the Father (see Lesson 91) to become a man. We are admonished to have the same mind of humility as the Savior.

God the Son changed his <u>visible</u> appearance from that of God (verse six) to that of a man (verse seven). More than that, he was born into the human race to become as fully <u>human</u> as He was fully <u>God</u>. All this was done for a purpose. He further humbled Himself to die for our sins on a cross. *"For as by one man's disobedience <Adam> many were made sinners, so by the obedience of one <man> shall many be made righteous." (Romans 5:19).*

Scripture to read: Philippians 2:1-8

Question to ponder: *If God the Son could so humble Himself to help me, is there any reason I should be too proud to identify with Him?*

Day 101   Date: _____

A Name Above Every Name

"Wherefore God also hath highly exalted him, and given him a name which is above every name" (Philippians 2:9)

The <u>name</u> of Jesus Christ is used in many ways today. Most of those ways are not honoring to Him. Many use His name as a curse word. Others throw it around casually without regard for Who it represents.

One day <u>every</u> person will bow his or her knee in reverence to that Holy name. God the Father has exalted the name of Jesus Christ above every other. At that day, <u>every</u> person will confess (admit) that Jesus Christ is <u>Lord</u>. This will bring glory to the Father, because He has chosen to exalt His Son in this way. It is only through His name that we find salvation (see Lesson 33).

The word "*Lord*" refers to a title of authority. Jesus told his disciples, "*All power <authority> is given unto me" (Matthew 28:18).*

Scripture to read: Philippians 2:9-11

Question to ponder: *What are some ways in which the <u>name</u> of Jesus Christ is dishonored today?*

Day 102   Date: _____

Pharaoh's Dream

"And Joseph said unto Pharaoh, The dream of Pharaoh is one: God hath shewed Pharaoh what he is about to do." (Genesis 41:25)

Soon after Joseph was put into prison by Potiphar (see Lesson 94) he impressed the keeper of the prison and was put in charge of the other prisoners. One day the king's butler and baker offended the king and were put into the same prison as Joseph. After some time each dreamed a dream which they could not interpret. Joseph replied that God was able to interpret dreams (*Genesis 40:8*). If they would tell him their dreams he would pray to God and give them the interpretation. This was done, and the interpretations given by Joseph proved to be true. The butler was restored back into Pharaoh's service, and the baker was hanged.

Today's scripture reading tells how, two years later, Pharaoh dreamed two dreams which troubled him. The butler remembered Joseph and he was called in to meet Pharaoh. Joseph interpreted his dream and was made second only to Pharaoh in all Egypt.

Scripture to read: Genesis 41:14-44

Question to ponder: *Could I remain faithful to God in such adverse circumstances as Joseph experienced?*

Day 103   Date: _____

A Great Nation

"And he said, I am God, the God of thy father: fear not to go down into Egypt; for I will there make of thee a great nation" (Genesis 46:3)

The famine foretold in Pharaoh's dream came, as God had said, after seven years of plenty. Egypt, because of Joseph's wise management, had storehouses full of food. All countries came to Egypt to purchase needed food from Joseph.

Joseph's family also was affected by the famine. Jacob (Israel) sent Joseph's ten older brothers to buy food for the family. Joseph recognized his brothers immediately, but they did not recognize him because he looked like an Egyptian. *Genesis, chapters 42 to 46*, tells the story of how Joseph tested his brothers to see if they were still as evil as before. He discovered that they had changed, he revealed himself to them, and he had Jacob and his entire family move to Egypt where he could provide for them. Today's text verse is God's promise to Jacob to bless his family while in Egypt. In Egypt, part of the promise originally made to Abraham (see Lesson 46) would become a reality.

Scripture to read: Genesis 45:16-28

Question to ponder: *How do you suppose Jacob felt when he learned that Joseph was still alive?*

Day 104   Date: _____

God Meant it Unto Good

"But as for you, ye thought evil against me; but God meant it unto good, to bring to pass, as it is this day, to save much people alive." (Genesis 50:20)

Jacob and his family settled in Egypt, in the fertile land of Goshen. The number that came from Canaan was 66; the total number including Joseph's wife and two sons was 70. Jacob lived another seventeen years in Egypt and died at the age of 147. The twelve sons carried his body back to Canaan to be buried where Abraham and Isaac were buried.

Upon returning to Egypt, Joseph's older brothers feared that he would now seek revenge against them. They approached him, begging for for-giveness, but Joseph had no plans to do evil against them. His reply, in our text verse above, showed his submission to the sovereign will of God. God had taken the evil deed of Joseph's brothers and turned it into good, for them and all Egypt. God's plans are not thwarted by our choosing to do wrong.

Scripture to read: Genesis 50:12-21

Question to ponder: *How does God's omniscience (Lesson 75) enable His plan to succeed in spite of our lack of cooperation?*

Day 105   Date: _____

A Virgin Shall Conceive

"Therefore the Lord himself shall give you a sign; Behold, a virgin shall conceive, and bear a son, and shall call his name Immanuel." (Isaiah 7:14)

The birth of Jesus Christ, which was God becoming man, was foretold many times by Old Testament prophets. Here, the prophet Isaiah revealed several circumstances of His birth over 700 years before it happened.

The fulfillment of this prophecy is recorded in today's scripture reading. A young virgin, <u>Mary</u>, *"was found with child of the Holy Ghost"*. <u>Joseph</u>, her betrothed husband, was not the father. This is important. It means Jesus was born of the seed of the woman (see Lesson 11) and that He did not have the sin nature that is passed on to all who are born of earthly fathers. This miraculous birth was a sign to the nation Israel that the promise originally given to Abraham (see Lesson 46) had been fulfilled.

The name "Immanuel" means "God with us". This is another Biblical proof of the deity of Jesus Christ.

Scripture to read: Matthew 1:18-25

Question to ponder: *How important is it to know that Mary was a virgin?*

Day 106   Date: _____

In Him Is No Sin

"And ye know that he was manifested to take away our sins; and in him is no sin." (I John 3:5)

Because He was God, Jesus Christ was sinless. Not only did He <u>never</u> commit any sins, He was not capable of committing any sin. This is called the <u>impeccability</u> of Christ. Contrary to what many teach today, it was <u>never</u> a possibility that Jesus would sin in any way.

When on earth Jesus was constantly confronted by many who sought to discredit Him. Over and over again He defended Himself against their groundless accusations, each time exposing the fallacy of their arguments. In today's scripture reading, Jesus openly challenged anyone to bring a credible charge of sin against Him. He said, in verse 46, *"Which of you convinceth me of sin?"* He followed up by asking why they did not believe in Him if they could prove no such charge against Him.

Scripture to read: John 8:34-46

Question to ponder: *Would I dare make such a challenge about myself?*

Day 107   Date: _____

Our Great High Priest

"Who being the brightness of his glory, and the express image of his person, and upholding all things by the word of his power, when he had by himself purged our sins, sat down on the right hand of the Majesty on high." (Hebrews 1:3)

When Christ's earthly ministry was finished He ascended back into Heaven and is today seated at the right hand of the Father. There He ministers to us as our High Priest. A priest is someone with a ministry of representing other persons before God. Prior to Christ's earthly ministry the priests of God, including the High Priests, were specially chosen men from a particular family.

Today, it is in the name of Jesus Christ that we have access to the Heavenly Father in prayer. Our scripture reading for today reminds us that Jesus, the Son of God, is a compassionate High Priest because He experienced every kind of temptation that we experience. The difference is that He never sinned!

Scripture to read: Hebrews 4:14- 5:10

Question to ponder: *Why does having Jesus Christ as our High Priest allow us to approach God the Father confidently?*

Day 108   Date: _____

One Mediator

"My little children, these things write I unto you, that ye sin not. And if any man sin, we have an advocate with the Father, Jesus Christ the righteous"
(I John 2:1)

John wrote to believers in very affectionate terms. His concern was to encourage them, and us, to keep from sinning. However, if (when) we sin after we have been born again we do not need to be afraid to approach our Heavenly Father. Jesus Christ is at His right hand to speak in our defense. The term "advocate" refers to the work of Jesus Christ acting as our "defense attorney": pleading our case, continually reminding the Father that He shed His blood to cleanse us from all our sin *(I John 1:7)*, and restoring us to fellowship with Him.

There is only one person qualified to perform this ministry. In today's scripture reading, taken from Paul's first letter to Timothy, we are instructed in the importance of prayer. In verse five, Paul writes that there is only one mediator between God and men. Contrary to what is taught by many today, the only mediator acceptable to the Father is His Son.

Scripture to read: I Timothy 2:1-5

Question to ponder: *Why do I need a mediator?*

Day 109   Date: _____

They Testify of Me

"Search the scriptures; for in them ye think ye have eternal life: and they are they which testify of me." (John 5:39)

The religious leaders of the day continually harassed Jesus, seeking to discredit all He did. They claimed He was not who He claimed to be. In this instance, Jesus directed their attention to the scriptures. They would have had the entire Old Testament available to them. He told them that if they would search the scriptures, they would discover that the scriptures supported His claims.

After His resurrection from the dead, Jesus appeared to two disciples who were perplexed by the reports coming out of Jerusalem. In today's scripture reading we see Jesus taking them on a tour of the Old Testament, showing them how the scriptures spoke of Him. <u>Jesus Christ is the central figure of the Bible, and of all history</u>!

Scripture to read: Luke 24:13-27

Question to ponder: *What do the initials B.C. and A.D. mean (i.e. 330 B.C. or 2002 A.D.)?*

Day 110   Date: _____

A New King Over Egypt

"And the children of Israel were fruitful, and increased abundantly, and multiplied, and waxed exceeding mighty; and the land was filled with them." (Exodus 1:7)

God kept His promise, and the family of Israel began to grow in number. Estimates at this point in their history, almost 400 years after their arrival in Egypt, are that they numbered over three million people.

The Bible tells that *"there arose up a new king over Egypt, which knew not Joseph"*. The Egyptians began to look on the children of Israel as a threat to their security. They made them slaves and made life hard for them. Still the Israelites multiplied. Pharaoh ordered their male children killed at birth.

The Book of *Exodus* is the story of the deliverance of the Jewish people from this bondage.

Scripture to read: Exodus 1:7-22

Question to ponder: *Why would God allow His chosen people to go through this hardship?*

Day 111   Date: _____

Moses

"And the child grew, and she brought him unto Pharaoh's daughter, and he became her son. And she called his name Moses: and she said, Because I drew him out of the water." (Exodus 2:10)

In spite of Pharaoh's order that all Jewish male children be killed at birth, one family took daring action to save their son. The mother made an ark of bulrushes, put her son into it, and set it in the river.

Pharaoh's daughter saw the baby boy, had compassion, and made him her adopted son. The boy's older sister, thinking quickly, arranged to have the boy's mother nurse him. The boy was named, Moses.

Moses received the finest Egyptian upbringing and education as the grandson of Pharaoh. He never forgot who his people were, however, and one day he had to flee from Egypt to save his own life after avenging one of his own people.

Scripture to read: Exodus 2:1-15

Question to ponder: *What would have happened to Moses if it were told that he had defended a slave?*

Day 112   Date: _____
The Angel of the LORD

"The angel of the LORD appeared unto him in a flame of fire out of the midst of a bush: and he looked, and, behold, the bush burned with fire, and the bush was not consumed." (Exodus 3:2)

When Moses fled from Egypt at the age of forty, he went into the land of Midian. There he was married, had a son, and lived for another forty years. Meanwhile God was looking upon the bondage of the children of Israel back in Egypt and was about to send a deliverer.

One day, while tending sheep, Moses' attention was caught by a bush burning with fire, but not consumed. As he approached the bush, God called out to him from the bush. The Bible says *"the angel of the LORD appeared unto him"*. In verse six of today's scripture reading, that same angel calls Himself *"the God of thy father"*. The "angel of the LORD" is an Old Testament appearance of Jesus Christ. This is called a *"theophany"*. Review Lesson 59 for another example.

Scripture to read: Exodus 3:1-12

Question to ponder: *Why could Jesus Christ appear as an angel in the Old Testament and not the New?*

Day 113   Date: _____

I AM THAT I AM

"And God said unto Moses, I AM THAT I AM: and he said, Thus shalt thou say unto the children of Israel, I AM hath sent me unto you." (Exodus 3:14)

Moses was afraid to return to Egypt. God told Moses to identify the God of Abraham, Isaac, and Jacob to the Jewish people by the name "I AM". It is the name by which He would be known to the Jewish people: <u>Jehovah</u>. The name means "the self-existent One". We owe our existence to God, and are dependent upon Him continually for even our very breath. God is dependent upon <u>no one</u> for His existence. He exists within Himself.

When questioned by some of His critics during his time on earth, Jesus responded, *"Before Abraham was, I am"*. He was claiming the name Jehovah ("I AM") as His own. The Jews knew what He was saying. They took up stones because the penalty for blasphemy was death by stoning. They understood Him, but did not believe Him.

Scripture to read: John 8:51-59

Question to ponder: *What would happen to me if God ceased to exist for even one instant?*

Day 114   Date: _____

I Will Come Again

"And if I go and prepare a place for you, I will come again, and receive you unto myself; that where I am, there ye may be also." (John 14:3)

One of the blessed truths of the Christian faith is that our Savior is coming back again someday. His disciples were troubled at His words that He would be leaving them. Jesus spoke words of comfort to them, and to us. He has left this earth, but is busy preparing a place for us to join Him in His Father's house (Heaven)!

<u>Thomas</u>, one of the disciples, questioned Jesus about how to get where he was going. Jesus responded that He <u>alone</u> is the way to the Father. The only way to dwell with the Father someday is to receive Christ as personal Savior. Accept the <u>truth</u> of His gospel, the eternal <u>life</u> He provides, and find the <u>way</u> to Heaven!

Scripture to read: John 14:1-6

Question to ponder: *Am I ready for Jesus Christ to return today?*

Day 115   Date: _____

The Alpha and Omega

"And when I saw him, I fell at his feet as dead. And he laid his right hand upon me, saying unto me, Fear not; I am the first and the last"
(Revelation 1:17)

People often wonder what Jesus looks like. Artists have their conceptions, but most are easily proved inaccurate from scripture. The apostle John saw a vision of Jesus Christ and recorded it in the last book of the Bible. He saw the Savior in his present glory.

Notice the description as given in our scripture reading today. *"His head and His hairs were white like wool, as white as snow; and His eyes were as a flame of fire"*. No wonder John's reaction was similar to Isaiah's when he saw a vision of God (see Lesson 6). Here we also see another title of the Lord, *"Alpha and Omega"*. These are the first and last letters of the Greek alphabet. Jesus Christ is the beginning and the ending, the sum total of all that can be written about God!

Scripture to read: Revelation 1:8-18

Question to ponder: *Why is there so much irreverence for Jesus Christ today?*

Day 116   Date: _____

Moses and Aaron

"And Moses and Aaron went and gathered together all the elders of the children of Israel" (Exodus 4:29)

When God appeared to Moses in the burning bush He told Moses that he had been chosen to lead the children of Israel out of Egypt. Moses had several objections and God answered them all. Still Moses persisted, so God told him He would use his older brother <u>Aaron</u> to do the speaking for Moses. Aaron joined Moses and the two of them went into Egypt to confront Pharaoh.

The Bible says in *Exodus 4:14* that God was <u>angry</u> with Moses because of his reluctance. Since we are made in His image, it should not be surprising to find that God displays many of the same emotions we are familiar with. The difference is that we often become angry over the wrong things, and often lose control over ourselves. God's anger is always a controlled emotion, used for a right purpose.

Scripture to read: Exodus 4:27-31

Question to ponder: *Do I make God angry by being unwilling to do what He asks of me?*

Day 117   Date: _____

Let My People Go

"And afterward Moses and Aaron went in, and told Pharaoh, Thus saith the LORD God of Israel, Let my people go, that they may hold a feast unto me in the wilderness." (Exodus 5:1)

Moses and Aaron went in to Pharaoh and delivered the message God had given them. Pharaoh responded that he did not know Israel's God. The Egyptians worshipped many gods, and Pharaoh would have believed his gods were more powerful than the God of Israel was because the Israelites were his slaves. He reasoned within himself that the Israelite people must have too much time on their hands, and increased the demands upon them.

This was not what Moses and Aaron expected, or hoped for. It made them very unpopular with the children of Israel. But God had a purpose in mind through all this.

Scripture to read: Exodus 5:1-23

Question to ponder: *Should we mistrust God when things do not go our way immediately?*

Day 118   Date: _____

Whom He Will He Hardeneth

"And the LORD said unto Moses, Pharaoh's heart is hardened, he refuseth to let the people go." (Exodus 7:14)

Moses and Aaron began to show Pharaoh the signs that God had given them. Pharaoh was unmoved.

Our scripture reading today is an interesting New Testament commentary on God's dealings with Pharaoh. God intended to use Pharaoh's hard heart to bring glory to Himself. Paul, in this passage in *Romans*, asks the question, how could Pharaoh be held accountable for his actions if it was God who hardened his heart? Or, if God (who knows everything) knows that a person is going to reject Him, how can we say that person has a free will? Is God unfair? The answer is that God is sovereign over His creation and has the right to do with it as He pleases. We must trust Him that He is good and has a good purpose to all that He does.

Scripture to read: Romans 9:14-23

Question to ponder: *If we could understand everything there is to understand about God would we be lesser or greater than He is?*

Day 119   Date: _____

None Like Unto the LORD our God

"And he said, To morrow. And he said, Be it according to thy word: that thou mayest know that there is none like unto the LORD our God."
  (Exodus 8:10)

As Pharaoh continued to refuse God's demands to *"Let my people go"*, God began to demonstrate His mighty power to him. God intended to show Pharaoh that the God of Israel was different than all the false gods the Egyptians worshipped. In this instance God had plagued Egypt with frogs. Pharaoh called Moses and told him to ask God to remove the frogs. Moses asked when he wanted this done. Interestingly, Pharaoh said *"to morrow"*.

In today's scripture reading the prophet Jeremiah describes the folly of false gods, and they that worship them (the heathen). He contrasts these gods, made with the hands of them that worship them, with the true and living God. Truly, there is none like unto our God!

Scripture to read: Jeremiah 10:1-16

Question to ponder: *What are some ways in which we "learn the way of the heathen" (verse 2) today?*

Day 120   Date: _____

The Plagues of Egypt

"And Pharaoh said unto him, Get thee from me, take heed to thyself, see my face no more; for in that day thou seest my face thou shalt die."
(Exodus 10:28)

God began to send plague after plague upon the land of Egypt. After each plague, Pharaoh would soften. Once the plague was removed, however, his heart would harden again and he would refuse to let the children of Israel go. God sent nine plagues before Pharaoh spoke the words of our text verse. River waters turned to blood, frogs, lice, flies, murrain (a pestilence affecting animals), boils, hail, locusts, and darkness. The tenth, and final, plague would be the worst.

In the *78th Psalm*, Asaph, a leading musician of Israel, reviews the history of Israel to his day. In today's scripture reading he refers to the plagues of Egypt.

Scripture to read: Psalms 78:42-52

Question to ponder: *Why does it often take so much to get us to listen to God?*

Day 121   Date: _____

The Passover Lamb

"The next day John seeth Jesus coming unto him, and saith, Behold the Lamb of God, which taketh away the sin of the world." (John 1:29)

The tenth and final plague would be the death of all the firstborn of Egypt. This plague would also be upon the children of Israel unless they followed God's instructions. A lamb, without blemish, was to be killed on the fourteenth day of the month. The meat of it was to be eaten, along with unleavened bread (without yeast), and the <u>blood</u> of it was to be applied to the side and upper door posts of the house. The plague would be executed upon all households where blood had not been applied in this manner. Where blood had been properly applied God would "pass over" and they would be spared. This event marked the beginning of the annual <u>Passover</u> feast of the children of Israel.

Over 1,500 years later John the Baptist applied the title, the Lamb of God, to Jesus Christ. If His shed blood has been applied to your heart, God will "pass over" you and you will not suffer eternal death.

Scripture to read: Exodus 12:1-14

Question to ponder: *Has His blood been applied to my heart?*

Unit Four Review
Lessons 89 to 121

List the key historical events found in these lessons:

Lesson 93: _____

Lesson 94: _____

Lesson 102: _____

Lesson 103: _____

Lesson 110: _____

Lesson 112: _____

Lesson 121: _____

Who is the first person of the Trinity? _____

List the exciting truths about Jesus Christ found in each of these lessons:

Lesson 96: _____

Lesson 97: _____

Lesson 98: _____

Lesson 105: _____

Lesson 106: _____

Lesson 108: _____

Lesson 114: _____

Unit Five

Lessons 122 to 155

Bible History

The Exodus
The Wilderness Wanderings

Bible Truths

God the Spirit
The Law

Day 122   Date: _____

Living Water

"Jesus answered and said unto her, If thou knewest the gift of God, and who it is that saith to thee, Give me to drink; thou wouldest have asked of him, and he would have given thee living water."
(John 4:10)

Jesus often used everyday objects to illustrate eternal truths. In today's scripture, He is seen at the scene of Jacob's well in a city called Sychar. A woman approached, who Jesus asked for a drink of water. In the exchange between them, Jesus presented Himself as the One who could satisfy spiritual thirst completely. He offered the woman "living water" to drink.

In verse 14, Jesus explained that the living water would "*be in him a well of water springing up into everlasting life*". This is a reference to the Spirit of God who "indwells" (lives inside) every person who is born again. The woman ended up believing and bringing many others to the Savior.

Scripture to read: John 4:5-14

Question to ponder: *Think of how you use water each day. What qualities and properties does water have that teaches us about God?*

Day 123   Date: _____

The Spirit of God

"The Spirit of God hath made me, and the breath of the Almighty hath given me life." (Job 33:4)

When God created man, the Bible says *"And the LORD God formed man of the dust of the ground, and breathed into his nostrils the breath of life; and man became a living soul"* (Genesis 2:7). In today's verse, from the book of Job, we see that the creative act is attributed to the Holy Spirit, the third person of the Holy Trinity. In today's scripture reading, in verse 30, the Holy Spirit is credited with creation of animal life.

Again, we see that God is three Persons in One. The Holy Spirit is as much God as the Father and the Son.

Scripture to read: Psalms 104:24-35

Question to ponder: Who *am I dependent upon for every breath that I take?*

Day 124   Date: _____

The Comforter

"Nevertheless I tell you the truth; It is expedient for you that I go away: for if I go not away, the Comforter will not come unto you; but if I depart, I will send him unto you." (John 16:7)

While Jesus was on earth, the Holy Spirit's primary residence was in Heaven. Jesus taught His disciples that it was for their benefit that He leave them. He was (willingly) subject to the limitations of a human body, including that of being in only one place at a time. The Spirit would not be limited in this way. The title, <u>Comforter</u>, literally means, "one called alongside to help". His is a multi-faceted ministry.

In today's scripture, Jesus outlines a three-fold work of the Spirit. First, He reproves the world of <u>sin</u>: He confronts people with their unbelief in Jesus Christ. Second, He reproves the world of <u>righteousness</u>. The righteous life that Jesus lived caused people to feel guilty of their own sinful lives. The Holy Spirit now does this through the lives of Christians. Third, He reproves the world of <u>judgment</u>. He causes people to understand that their sin will not go unpunished.

Scripture to read: John 16:7-11

Question to ponder: *In what ways is the Holy Spirit's ministry a comfort to Christians?*

Day 125   Date: _____

The Spirit of Truth

"But when the Comforter is come, whom I will send unto you from the Father, even the Spirit of truth, which proceedeth from the Father, he shall testify of me" (John 15:26)

Notice that the Spirit proceeds from the Father, and is sent by the Son. The Spirit's primary ministry is to testify of the Son. Here again, we see order within the Trinity (see Lesson 89).

In today's scripture reading we see that the Holy Spirit *"shall not speak of himself"*. He shall testify of the Son, and glorify the Son. This is a key point in evaluating the Biblical accuracy of a ministry or movement. If the Holy Spirit deflects attention from Himself to Jesus Christ, then we should as well. Any person or ministry that focuses more attention on the Holy Spirit than on Jesus Christ is out of balance. He is called the *"Spirit of Truth"*, but Jesus Christ is the Way, the Truth and the Life (*John 14:6*).

Scripture to read: John 16:12-15

Question to ponder: *Which person of the Trinity is to be exalted above the other two (see Lesson 101)?*

Day 126   Date: _____

Born of the Spirit

"Jesus answered, Verily, verily, I say unto thee, Except a man be born of water and of the Spirit, he cannot enter into the kingdom of God."
(John 3:5)

When a person confesses Jesus Christ as Savior, and is born again, it is the Holy Spirit that gives spiritual life. That person is said to be born *"of the Spirit"*. To be born *"of water"* refers to the physical birth *"of the flesh"*.

The apostle Paul wrote a letter to a young pastor named Titus. In this letter he refers to this birth as *"the washing of regeneration, and renewing of the Holy Ghost"*. The Holy Spirit cleanses (washes) us from the stain of our sin, thereby giving us new birth (regeneration, "born again") and we are made a new creature (renewed, see Lesson 51). Notice the contrast in today's scripture reading between our old life before salvation and our new condition after God's grace has saved us.

Scripture to read: Titus 3:1-6

Question to ponder: *Why isn't our salvation "through works of righteousness which we have done"?*

Day 127   Date: _____

The Red Sea

"And Moses said unto the people, Fear ye not, stand still, and see the salvation of the LORD, which he will shew to you to day: for the Egyptians whom ye have seen to day, ye shall see them again no more for ever." (Exodus 14:13)

When the Egyptians realized that the firstborn of every house was dead, there was a great cry, and Pharaoh sent word to Moses to *"be gone"*. The Israelite people asked of their Egyptian neighbors, who gave them jewels of gold and silver, and much clothing. The family of Israel had been in Egypt 430 years, most of that as slaves.

As they left Egypt, God Himself went before them in the form of a *"pillar of a cloud"* during the day and a *"pillar of fire"* at night. Soon, however, Pharaoh changed his mind, gathered his army, and pursued after them. They came to the Red Sea, and appeared to be trapped. Pharaoh's army was behind, and the Red Sea was ahead. The people were terrified, and began to complain. The response of Moses is today's text verse. Today's scripture tells the story of God's miraculous deliverance.

Scripture to read: Exodus 14:13-31

Question to ponder: *After such a great experience, would the people ever doubt God again?*

Day 128   Date: _____

The Bread of Life

"And Jesus said unto them, I am the bread of life: he that cometh to me shall never hunger; and he that believeth on me shall never thirst."
(John 6:35)

After God delivered the children of Israel at the Red Sea, they continued on their journey into the wilderness of the Sinai Peninsula. Soon they were without water. When they did find water, it was too bitter to drink. God made the waters drinkable when Moses cast a tree into the waters. After a month and a half, the people began to complain of hunger. God caused the camp to be filled with quails, which He sent for meat.

At that time God began to supply the people each morning with *"a small round thing"*. This was called *"manna"* which literally means, "what is it?" The manna was good for food. God continued to supply them with manna, day by day, for forty years. When Jesus was on earth, He taught that the manna, which the children of Israel gathered each day, was a picture of Himself, the Bread of Life.

Scripture to read: Exodus 16:1-22

Question to ponder: *What things does the manna teach us about our relationship to Jesus Christ?*

Day 129   Date: _____

Water from the Rock

"And did all drink the same spiritual drink: for they drank of that spiritual Rock that followed them: and that Rock was Christ." (I Corinthians 10:4)

The children of Israel continued their journey through the wilderness, being led by God. Again they reached a place where there was no water to drink. Again the people complained bitterly against Moses. Moses appealed to God and was told to take the rod in his hand and strike the rock in Horeb. When he did so, water gushed out from the rock and the people drank.

In many of the Psalms, God is likened to a rock. In the *62nd Psalm* David wrote of God, "*He only is my rock and my salvation*". A rock speaks of something solid and unmovable. The rock that Moses struck pictures the Savior, who was smitten on the cross that we might drink freely of the water of life.

Scripture to read: Exodus 17:1-7

Question to ponder: *Why would the people be so quick to complain after all they had seen thus far?*

Day 130   Date: _____

The Law

"Now therefore, if ye will obey my voice indeed, and keep my covenant, then ye shall be a peculiar treasure unto me above all people: for all the earth is mine: And ye shall be unto me a kingdom of priests, and an holy nation." (Exodus 19:5-6a)

In three months' time the children of Israel came to the same mountain where Moses had been called of God out of the burning bush, Mount Sinai. While the people camped at the base of the mountain, Moses went up to the top of the mountain to meet with God. At this time, God gave to Moses the Law, including the Ten Commandments (see Lessons 13 and 14), that would set the Israelite people apart from all others on the face of the earth.

In today's text verse we read God's words explaining the purpose in giving Israel the Law. They were to use this knowledge to lead all peoples of the earth in worship and service of God. Instead, they would neglect this tremendous opportunity and ultimately have it removed from them.

Scripture to read: Exodus 19:1-25

Question to ponder: *Do we take full advantage of the knowledge we have of God today?*

Day 131   Date: _____

The Tabernacle

"And let them make me a sanctuary; that I may dwell among them." (Exodus 25:8)

Moses was on the mountain talking with God for forty days and forty nights. God gave him a codified law governing the everyday life of the people, in preparation for dwelling in the Promised Land. He instituted three national feasts: the feast of <u>unleavened bread</u> (observed in connection with the Passover), the feast of <u>harvest</u> (firstfruits), and the feast of <u>ingathering</u> (end of the harvest).

God then expressed a desire to dwell among His people. In chapters 25 to 27, and 30 to 31, He outlines detailed instructions for a "<u>tabernacle</u>" to be built. This tabernacle is rich in meaning. Every detail of it pictures Jesus Christ and His death on the cross for our sins. The tabernacle was built to be portable, easily disassembled and reassembled as the people journeyed through the wilderness. God even prepared some special men with the specific skills needed to build the tabernacle.

Scripture to read: Exodus 31:1-11

Question to ponder: *Could any other people say that their god(s) dwelt among them?*

Day 132   Date: _____

God Dwelleth In You

"Know ye not that ye are the temple of God, and that the Spirit of God dwelleth in you?" (I Corinthians 3:16)

When a person accepts Jesus Christ as Savior, the Spirit of God takes up residency inside him. This is called the "indwelling" of the Spirit. Jesus, when on earth, had prophesied of this (see Lesson 122), and spoken of the necessity of it (see Lesson 124).

This indwelling has some very practical advantages for the believer. It also has some very sobering aspects to it. If God dwells inside your body, then you take Him with you every where you go! He participates in every activity you participate in! Ephesians 4:30 warns us, *"grieve not the holy Spirit of God"*, after listing many ungodly practices which believers should separate themselves from. Let's rejoice in the infinite benefits that come from the Spirit's indwelling, and be careful to glorify God in our bodies that we *"grieve not the holy Spirit of God"*.

Scripture to read: I Corinthians 6:19-20

Question to ponder: *What things that I do might grieve God's Spirit within me?*

Day 133   Date: _____

Sealed

"In whom ye also trusted, after that ye heard the word of truth, the gospel of your salvation: in whom also after that ye believed, ye were sealed with that holy Spirit of promise" (Ephesians 1:13)

The indwelling Holy Spirit is God's <u>seal</u> upon the life of a believer. That seal is the earnest (down payment) of an inheritance we will later receive from God.

The people of Ephesus, to whom this letter was written, were very familiar with this concept. Logs cut in the mountains above the city would be floated down the river to the harbor city of Ephesus. Lumber companies would pick out the logs they wanted, and place the mark (seal) of their company on them. At a later date, the "day of redemption", they would come and pick up the logs with their seal on them. God used this familiar business activity to illustrate to the Ephesian people how He places His seal upon us, until the "day of redemption", when He claims us and takes us to be with Him forever!

Scripture to read: Ephesians 1:3-14

Question to ponder: Can *Satan ever claim me if God has His seal upon me?*

Day 134   Date: _____

The Spirit Beareth Witness

"The Spirit itself beareth witness with our spirit, that we are the children of God" (Romans 8:16)

The Holy Spirit's indwelling ministry in the life of the believer <u>secures</u> (seals) the believer's eternal destiny. The Spirit has another very important role in the life of the believer. He <u>communicates</u> with the spirit of man to assure him that he is God's child. Our text verse explains that the Spirit bears witness, or testifies, to our spirit within us. This brings a peace within that did not exist prior to salvation.

This peace allows a personal relationship with the Father that enables us to cry, "*Abba, Father*". "Abba" is a term of endearment similar to "Daddy". The Spirit's ministry within causes us to have that kind of an intimate relationship with our Heavenly Father.

Scripture to read: Romans 8:14-16

Question to ponder: *If the Holy Spirit is testifying of our relationship to God, can anything or anyone speak against Him?*

Day 135   Date: _____

The Aaronic Priesthood

"And take thou unto thee Aaron thy brother, and his sons with him, from among the children of Israel, that he may minister unto me in the priest's office, even Aaron, Nadab and Abihu, Eleazar and Ithamar, Aaron's sons." (Exodus 28:1)

After giving Moses instructions for the tabernacle, God gave instructions for a priesthood to be established. The men of Aaron's family would be "set aside" for the special purpose of serving God as priests. The only way to become a priest was to be born as a male child into Aaron's family. Aaron would serve as high priest, and would one day be succeeded in that position by his son, Eleazar (*Numbers 20:23-29*).

Chapters 28 and 29 give instructions for the special garments worn by the priests. There was even instruction given concerning the food that they would eat.

Scripture to read: Exodus 28:1-4

Question to ponder: *Why does God say, in the text verse, that Aaron would "minister unto me" in the priest's office?*

Day 136 Date: _____

An Unchangeable Priesthood

"For such an high priest became us, who is holy, harmless, undefiled, separate from sinners, and made higher than the heavens" (Hebrews 7:26)

Today the priesthood of Aaron's family has been forever <u>replaced</u> by that of Jesus Christ. Although the Aaronic priesthood illustrated in pattern form the priesthood of Jesus Christ, there are many important differences.

The high priesthood of Aaron's family was constantly changing of necessity, due to death. Our Great High Priest has an <u>unchangeable</u> priesthood because He lives forever! Aaron, and his sons, had to offer sacrifices for their own sins first. Jesus Christ, because He is <u>sinless</u>, did not need to offer a sacrifice for Himself (see Lesson 107). He was fully qualified to die (sacrifice Himself) for <u>our</u> sins.

Scripture to read: Hebrews 7:23-28

Question to ponder: *Will the priesthood of Jesus Christ ever end?*

Day 137   Date: _____

The Priesthood of the Believer

"But ye are a chosen generation, a royal priesthood, an holy nation, a peculiar people; that ye should shew forth the praises of him who hath called you out of darkness into his marvellous light" (I Peter 2:9)

When Jesus died on the cross, and rose again from the dead the third day, He ended forever the old Aaronic priesthood. He, Himself, is our Great High Priest. He established a new priesthood, in which all believers serve as priests before God. All who are born again have <u>direct</u> access to God through Jesus Christ (*Hebrews 4:16*)! There is <u>no</u> human mediator, or priest, to go through. Also, all believers have <u>equal</u> standing before God. No man has a greater access to God than any other man.

Just as the Aaronic priests offered sacrifices, we have sacrifices to offer today. Ours, however, are "spiritual sacrifices". These include praise (Hebrews 13:15), humility (*I Peter 2:20*), our bodies in service (*Romans 12:1*), faith (*Philippians 2:17*), time (*Ephesians 5:16*), among others.

Scripture to read: I Peter 2:1-10

Question to ponder: *Should the pastor of any church take exclusive claim to the title of "priest"?*

Day 138   Date: _____

The Spirit's Intercession

"Likewise the Spirit also helpeth our infirmities: for we know not what we should pray for as we ought: but the Spirit itself maketh intercession for us with groanings which cannot be uttered." (Romans 8:26)

It is exciting to know that when we pray all three persons of the Trinity are actively involved with us! We pray to the Father, in Jesus' name. The Holy Spirit helps us communicate our deepest yearnings and concerns to the Father, even those things we find hard to adequately express. Intercession is pleading with another person on someone else's behalf. God the Spirit does this for us with the Father. He takes what is on our heart and pleads it to the Father on our behalf.

For a human example of intercession read today's scripture. Abraham is interceding with God on behalf of his nephew, Lot. God was about to destroy Sodom and Gomorrah (see Lesson 54). This is also an example of a theophany – an Old Testament appearance of Jesus Christ.

Scripture to read: Genesis 18:17-33

Question to ponder: *Do we ever use intercessors in earthly matters?*

Day 139   Date: _____

Revealed by His Spirit

"For what man knoweth the things of a man, save the spirit of man which is in him? even so the things of God knoweth no man, but the Spirit of God."
(I Corinthians 2:11)

When believers try to explain their new life in Christ to unbelievers, they are usually brushed off as having "gotten religion" or some similar put off. The new believer is excited because he is experiencing something he had no clue about prior to his conversion. He may have seen it evidenced in the life of another believer, even to the point of wanting what that person had.

Verse nine explains that man cannot even imagine the things God has prepared for them that love Him. Verse fourteen further explains that they cannot be explained to an unbeliever, for he will think them to be foolishness. These things can only be understood <u>spiritually</u>. It is the ministry of the Holy Spirit in the life of a believer that causes him to understand and enjoy the things of God (verse ten).

Scripture to read: I Corinthians 2:1-14

Question to ponder: *Is the Bible easier to understand, now that you are saved?*

Day 140   Date: _____

The Golden Calf

"And the LORD said unto Moses, Go, get thee down; for thy people, which thou broughtest out of the land of Egypt, have corrupted themselves" (Exodus 32:7)

The people grew impatient waiting for Moses to come down off the mountain (see Lesson 131). They pressured Aaron to make them "gods" that they could worship. The Egyptian people had many gods, and the children of Israel wanted to return to something familiar to them. Aaron collected golden earrings from the people, and molded them into an image of a calf. The people then began to indulge themselves in nakedness and dancing. God told Moses what was happening, and Moses confronted the people. In his anger he threw the stone tablets containing the Ten Commandments to the ground, breaking them. As a result of this sin, about three thousand men died.

We need to be careful that we do not lose sight of God in our lives, and seek to return to former days of enslavement to sin.

Scripture to read: Exodus 32:1-28

Question to ponder: *Could I ever be so easily enticed to turn back to former ways of sin?*

Day 141   Date: _____

The Goodness of God

"O taste and see that the LORD is good: blessed is the man that trusteth in Him." (Psalms 34:8)

The responsibility of leading a nation of over three million people through the wilderness was very burdensome to Moses, especially since they often complained against him. Moses desired to know God in a more intimate way, so he requested that God show him His glory. God responded that He would *"make all my goodness pass before thee"*.

The <u>goodness</u> of God is His infinite capacity to bless people with kindness and benevolence. It is the attribute of God that motivates all the blessings we receive from Him. God is good. He can be trusted because He always has our best interests at heart.

God rewarded Moses' request with an extraordinary vision of His glory. In response, Moses bowed his head toward the ground and worshipped.

Scripture to read: Exodus 33:11 – 34:8

Question to ponder: *Would God be pleased today with someone who desired to know Him better?*

Day 142   Date: _____

The Sabbath

"Six days shall work be done, but on the seventh day there shall be to you an holy day, a sabbath of rest to the LORD: whosoever doeth work therein shall be put to death." (Exodus 35:2)

The fourth of the Ten Commandments is the prohibition against working on the Sabbath Day. The counterpart to that (often overlooked) is the command to work six days of the week. The <u>Sabbath</u> was to be a day set aside for rest from labor, and for worship unto the LORD. Notice also, that with this commandment God explicitly tells us that <u>all</u> of God's creative work occurred within six days (*Exodus 20:11; 31:17*).

The Sabbath was given specifically to <u>Israel</u> (verse seventeen) as a sign between God and their nation. No other nation had a similar observance. Today, we worship on the <u>first</u> day of the week (Sunday) in observance of the resurrection of Christ.

Scripture to read: Exodus 31:12-17

Question to ponder: *Why do you suppose the penalty for breaking the Sabbath was so severe?*

Day 143   Date: _____

A Willing Offering

"I have shewed you all things, how that so labouring ye ought to support the weak, and to remember the words of the Lord Jesus, how he said, It is more blessed to give than to receive." (Acts 20:35)

The time came to implement the instructions given to Moses on Mount Sinai. Moses gathered the people and asked them to bring an <u>offering</u> of the things that would be needed to build the tabernacle and the instruments of worship. God pointed Moses to two men, <u>Bezaleel</u> and <u>Aholiab</u>, who He had filled with wisdom and skill for the needed work.

When all was received, the people had to be told to stop giving! There was more than enough! The generous spirit of the children of Israel illustrates the kind of attitude that is pleasing to God. Jesus taught this when He was on earth. Where did people who had been slaves for so long find so much to give? Review Lesson 127 for the answer. The gifts they gave to God were theirs because God had first given them to them!

Scripture to read: Exodus 36:1-7

Question to ponder: *Where do the gifts that we give to God today come from?*

Day 144   Date: _____

One Sacrifice Forever

"But this man, after he had offered one sacrifice for sins for ever, sat down on the right hand of God" (Hebrews 10:12)

The Book of *Leviticus* records the detailed instructions given to Moses by God concerning the daily life of the people and their worship and service to God. The book begins by explaining the different kinds of offerings and sacrifices the people could bring to the priests with which to worship God. Many of the sacrifices were made in acknowledgment of personal sin. These sacrifices did not remove the guilt of sin; they only "covered" the sin. They had to be continually repeated. They were made in faith to God because they were the prescribed way for that time.

When Jesus Christ died on the cross, the Old Testament system of sacrifices ceased. This was because, for the first time, sin had been completely dealt with. There is nothing that can be added to what the Savior did on the cross. Any attempt at a sacrifice for sin today is in error.

Scripture to read: Hebrews 10:1-18

Question to ponder: *How do you think God regards any attempt at a sacrifice for sin today?*

Day 145   Date: _____

The Blood

"For the life of the flesh is in the blood: and I have given it to you upon the altar to make an atonement for your souls: for it is the blood that maketh an atonement for the soul." (Leviticus 17:11)

The Book of *Leviticus* includes a listing of foods that were permissible for the children of Israel to eat, and foods that God called unclean. Even the diet of the people was important to God and would be used to distinguish them from all other peoples of the earth. Included in the restrictions was a prohibition against the eating of blood. God has set the blood aside for a special purpose. It is to be offered as a sacrifice for sin to purge away (make an atonement for) the guilt of sin.

Of course the blood of the animals offered by the Israelite people could not take away sin (*Hebrews 10:4*). Yet God has said, *"without shedding of blood is no remission"* (*Hebrews 9:22*). It is the shed blood of Jesus Christ that cleanses us from our sin (*I John 1:7*).

Scripture to read: Leviticus 17:10-14

Question to ponder: *What was the difference between the two offerings of Cain and Abel (see Lesson 17)?*

Day 146 Date: _____
The Feast of Tabernacles

"In the last day, that great day of the feast, Jesus stood and cried, saying, If any man thirst, let him come unto me, and drink." (John 7:37)

The 23rd chapter of *Leviticus* gave the children of Israel seven feasts to be observed. These are the Passover, the feast of Unleavened Bread, the feast of First-fruits, the feast of Pentecost, the feast of Trumpets, the Day of Atonement, and the feast of Tabernacles. Each of these feasts spoke of some aspect of their relationship to God.

The feast of Tabernacles was to be observed in remembrance of their time in the wilderness. During this seven-day observance they were to make "booths" out of tree branches and live in them. By the time of Jesus many rituals had been added to this feast. One such addition was a daily procession, led by the priests, to gather water from the Pool of Siloam and bring it into the Temple. Jesus used this occasion to invite the people to be satisfied with the "living water" that only He could give (see Lesson 122).

Scripture to read: Leviticus 23:33-44

Question to ponder: *What are some observances we have today to remember key events in our past?*

Day 147   Date: _____

The Fruit of the Spirit

"But the fruit of the Spirit is love, joy, peace, longsuffering, gentleness, goodness, faith, Meekness, temperance: against such there is no law." (Galatians 5:22-23)

The Book of *Numbers* is so named because it has several passages that number the Israelites. It also records much history of the time spent in the wilderness between Egypt and the Promised Land. Today's scripture reading tells the story of Miriam and Aaron speaking out against Moses. They complained that they, too, deserved credit for leading the people. God came to the defense of Moses, reminding all the people that He was the One who would identify His leaders. Moses wound up interceding for his brother and sister.

Verse three records that Moses was very meek. We see in this story an illustration of what is meant by meekness. Moses was being attacked, but he did not speak to defend himself. That is meekness. He kept quiet and let God defend him. Meekness is listed in our text verses as one of the "fruits" that the Holy Spirit produces in the life of a believer.

Scripture to read: Numbers 12:1-16

Question to ponder: *Could Moses defend himself as ably as God could?*

Day 148   Date: _____

The Twelve Spies

"After the number of the days in which ye searched the land, even forty days, each day for a year, shall ye bear your iniquities, even forty years, and ye shall know my breach of promise." (Numbers 14:34)

The children of Israel finally came to the border of the Promised Land, Canaan. The LORD commanded Moses to send twelve men, one from each tribe, into the land to search it out and bring back a report. The men were chosen and inspected the land for forty days. When they returned they carried with them some of the fruit of the land.

When the report was given, ten of the spies said that they would be unable to possess the land because of the strength, and size, of the inhabitants. Two of the spies, Joshua and Caleb, encouraged the people that with God's help they would be well able. The people were swayed by the evil report of the ten spies, and started to complain and even wanted to kill Joshua and Caleb. God again intervened, and judgment was pronounced. The people would wander for forty years in the wilderness.

Scripture to read: Numbers 13:21-14:10

Question to ponder: *How could the people react like this after seeing God's power over the Egyptians?*

Day 149   Date: _____

Speak Ye Unto the Rock

"And Moses lifted up his hand, and with his rod he smote the rock twice: and the water came out abundantly, and the congregation drank, and their beasts also." (Numbers 20:11)

Again the children of Israel came to a place with no water. Again they complained. Again Moses and Aaron appealed to God for help. God told Moses to take his rod, gather the people, and speak unto the rock. It would give forth water.

Moses had had enough, however. The constant complaining of the people had finally gotten to him. Instead of speaking to the rock, he struck it twice with his rod. God allowed water to come out, but Moses would be disciplined by not being allowed to enter the Promised Land. Why was God so severe? God expects a higher standard from those He has placed in leadership. More than this, however, the rock was a picture of the Savior. Jesus was smitten once for our sin. Moses had already struck the rock (see Lesson 129). Once smitten (crucified), Jesus needs only to be spoken to for Him to provide the living water of salvation (see Lesson 34).

Scripture to read: Numbers 20:1-13

Question to ponder: *How important is obedience to God?*

Day 150   Date: _____

The Serpent of Brass

"And as Moses lifted up the serpent in the wilderness, even so must the Son of man be lifted up" (John 3:14)

The people were led through a rough part of the wilderness, and became discouraged. Again, they began to complain. This time God sent fiery serpents among the people, and many people died. Moses prayed for the people, and God told him to make a serpent of brass and lift it up on a pole. Any person, having been bitten by a serpent, who looked upon that serpent of brass, would live.

When Jesus was visited by Nicodemus (see Lessons 30 and 39), He referred to this incident as a picture of Himself. He would be lifted up, and any person, having been bitten by sin, who would look upon Him in faith, would be saved.

Scripture to read: Numbers 21:4-9

Question to ponder: *In what way would Jesus be lifted up from the earth (see John 12:32-33)?*

Day 151   Date: _____

The Doctrine of Balaam

"But I have a few things against thee, because thou hast there them that hold the doctrine of Balaam, who taught Balac to cast a stumblingblock before the children of Israel, to eat things sacrificed unto idols, and to commit fornication." (Revelation 2:14)

As the children of Israel moved through the wilderness, they began to be engaged in battle by the people of the land. God gave Israel victory after victory. One king in the way, Balak (or Balac), was afraid of the Israelites. He sent for a prophet by the name of Balaam, who he wanted to curse the Israelites for him. God told Balaam not to go, because the people were a blessed people. But, Balak had promised Balaam a handsome reward and he persisted in going. God never allowed Balaam to curse the children of Israel, but we learn in the New Testament that afterward he taught Balak how to lure the Israelites into sin. Today's scripture reading is an account of God giving Balaam's donkey the ability to speak in warning to Balaam.

Scripture to read: Numbers 22:21-35

Question to ponder: *Would I be willing to disobey God for money?*

Day 152   Date: _____

The Heart of God

"O that there were such an heart in them, that they would fear me, and keep all my commandments always, that it might be well with them, and with their children for ever!" (Deuteronomy 5:29)

God used Moses to write the first five books of the Bible. The fifth book, of *Deuteronomy*, contains final instructions from God, through Moses, to the children of Israel in preparation to enter the Promised Land. Chapter five contains a review of the Ten Commandments.

Today's verse is a touching look into the heart of God. The commandments He gives are for our good. They instruct us in the way that leads to the blessings of God. He has given them to us that we might know how to have those blessings. God not only gives us this needed instruction, but also deeply longs for us to keep it that He might pour out those same blessings on our lives. The fear of God as mentioned in the Old Testament is the equivalent of faith as mentioned in the New Testament.

Scripture to read: Deuteronomy 5:22-33

Question to ponder: *Why does God allow obedience to His commandments to be our choice?*

Day 153   Date: _____

The Great Commandment

"And Jesus answered him, The first of all the commandments is, Hear, O Israel; The Lord our God is one Lord: And thou shalt love the Lord thy god with all thy heart, and with all thy soul, and with all thy mind, and with all thy strength: this is the first commandment." (Mark 12:29-30)

One day Jesus was approached by a man with a question. He asked, *"Which is the first* (or, greatest) *commandment of all?"* In answering, Jesus quoted from Deuteronomy, chapter six. He explained that whoever kept this commandment would, in so doing, be keeping all the others as well.

Today's scripture reading is the full reading of this greatest commandment. Notice the manner in which parents are to teach their children the commandments of God. It is to be a continual process in which all daily activities are used as teaching opportunities.

Scripture to read: Deuteronomy 6:4-12

Question to ponder: *What are some ways that I can create daily opportunities to teach my children (or myself) about God?*

Day 154   Date: _____

The Purpose of Trials

"And thou shalt remember all the way which the LORD thy God led thee these forty years in the wilderness, to humble thee, and to prove thee, to know what was in thine heart, whether thou wouldest keep his commandments, or no. And he humbled thee, and suffered thee to hunger, and fed thee with manna, which thou knewest not, neither did thy fathers know; that he might make thee know that man doth not live by bread only, but by every word that proceedeth out of the mouth of the LORD doth man live." (Deuteronomy 8:2-3)

The children of Israel wandered in the wilderness for forty years, until every person who was over 20 years old at the time they refused to enter the Promised Land was dead (see Lesson 148). Only Joshua and Caleb, the two faithful spies, remained of those who were over 20 years at that time. Why does God allow His people (then and now) to endure trials and hardships? The answer is in today's text verses. To reveal to us (not God, He already knows) what is in our hearts, and to help us see our utter dependence upon God.

Scripture to read: Psalms 78:12-41

Question to ponder: *What happens to us when things are too easy?*

Day 155   Date: _____

A Prophet From Among Them

"I will raise them up a Prophet from among their brethren, like unto thee, and will put my words in his mouth; and he shall speak unto them all that I shall command him." (Deuteronomy 18:18)

In the midst of giving the children of Israel instructions for living in the Promised Land, God paused to tell of a Prophet He would send them someday. This Prophet came over 1,400 years later, and was none other than God Himself in the person of Jesus Christ!

When John the Baptist began his ministry, he was asked if he was "that prophet" (*John 1:21*). He answered, "No". Jesus came at a time when people were anticipating the coming of "that prophet" and He was rejected. Notice the test for determining if a prophet was sent from God, or not (verses 20-22). Today, the test of a preacher is whether or not they agree with the completed Word of God.

Scripture to read: Deuteronomy 18:15-22

Question to ponder: What *nation would this Prophet be from?*

Unit Five Review
Lessons 122 to 155

List the key historical events from the period after the Egyptian captivity as found in these lessons:

Lesson 127: _____

Lesson 130: _____

Lesson 140: _____

Lesson 143: _____

Lesson 148: _____

Lesson 149: _____

Lesson 150: _____

What <u>alone</u> can take away sin (145)? _____

What titles of the Holy Spirit are found in the text verses of each of these lessons:

Lesson 123: _____

Lesson 124: _____

Lesson 125: _____

Lesson 133: _____

List some ways the Holy Spirit helps you as found in these lessons:

Lesson 124: _____

Lesson 134: _____

Lesson 138: _____

Lesson 139: _____

Lesson 147: _____

Unit Six

Lessons 156 to 183

Bible History

Joshua & Caleb
The Judges
Ruth

Bible Truths

Sin
Angels
Satan

Day 156   Date: _____

Meditate Therein Day and Night

"This book of the law shall not depart out of thy mouth; but thou shalt meditate therein day and night, that thou mayest observe to do according to all that is written therein: for then thou shalt make thy way prosperous, and then thou shalt have good success." (Joshua 1:8)

Moses lived to the age of 120 years, and died. Before he died, God took him to the top of a mountain and allowed him to see the Promised Land (*Deuteronomy 34:1-4*). Moses was not allowed to enter it, because of the sin he had committed in striking the rock (see Lesson 149).

In his place God raised up Joshua, one of the two faithful spies (see Lesson 148), as leader. God encouraged Joshua to *"be strong and of a good courage"*. The source of his success as a leader would be his attention to the Word of God, which to this point in time was the Law. Joshua proved to be a strong and courageous leader.

Scripture to read: Joshua 1:1-18

Question to ponder: *In what ways will meditating on the Bible and doing the things found in it make us successful?*

Day 157   Date: _____

Crossing Jordan

"And the priests that bare the ark of the covenant of the LORD stood firm on dry ground in the midst of Jordan, and all the Israelites passed over on dry ground, until all the people were passed clean over Jordan." (Joshua 3:17)

The time came to enter Canaan, the Promised Land. In order to accomplish this, the children of Israel had to cross the River Jordan at a time when it was flooded over its banks. The priests led the way, carrying the Ark of the Covenant that contained the stone tablets of the Ten Commandments. As soon as the priests' feet touched the waters of the river, God caused the waters from upstream to stand in a heap, and the Israelites crossed on dry land!

Two memorials were set up containing twelve stones each. One at the point where the priests entered the water, and one at the point the people camped on the other side.

Scripture to read: Joshua 3:1-17

Question to ponder: *Could I benefit by setting up "memorials" in my life that remind me of things God has done for me?*

Day 158   Date: _____

The Battle of Jericho

"And it came to pass at the seventh time, when the priests blew with the trumpets, Joshua said unto the people, Shout; for the LORD hath given you the city." (Joshua 6:16)

The first city of Canaan to be conquered was Jericho, a city surrounded by a great wall. The battle plan given to Joshua by God was rather unusual. For six consecutive days the people marched around Jericho, led by the priests and the Ark of the Covenant. On the seventh day, the people marched around the city seven times. After the seventh time, the priests blew their trumpets, Joshua shouted, and the walls fell flat.

The only residents of Jericho allowed to live were the family of a harlot (prostitute) named Rahab. She had protected two men that Joshua had sent ahead to spy out Jericho. Because of her faith in God (*Hebrews 11:31*), her life was spared, she became an Israelite and an earthly ancestor of the Lord Jesus Christ (*Matthew 1:5* "Rachab").

Scripture to read: Joshua 6:1-27

Question to ponder: *Why do you suppose God used such an unusual method to defeat Jericho?*

Day 159 Date: _____

Israel Hath Sinned

"Israel hath sinned, and they have also transgressed my covenant which I commanded them: for they have even taken of the accursed thing, and have also stolen, and dissembled also, and they have put it even among their own stuff." (Joshua 7:11)

The next Canaanite city to be conquered was the smaller city of Ai. The Israelites decided to send only a few men to take Ai; and they were defeated. When Joshua cried unto the LORD, he received the response of our text verse. God had commanded that the silver and gold of Jericho, along with the vessels of brass and iron, be kept for the LORD. All else was to be destroyed.

A man of the tribe of Judah, by the name of Achan, had taken a garment and some silver and gold, and kept them for himself. God revealed him to Joshua, and he and his family were stoned to death. Ai was then defeated in the next battle. God wanted Israel to learn the importance of obedience to His word right away as they took possession of Canaan.

Scripture to read: Joshua 7:1-26

Question to ponder: *How does God view sin?*

Day 160   Date: _____

Filthy Rags

"But we are all as an unclean thing, and all our righteousnesses are as filthy rags; and we all do fade as a leaf; and our iniquities, like the wind, have taken us away." (Isaiah 64:6)

We can understand that the evil things that we do are repulsive to God. These things are detestable to us as well. We don't like them in others and we don't like to find them in ourselves. However, in God's eyes, even the good (righteous) things that we do are as filthy rags in His sight! Aside from the righteous works that God Himself produces in us after our salvation (see Lesson 147), we are incapable of doing good in God's eyes.

Why is this? Any such act by an unbeliever is seen as an attempt to <u>earn</u> salvation aside from the work of Jesus Christ on the cross of Calvary (see Lesson 31). It is a rejection of God's plan of salvation.

Scripture to read: Romans 7:14-25

Question to ponder: *What is the only way that I can be seen as righteous (truly good; right) in God's eyes (II Corinthians 5:21)?*

Day 161   Date: _____

Too Heavy for Me

"For mine iniquities are gone over mine head: as an heavy burden they are too heavy for me." (Psalms 38:4)

Because we are made in God's image we have a natural conscience that causes us to feel <u>guilty</u> when we have done wrong. Modern psychologists try to eliminate <u>guilt</u> from contemporary vocabulary, teaching that it is a man-made concept that comes from out-dated ideas of right and wrong. The truth is that guilt is <u>God-given</u> and is intended to motivate us to take action regarding our sin. It is the Holy Spirit speaking to our hearts that brings consciousness of sin (conviction) and the resulting feelings of guilt (see Lesson 124). He brings conviction to unbelievers, seeking to turn them to Christ. Because He indwells believers, He brings conviction to them, seeking to turn them back to full fellowship with the Father.

In today's scripture, David writes of the conviction he felt when out of fellowship with God. <u>Iniquity</u> is another word for sin, speaking of its lawlessness.

Scripture to read: Psalms 38:1-22

Question to ponder: *Is <u>guilt</u> a good or a bad thing?*

Day 162   Date: _____

The Sin of Omission

"Therefore to him that knoweth to do good, and doeth it not, to him it is sin." (James 4:17)

We often define sin by listing actions and emotions that we consider to be wrong. There is another category of sin, however, that goes beyond the wrongs we commit. This sin is aptly described in today's verse. To fail to do right, when it was possible to do so, is called the sin of omission.

The victories won at Jericho and Ai, coupled with previous stories of the Red Sea, the wilderness journeys, and the crossing of the Jordan, caused a stir in the land of Canaan. The kings of the land banded together to fight off these new invaders. One people, of Gibeon, decided to use trickery instead. They feigned themselves to be from a far distant land and sought a peace treaty with Joshua. Without consulting God, Joshua accepted their offer.

Scripture to read: Joshua 9:1-27

Question to ponder: *How can I keep myself from the sin of omission?*

Day 163   Date: _____

Caleb

"Now therefore give me this mountain, whereof the LORD spake in that day; for thou heardest in that day how the Anakims were there, and that the cities were great and fenced: if so be the LORD will be with me, then I shall be able to drive them out, as the LORD said." (Joshua 14:12)

God continued to give the inhabitants of Canaan into the hands of Joshua and the armies of Israel. Soon Israel was in possession of the whole land, and it was time to divide the land to the eleven tribes. The family (tribe) of Levi would not receive an inheritance of land because their inheritance was the service of the LORD in the tabernacle.

At this time Caleb asked for the inheritance promised him by Moses, 45 years earlier. In particular he asked for the portion of land inhabited by the Anakims (*Numbers 13:33*). It was their stature that had caused the ten unfaithful spies to bring an evil report of the land. Caleb received that land and drove the Anakims out (*Joshua 15:14*).

Scripture to read: Joshua 14:1-15

Question to ponder: *Is there some "mountain" in my life I need to claim for God?*

Day 164   Date: _____

Choose You This Day

"And if it seem evil unto you to serve the LORD, choose you this day whom ye will serve; whether the gods which your fathers served that were on the other side of the flood, or the gods of the Amorites, in whose land ye dwell: but as for me and my house, we will serve the LORD." (Joshua 24:15)

The land was divided out to the tribes, and the people were settled in. Unfortunately, the children of Israel did not completely expel the Canaanites from the land as God had instructed them. This incomplete obedience would be the cause of much grief in the years that followed.

Joshua led the children of Israel for thirty years. Before he died he called the people together to give them one last charge. He reminded them of all God had done for them, and encouraged them to complete the work of possessing the land. He warned them of the cost of disobedience. In today's verse we read Joshua's challenge to the people to make a choice, and Joshua's example that *"as for me and my house, we will serve the LORD"*.

Scripture to read: Joshua 24:1-28

Question to ponder: *Will I follow Joshua's example?*

Day 165   Date: _____

The Judges

"Nevertheless the LORD raised up judges, which delivered them out of the hand of those that spoiled them." (Judges 2:16)

After the death of Joshua the children of Israel lived a roller coaster existence. They would depart from worshipping and serving God and serve the false gods of the land of Canaan. As a result God would send oppressors against them that would cause them to cry out to God for deliverance. God raised up a series of leaders, called judges, who led the children of Israel out of bondage and back into an obedient relationship with Him.

Over and over again the sequence was repeated. Time and time again God forgave His people and sent a deliverer to lead them. This entire period of time, covering about 300 years, is best summed up in the closing words of the Book of *Judges*, "every man did that which was right in his own eyes."

Scripture to read: Judges 2:7-23

Question to ponder: *Do people today ignore God until tragedy comes, then cry out to Him for help?*

Day 166   Date: _____

Deborah and Barak

"And she said, I will surely go with thee: notwithstanding the journey that thou takest shall not be for thine honour; for the LORD shall sell Sisera into the hand of a woman. And Deborah arose, and went with Barak to Kedesh." (Judges 4:9)

The children of Israel were being oppressed by Jabin, a king of the land of Canaan, because of their sin. This had gone on for twenty years; and the Israelites cried unto the LORD. God used a prophetess by the name of Deborah to deliver a message to a man by the name of Barak. God had chosen him to lead a victory over Jabin and his military captain, Sisera. Barak agreed to answer the call, but only if Deborah went with him. Deborah responded as cited in today's verse.

God did indeed give the victory as He said. Sisera, however, was killed by a woman. A brave woman named Jael lured Sisera into her tent, used milk to put him into a deep sleep, and drove a tent stake (nail) into the temple of his forehead.

Scripture to read: Judges 4:1-24

Question to ponder: *Why did God keep Barak from receiving full credit for this military victory?*

Day 167   Date: _____

Gideon

"And the LORD said unto Gideon, The people that are with thee are too many for me to give the Midianites into their hands, lest Israel vaunt themselves against me, saying, Mine own hand hath saved me."
(Judges 7:2)

After the victory led by Deborah and Barak, the children of Israel again fell away from serving God and found themselves serving the Midianites for seven years. The angel of the LORD (see lesson 112) visited a man by the name of <u>Gideon</u> to tell him he would be used to save Israel from the Midianites. Chapter 6 tells the story of Gideon's encounter with the LORD.

Gideon raised an army of 32,000 men to fight the larger army of the Midianites. God reduced his army to 10,000 and then to 300 men. Then, using trumpets and pitchers, God gave this small army the victory.

Scripture to read: Judges 7:1-25

Question to ponder: *Why did God reduce Gideon's army so drastically?*

Day 168   Date: _____

Samson

"And the angel of the LORD appeared unto the woman, and said unto her, Behold now, thou art barren, and bearest not: but thou shalt conceive, and bear a son." (Judges 13:3)

After Gideon, God raised a series of men to judge Israel. Israel continued to return to evil after each judge. When Israel had served the Philistines for 40 years, God answered the prayers of one couple who was childless. The angel of the LORD (see Lesson 112) appeared to them to announce that they would have a special son. He would be a "Nazarite" unto the LORD "from the womb".

Numbers, chapter six, records the instructions given for a person living under a Nazarite vow. Among other things, they would vow to keep themselves from anything made of the fruit of the vine, they would not cut their hair or shave, and they would not touch any dead body. Samson, their son, was to live under the restraints of the Nazarite vow for his entire life. God used Samson to judge Israel for twenty years, and to single-handedly win many battles against the Philistines.

Scripture to read: Judges 15:1-20

Question to ponder: *What was the secret of Samson's great strength?*

Day 169   Date: _____

The Elect Angels

"I charge thee before God, and the Lord Jesus Christ, and the elect angels, that thou observe these things without preferring one before another, doing nothing by partiality." (I Timothy 5:21)

The apostle Paul, when writing to Timothy, made reference to *"the elect angels"* in the middle of this instruction to be impartial in his dealings with people. <u>Angels</u> are created spiritual beings; created as messengers (the meaning of the word "angels") and *"ministering spirits"* (verse 14 of today's scripture). The Bible does not specifically state when angels were created except to say that God created <u>everything</u> within six days (*Exodus 20:11*).

The "elect angels" refers to those angels who refused to follow Satan in rebellion against God. Their decision is sealed and they are God's forever. Today's scripture compares the revelation of God through His Son to His previous revelation of Himself through the words of angels.

Scripture to read: Hebrews 1:1-14

Question to ponder: *In what ways does today's scripture show that Jesus Christ is superior to the angels?*

Day 170   Date: _____

Not Given in Marriage

"For when they shall rise from the dead, they neither marry, nor are given in marriage; but are as the angels which are in heaven." (Mark 12:25)

Jesus was being confronted with a question from some <u>Sadducees</u>, a sect that did not believe in the resurrection. In answer to a question they posed trying to entrap Him, Jesus rebuked them for not knowing the scriptures and taught that in Heaven there will be no marriage among people or angels. Angels, though identified with masculine names, are sexless. They do not marry or reproduce.

When God created man, He created Adam from the dust of the ground. Then He took Eve from Adam, and since that time we all come from a biological father and mother. Hence, we were all <u>in</u> Adam. When he sinned, we all sinned because we were in him. That is why Jesus could die <u>once</u> for all mankind. The angels, on the other hand, were each created individually. There can be no plan of salvation for them because there would have to be a separate provision for each angel.

Scripture to read: Mark 12:18-27

Question to ponder: *Who has the greater blessing, men or angels?*

Day 171   Date: _____

Michael the Archangel

"Yet Michael the archangel, when contending with the devil he disputed about the body of Moses, durst not bring against him a railing accusation, but said, The Lord rebuke thee." (Jude 1:9)

The second to the last book of the Bible is a small letter of only one chapter, written by one of the earthly half-brothers of Jesus. <u>Jude</u> wrote this letter to encourage believers to contend (battle) for the faith of Jesus Christ. In it he refers to <u>Michael</u> the archangel.

Michael is one of only two angels (not including Satan) mentioned by name in the Bible. As archangel, he apparently has responsibility over the other angels and appears to have a special ministry to the children of Israel. Here, he is described as doing battle with the devil over the body of Moses. Even with all his power, Michael would not accuse Satan in his own name, but the Lord's.

Scripture to read: Jude 1:1-25

Question to ponder: *If Michael the archangel is careful in his dealings with Satan, how much more should we be?*

Day 172   Date: _____
Seraphims and Cherubims

"Above it stood the seraphims: each one had six wings; with twain he covered his face, and with twain he covered his feet, and with twain he did fly." (Isaiah 6:2)

The prophet Isaiah was privileged to be given a vision of the throne room of Heaven (see Lesson 6). He saw the Lord sitting upon a throne, and angelic beings above. These angels, called the Seraphims, are mentioned only this once in the Bible. They spend their time praising God for His holiness.

When God expelled Adam and Eve from the Garden of Eden He placed Cherubims, another kind of angelic being, at its entrance to guard it. Cherubims are mentioned several times in the Bible. A description of them is given in today's scripture.

Scripture to read: Ezekiel 1:1-28

Question to ponder: *If the angels, who can see God, praise Him continually, what should we do?*

Day 173   Date: _____

The Fallen Angels

"And his tail drew the third part of the stars of heaven, and did cast them to the earth: and the dragon stood before the woman which was ready to be delivered, for to devour her child as soon as it was born." (Revelation 12:4)

The twelfth chapter of Revelation tells the story of the nation Israel in summary form, with Israel characterized as a woman. Satan is introduced into the story as a great red dragon who, having rebelled against God, seeks to destroy the woman and her child (Jesus Christ). In his rebellion, Satan draws *"the third part of the stars of heaven"* and casts them to earth. This indicates that Satan has led one third of the created angels to rebel against their Creator. These "fallen angels" are called demons. Like the elect angels, their eternal destiny is sealed.

Jesus, in His earthly ministry, was often confronted by demons. He clearly demonstrated that He had power over them. Today's scripture is one such instance.

Scripture to read: Matthew 8:28-34

Question to ponder: *Were the demons who confronted Jesus able to resist Him in any way?*

Day 174   Date: _____

Samson and Delilah

"And it came to pass afterward, that he loved a woman in the valley of Sorek, whose name was Delilah." (Judges 16:4)

Although Samson was greatly used of God at times, he mostly lived his life for his own passions. One of his weaknesses was his attraction toward ungodly women. One such woman, Delilah, was hired by the Philistines to discover the secret of Samson's great strength. The Philistines had tried on numerous occasions to rid themselves of Samson, but he prevailed each time.

Samson lied to Delilah three times as she sought to entrap him. Still she persisted until Samson could bear her words no longer. He told her the secret of his strength. Delilah told the Philistines and they successfully captured him. His eyes were put out and he became a slave. In his death, however, God used Samson one last time to win a great victory over the Philistines.

Scripture to read: Judges 16:1-31

Question to ponder: *Was the length of his hair the real source of Samson's strength?*

Day 175   Date: _____

The Strange Woman

"That they may keep thee from the strange woman, from the stranger which flattereth with her words." (Proverbs 7:5)

Samson was a man who gave into the flattery of women and seemed to go out of his way to find temptation. Contrast him with Joseph, who resisted temptation and fled when it came to him (see Lesson 94).

The seventh chapter of *Proverbs* describes a young man, a "simple one", who deliberately puts himself in the path of temptation. When a deceitful woman seduces him he charges ahead, not aware that he is going after his own destruction. The chapter describes in graphic language the words used by the "strange woman" to lure the simpleton into sin. Who is this strange woman? She may be any woman you are not married to!

Scripture to read: Proverbs 7:1-27

Question to ponder: *What instruction is given in Proverbs chapter seven to help a man avoid falling in this way?*

Day 176   Date: _____

The Anointed Cherub

"Thou wast perfect in thy ways from the day that thou wast created, till iniquity was found in thee." (Ezekiel 28:15)

The prophet Ezekiel was used to pronounce judgment on many of Israel's enemies. In the case of the king of Tyrus (from today's scripture reading), the wording extends beyond the earthly king to a rebuke of Satan himself (this kind of double meaning is often used in scripture). The king of Tyrus could not have been in the Garden of Eden, but we know that Satan was – as the serpent (see Lesson 10). From this passage we learn much about the devil.

He was created an angelic being of supreme beauty and wisdom. He apparently was the highest, the anointed, of the Cherubim. From the wording of verse thirteen of today's scripture we see that Satan was created with musical qualities (tabrets, pipes). But, one day, iniquity was found in Satan and he rebelled against God.

Scripture to read: Ezekiel 28:11-19

Question to ponder: *Wouldn't you think that someone with such beauty and wisdom would be thankful rather than filled with pride?*

Day 177   Date: _____

Lucifer

"How art thou fallen from heaven, O Lucifer, son of the morning! how art thou cut down to the ground, which didst weaken the nations!"
(Isaiah 14:12)

In the book of the prophet Isaiah we find what happened that caused Satan to fall from his exalted position as the anointed cherub. We also read of Satan's original name, Lucifer.

It began with a heart lifted up with pride (*Ezekiel 28:17*, Lesson 176). From there, Lucifer began to imagine in the privacy of his own heart that he could exalt himself above his Creator. The thoughts of his heart led to committing the act that caused him to be the author of sin. Notice in this brief passage, five "I wills" of Lucifer's sin. Notice in the scripture reading of Lesson 176, six "I wills" of God's judgment upon him.

Scripture to read: Isaiah 14:12-17

Question to ponder: *What is the primary difference between the "I wills" of Lucifer and God?*

Day 178   Date: _____

The Wiles of the Devil

"Be sober, be vigilant; because your adversary the devil, as a roaring lion, walketh about, seeking whom he may devour." (I Peter 5:8)

Both the apostle Peter and the apostle Paul were used of God to warn us to beware of the devil. Peter cautions us that the devil restlessly searches for Christians to destroy. He is not a person to be taken lightly, as a cartoon character, but is as dangerous as a hungry lion about to attack. Whether we regard him as our enemy or not, he certainly regards us as his!

Paul warns us of the *"wiles of the devil"*. Satan is highly intelligent and does not play fair. He will use every dirty trick available to trip us up. He describes our battle with the devil as a wrestling match; <u>close</u> combat, not distant. In the Garden of Eden he caught Eve away from Adam, disguised himself, lied to her, and tricked her into sinning. He uses the same deceitful tactics today!

Scripture to read: Ephesians 6:10-12

Question to ponder: *Should we seek out battles with such an opponent, or avoid them?*

Day 179   Date: _____

The Accuser of Our Brethren

"And I heard a loud voice saying in heaven, Now is come salvation, and strength, and the kingdom of our God, and the power of his Christ: for the accuser of our brethren is cast down, which accused them before our God day and night." (Revelation 12:10)

In this verse in *Revelation*, Satan is referred to as the *"accuser of our brethren"*. A good illustration of this is the story of Job (see Lesson 45). Job was a man who pleased God by the way he lived. God pointed this out to Satan, who set about to discredit him.

Satan contended that the only reason Job served God was because God had blessed him materially. God allowed Satan to remove his material wealth, and still Job honored God by his life. Again, Satan accused Job by claiming he would curse God if only his health was taken away. God allowed that as well, and Job still remained faithful to God.

Scripture to read: Job 1:1 – 2:10

Question to ponder: *How long did it take Satan to attack Job when God granted permission?*

Day 180   Date: _____

An Angel of Light

"And no marvel; for Satan himself is transformed into an angel of light."
(II Corinthians 11:14)

In the Garden of Eden, Satan presented the forbidden fruit to Eve as *"a tree to be desired to make one wise"*. He took something that would ultimately destroy the fellowship Eve, and Adam, enjoyed with God and portrayed it as something that would improve their situation. He presented himself as a *"minister of light"* to Eve – a messenger with a message of hope. Instead, his was a message of death!

In this second letter to the church at Corinth, the apostle Paul warned the believers that Satan does not always <u>appear</u> as evil. He has the ability to imitate God, and his messengers the ability to imitate the way of truth. These *"false apostles"* present themselves as representing Christ, but deny Him in works and message.

Scripture to read: II Corinthians 11:1-15

Question to ponder: *What test can we apply to tell the difference between these "false apostles" and God's true messengers?*

Day 181   Date: _____

The Devil's Doom

"And the devil that deceived them was cast into the lake of fire and brimstone, where the beast and false prophet are, and shall be tormented day and night for ever and ever." (Revelation 20:10)

Although Satan refuses to admit it, his final destiny is <u>sealed</u>. He will fight to the bitter end, but there will come a day when he will be cast into everlasting fire. The victory has <u>already</u> been won; that happened when Jesus rose from the dead!

Jesus was answering some questions His disciples had asked Him about the future and He made an interesting statement. In today's scripture we read that Hell (the lake of fire, everlasting fire) <u>was prepared for the devil and his angels</u>. God did not prepare Hell as a place for people! He is *"not willing that <u>any</u> should perish"* (II Peter 3:9). The people that reject Christ and end up in Hell will have gone to a place not intended for them!

Scripture to read: Matthew 25:31-46

Question to ponder: *Is there anyone who <u>cannot</u> call on the name of Jesus Christ for salvation?*

Day 182   Date: _____

Ruth and Naomi

"And Ruth said, Intreat me not to leave thee, or to return from following after thee: for whither thou goest, I will go; and where thou lodgest, I will lodge: thy people shall be my people, and thy God my God" (Ruth 1:16)

The book of *Ruth* tells the story of a family that lived during the time of the judges in Israel. Elimelech and his wife, Naomi, left Israel due to a famine. They moved to the land of Moab, where Elimelech died. In Moab, their two sons married and died, leaving their young widows behind.

Naomi heard that the famine was over, and decided to return to Israel. She counseled her two daughters-in-law to stay behind and remarry from among their own people. One of them, Orpah did so. The other, Ruth, would not leave Naomi. The beautiful words of today's verse are those of Ruth as she pledged her loyalty to her mother-in-law. Her decision to remain with Naomi would prove to have an important place in the history of Israel.

Scripture to read: Ruth 1:1-22

Question to ponder: *What greater decision was Ruth making beyond that to stay with Naomi?*

Day 183   Date: _____

The Kinsman Redeemer

"Tarry this night, and it shall be in the morning, that if he will perform unto thee the part of a kinsman, well; let him do the kinsman's part: but if he will not do the part of a kinsman to thee, then will I do the part of a kinsman to thee, as the LORD liveth: lie down until the morning." (Ruth 3:13)

When Naomi and Ruth returned to Bethlehem in Israel, Ruth went out into the fields to gather whatever barley was left behind by the reapers. God directed her to the field of a man by the name of Boaz. Boaz, a wealthy man, was a close relative of Elimelech. Boaz was attracted to Ruth and took steps according to the law of Moses to purchase a piece of land from Naomi to keep it in the family, marry the young widow Ruth, and raise up children by her in the place of his dead relative. Only one who was "next of kin" could perform this role of a "kinsman-redeemer".

Over one thousand years later, God's Son would leave Heaven to become "next of kin" to us (a man), in order to redeem us out of the bondage of sin!

Scripture to read: Ruth 2:1 – 4:22

Question to ponder: *According to Ruth 4:22, who became the great-grandson of Boaz and Ruth?*

Unit Six Review
Lessons 156 to 183

List the key historical people found in these lessons:

Lesson 156: _____

Lesson 158: _____

Lesson 159: _____

Lesson 163: _____

Lesson 166: _____

Lesson 167: _____

Lesson 168: _____

Lesson 174: _____

Lesson 182: _____

Lesson 183: _____

List some reasons to be wary of Satan as found in each of these lessons:

Lesson 176: _____

Lesson 178: _____

Lesson 179: _____

Lesson 180: _____

What will be the final end of Satan?

Lesson 181: _____

Unit Seven

Lessons 184 to 213

Bible History

Samuel
Saul
David

Bible Truths

Hell
Government
Heaven

Day 184   Date: _____

A Real Place of Torment

"And in hell he lift up his eyes, being in torments, and seeth Abraham afar off, and Lazarus in his bosom." (Luke 16:23)

Jesus told this story of "The rich man and Lazarus" to teach us about the reality of Hell. Unlike many of His stories, this one is believed to be an actual account of a real event. In his "parables" (see Lesson 36), Jesus never identified the characters by name as He does in this story.

Prior to the resurrection of Christ, the souls of the dead abode in <u>Hades</u> (also called "Hell"). Hades had two compartments, <u>Paradise</u> (the abode of the saved) and <u>Hell</u> (the abode of the lost). Since the resurrection of Christ, Paradise has been emptied and only Hell remains. In this true story we learn that Hell is <u>real</u>, a place of extreme <u>torment</u>, and <u>inescapable</u>. We also learn that the lost dead have a consciousness of existence that continues.

Scripture to read: Luke 16:19-31

Question to ponder: *What is Abraham referring to by his reference to "Moses and the prophets" in verse 29 (see Lesson 152 for a clue)?*

Day 185   Date: _____

The Fire Is Not Quenched

"And if thy hand offend thee, cut it off: it is better for thee to enter into life maimed, than having two hands to go into hell, into the fire that never shall be quenched" (Mark 9:43)

While on earth, Jesus actually had a lot more to say about Hell than He did about Heaven. In today's scripture He warned his listeners that they should rid themselves of anything that might be a hindrance to faith. Whatever the loss, if it is an obstacle to saving faith it is better to suffer the loss temporarily in this life than to have comfort in this life and suffer loss forever in Hell.

In this scripture we see that Hell is real, that it is everlasting, that it is a place of everlasting fire, and that the fires of Hell never consume their victims. People often will liken trials on earth to Hell (i.e. "he is going through Hell on earth"), but in reality nothing on earth could compare to the torments of Hell.

Scripture to read: Mark 9:42-48

Question to ponder: *Does this sound like the party atmosphere often ascribed to Hell?*

Day 186   Date: _____

Everlasting Punishment

"And these shall go away into everlasting punishment: but the righteous into life eternal." (Matthew 25:46)

The worst thing about Hell is that it is <u>everlasting</u>. The punishment will never end! In his second of two letters to the local church at the eastern European city of Thessalonica, the apostle Paul spoke of *"everlasting destruction from the presence of the Lord"*. The term "destruction" does not refer to annihilation, as in ceasing to exist, but to <u>ruin</u> or eternal <u>loss</u>.

Today's scripture also refers to the Lord Jesus *"taking vengeance on them that know not God, and that obey not the gospel of our Lord Jesus Christ"*. It must be remembered that the rejection of Jesus Christ as Savior is an <u>infinite</u> offence against the Holy God that sent Him to earth to die in our place. That is why the punishment is <u>everlasting</u> – it must match the offence!

Scripture to read: II Thessalonians 1:5-9

Question to ponder: *Since God provided all that is necessary to be done for our salvation, and offers it to all as a free gift, is He not justified in punishing those who reject His Son so severely?*

Day 187   Date: _____

The Residents of Hell

"But the fearful, and unbelieving, and the abominable, and murderers, and whoremongers, and sorcerers, and idolators, and all liars, shall have their part in the lake which burneth with fire and brimstone: which is the second death." (Revelation 21:8)

People often make light of Hell saying, "all my friends will be there". The list of residents given above does not sound like the kind of friends anyone would want to spend eternity with. Especially when you add to that list the devil and his angels. Jesus said often that when the unbelievers are cast into Hell, *"there shall be weeping and gnashing of teeth"*.

Another sobering truth is that Hell will be filled with many people who were religious, but did not know the Savior personally. *Isaiah 64:6* tells us that even our *"righteousnesses are as filthy rages"* in God's sight. Jesus warned that, by comparison, there will be far more people lost in Hell than saved with Him in eternity.

Scripture to read: Luke 13:22-28

Question to ponder: *Does religion save a person?*

Day 188   Date: _____

Hannah's Vow

"Wherefore it came to pass, when the time was come about after Hannah had conceived, that she bare a son, and called his name Samuel, saying, Because I have asked him of the LORD." (I Samuel 1:20)

About 140 years after Ruth and Boaz lived God gave a son to a woman named Hannah. She had been unable to have children and had prayed earnestly for a son. She promised God that if He would give her a son she would raise him as a Nazarite (see Lesson 168) and give him to the LORD at the earliest possible age.

The LORD granted her request and the boy was named Samuel. Samuel grew to be a judge of Israel and a mighty prophet of the LORD. Two books of the Bible, *I & II Samuel*, bear his name although his death is recorded in the first book.

Scripture to read: I Samuel 1:1-28

Question to ponder: *What blessings would have been missed if the fertility drugs of today had been available to Hannah?*

Day 189   Date: _____

Samuel, Samuel

"And the LORD came, and stood, and called as at other times, Samuel, Samuel. Then Samuel answered, Speak; for thy servant heareth."
(I Samuel 3:10)

Eli the priest had two sons that were wicked men. Eli, however, did nothing to restrain his sons. Meanwhile, the boy Samuel had been given by his mother, Hannah, to Eli to raise after he was weaned. Samuel lived with Eli and ministered in the tabernacle (see Lesson 131).

Today's scripture tells the story of God calling the young boy Samuel into the ministry of a prophet. After Samuel, with Eli's help, responded to God's call, God gave him his first message. Samuel was to inform Eli of God's judgment upon him for allowing his two sons to live such openly wicked lives without restraining them.

Scripture to read: I Samuel 3:1-21

Question to ponder: *Would I recognize God's voice if He called me?*

Day 190   Date: _____

The Ark of God Taken

"And the ark of God was taken; and the two sons of Eli, Hophni and Phinehas, were slain." (I Samuel 4:11)

The Philistines again attacked the Israelites, and the Israelites were defeated in the battle. The Israelites decided they could win if the Ark of the Covenant (see Lesson 157) was brought into their camp. It was, and Eli's two sons came with it.

In the battle that followed, the Israelites were defeated in a very great slaughter. Eli's two sons were killed as God had previously told Eli they would be. The Philistines also stole the Ark of the Covenant, which represented God's presence among the Israelites. When Eli heard the news, he fell to his death.

Scripture to read: I Samuel 4:1-22

Question to ponder: *Why do you think Eli's family paid such a terrible price for their sins?*

Day 191　　Date: _____

Make Us A King

"And the LORD said unto Samuel, Hearken unto the voice of the people in all that they say unto thee: for they have not rejected thee, but they have rejected me, that I should not reign over them." (I Samuel 8:7)

Samuel served as judge over Israel all the days of his life, but in time the people began to cry out for a king to rule over them. The source of this complaint seemed to be a desire to be like the nations around them. Samuel was displeased, and probably personally offended by their demands.

God told Samuel to grant the request of the people, but to warn them of the consequences. In the words that God spoke to Samuel we see a basic principle of <u>authority</u> illustrated. The people were rejecting Samuel as their leader. Samuel, however, had been placed in that position by God. Therefore, the people were not only rejecting Samuel, but also God, the One who had <u>delegated</u> his position and authority to him.

Scripture to read: I Samuel 8:1-22

Question to ponder: *Is this principle true of any person in authority who we may obey or disobey?*

Day 192   Date: _____

Ordained of God

"Let every soul be subject unto the higher powers. For there is no power but of God: the powers that be are ordained of God." (Romans 13:1)

When Noah and his family started over again after the flood, God gave them instructions for living that made man accountable to man for the first time (see Lesson 43). Since that time the peoples of the earth have been identified by the <u>governments</u> they live under. There are many differing systems of government, but they all have one thing in common – they derive their authority to govern from God.

Today's scripture makes no distinction between differing forms of government, but calls all people to obey the authorities ("powers") they live under. Notice God calls these dignitaries His "ministers". He has "ordained" them and given them a job to do, to punish evildoers and reward doers of good works. Again, notice that if you resist one to whom authority has been given, you resist the One who has delegated that authority to them.

Scripture to read: Romans 13:1-7

Question to ponder: *According to this scripture, are we responsible to obey good rulers <u>only</u>?*

Day 193   Date: _____

To Whomsoever He Will

"This matter is by the decree of the watchers, and the demand by the word of the holy ones: to the intent that the living may know that the most High ruleth in the kingdom of men, and giveth it to whomsoever he will, and setteth up over it the basest of men." (Daniel 4:17)

One of the hardest things for a believer to understand is how God allows some of the most wicked of men to rise to places of prominence. Believers suffering under the persecution of ungodly leaders have often wavered in their faith, wondering if God was still in control. The above verse, taken from the book of the prophet *Daniel*, clearly states that God is sovereign over the affairs of men and often places wicked men in high places.

Perhaps the most dramatic illustration of this is found in today's scripture. When Jesus was arrested and tried He found Himself before Pilate, the governor of Judea. Pilate tried to impress Jesus with the power he thought he had over Him, but Jesus reminded Pilate that he did not receive his position by his own doing, but by God.

Scripture to read: John 19:1-11

Question to ponder: *Can an ungodly leader serve a godly purpose?*

Day 194   Date: _____

King Saul

"And they ran and fetched him thence: and when he stood among the people, he was higher than any of the people from his shoulders and upward."
(I Samuel 10:23)

After Samuel warned the people of the problems they would face in the future because of their demand to have a king, he dismissed the people. God sent him to a young man by the name of Saul to privately anoint him as king.

Samuel again called the people together and lots were cast to reveal the man who God had chosen to be the first king over Israel. During Old Testament times, God often revealed His will through the casting of lots (see *Proverbs 16:33*). The practice is not condoned for us today. We are to rely on God's Word and prayer to determine His will. Today's scripture tells this story and the reaction of the people to Saul.

Scripture to read: I Samuel 10:17-27

Question to ponder: *Why does God allow us the freedom to make choices He knows will ultimately hurt us?*

Day 195   Date: _____

Three Branches of Government

"For the LORD is our judge, the LORD is our lawgiver, the LORD is our king; he will save us." (Isaiah 33:22)

When the founders of our country were struggling to write the documents that would form the basis for a new experiment in government, they took many of their ideas directly from scripture. One scriptural teaching they took into account was the existence of the sin nature of man. They knew that all men, they included, need systems in place to check their natural attraction toward sinning. They found one such formula in today's verse.

This verse gives a threefold duty of government, which our founding fathers molded into a pattern for government that has three branches. Each branch (judicial, legislative, and executive) has distinct responsibilities, and each is "checked" by the powers of the other two.

Scripture to read: Psalms 24:1-10

Question to ponder: *What things can each branch of government learn about their responsibilities from the LORD's example as judge, lawgiver, and king?*

Day 196   Date: _____

Saul Rejected

"And Samuel said to Saul, Thou hast done foolishly: thou hast not kept the commandment of the LORD thy God, which he commanded thee: for now would the LORD have established thy kingdom upon Israel forever." (I Samuel 13:13)

Once again, the Israelites were battling the Philistines. Saul had sent for Samuel to come offer burnt offerings to the LORD, and Samuel had set a time he would arrive. When the time passed and Samuel had not arrived, Saul offered the burnt offering himself. God had forbid anyone other than one of the priests to offer burnt offerings to Him. When Samuel arrived he rebuked Saul and informed him that his disobedience had cost his family the throne of Israel. God would give it to another more deserving man.

In this incident we learn that God has set a distinction between the institutions of government and of religion (the priesthood in this case). They are both ordained of God, but have separate functions and ought not to be commingled.

Scripture to read: I Samuel 13:1-14

Question to ponder: *Should the church be controlled by the government?*

Day 197　Date: _____

Should We Pay Taxes?

"They say unto him, Caesar's. Then saith he unto them, Render therefore unto Caesar the things which are Caesar's; and unto God the things that are God's." (Matthew 22:21)

The Jewish religious rulers were trying to entrap Jesus in His words. They asked Him what they thought was a trick question, designed to get Him into trouble regardless of which way He answered. Should a Jew pay taxes to the Roman emperor? If He said yes, they could turn the people against Him. If He said no, they could accuse Him before the Romans. Surely they had Him this time!

In His answer, Jesus pointed out that government and God are not mutually exclusive. A person can serve God and the government at the <u>same</u> time.

Scripture to read: Matthew 22:15-22

Question to ponder: *According to today's text verse, would you say that a Christian could be involved in government?*

Day 198   Date: _____

Every Ordinance of Man

"Submit yourselves to every ordinance of man for the Lord's sake: whether it be to the king, as supreme; Or unto governors, as unto them that are sent by him for the punishment of evildoers, and for the praise of them that do well." (I Peter 2:13-14)

The book of *I Peter* was written by Peter to believers who were experiencing very hard trials. Many of them were suffering at the hand of the very governments they were living under. Peter himself had suffered as they had for the cause of Jesus Christ.

In spite of all this, Peter's counsel to these believers was to submit to every ordinance of man. The municipalities we live in have many ordinances (laws) governing their citizens. We are to obey these *"for the Lord's sake"*. In other words, the Lord can use our obedience to these ordinances for His purpose – to bring glory to God!

Scripture to read: I Peter 2:11-17

Question to ponder: *According to verse 15, what will our good works do to the accusations which unbelievers bring against us?*

Day 199   Date: _____

Incomplete Obedience

"And Samuel said, Hath the LORD as great delight in burnt-offerings and sacrifices, as in obeying the voice of the LORD? Behold, to obey is better than sacrifice, and to hearken than the fat of rams."
(I Samuel 15:22)

When the children of Israel were on their way out of Egypt, shortly after the victory at the Red Sea (see Lesson 127), they were attacked by the Amalekites. God now gave instruction to King Saul to totally destroy them, saving nothing alive. Saul led his army in a great victory, but saved the Amalekite King and some of the livestock alive. When confronted by Samuel, Saul blamed his people and explained that they saved the livestock in order to sacrifice them to the LORD.

Today's verse records Samuel's response to Saul. <u>Obedience</u> is more important to God than religious activity. This is a key message of the Bible. The person who simply <u>obeys</u> what God has asked has delighted his God more than the one who busies himself in church work.

Scripture to read: I Samuel 15:1-23

Question to ponder: *To what is disobedience compared to in verse 23?*

Day 200   Date: _____

The LORD Looketh On the Heart

"But the LORD said unto Samuel, Look not on his countenance, or on the height of his stature; because I have refused him: for the LORD seeth not as man seeth: for man looketh on the outward appearance, but the LORD looketh on the heart."
(I Samuel 16:7)

In today's scripture we have the story of Samuel anointing the next king of Israel, David. Samuel went to the household of Jesse, the grandson of Boaz and Ruth (see Lesson 183). Samuel assumed the eldest son would be God's chosen, but God directed him to the youngest of the eight sons.

In today's verse, we see God's instruction to Samuel as he looked upon the outward appearance of the eldest son. Eliab looked the part, but his heart was not suitable to God. When we make choices pertaining to people we do well to remember this verse and ask for God's help. On the other hand, we ourselves need to remember that people do look on the outward appearance; therefore we need to make our own outward appearance testify of God's inward presence in our lives.

Scripture to read: I Samuel 16:1-13

Question to ponder: *What kind of outward appearance would help people see our Savior in us?*

Day 201   Date: _____

David and Goliath

"And all this assembly shall know that the LORD saveth not with sword and spear: for the battle is the LORD's, and he will give you into our hands." (I Samuel 17:47)

This is the famous story of the battle between the young boy <u>David</u> and the giant <u>Goliath</u>. Goliath stood approximately 9 ½ feet tall. David was a shepherd boy.

There are many lessons in this story. The best is given in today's text verse. In verses 28 and 29 we see a stark contrast between David and his older brother Eliab which reveals the reason for the choice made between the two (see Lesson 200). David's response, "Is there not a cause?", challenges us today to leave the sidelines of fear and venture out in faith to fight the battle for the Lord!

Scripture to read: I Samuel 17:1-58

Question to ponder: *What was the true source of David's astounding victory?*

Day 202   Date: _____

David and Jonathan

"And Saul cast a javelin at him to smite him: whereby Jonathan knew that it was determined of his father to slay David." (I Samuel 20:33)

After his victory over the giant Goliath, Saul exalted David and set him over his army. Meanwhile, David became a close friend with Saul's son Jonathan. Soon, however, Saul became jealous of David as he became a national hero. He tried several times to kill David, but failed each time.

At first, Jonathan did not believe David when he told him of Saul's intent to kill him. The two friends devised a plan to reveal the truth to Jonathan. David would purposely miss the required meal at the time of the new moon. Today's scripture tells the story of what happened when David's absence was discovered.

Scripture to read: I Samuel 20:24-42

Question to ponder: *What kinds of things is a man capable of when he is overcome with jealousy and hatred?*

Day 203   Date: _____

David's Mighty Men

"And every one that was in distress, and every one that was in debt, and every one that was discontented, gathered themselves unto him; and he became a captain over them: and there were with him about four hundred men." (I Samuel 22:2)

David spent the next several years of his life hiding and running from Saul. Much of that time was spent living amongst the enemies of Israel. During this time, David gathered around him men who had similar needs. His own family would have to roam with him, since their lives were in jeopardy as well.

In David, we see a picture of what the Savior does for us who are hunted by the king of this world, Satan. Satan seeks to destroy our lives, but we find acceptance and refuge with Christ our Savior!

Scripture to read: I Samuel 22:1-23

Question to ponder: *How did God use this difficult time in David's life to prepare him to be king?*

Day 204   Date: _____

In God Have I Put My Trust

"In God have I put my trust: I will not be afraid what man can do unto me." (Psalms 56:11)

Many of the *Psalms* were written by David to express his emotions in the perils and triumphs of his life. Today's scripture is such a psalm. David was fleeing from Saul's presence, fearing for his life. *I Samuel 21:10-15* records David's flight to the city of Gath. There he would be safe from Saul. The problem was that Gath was a city of the Philistines whom David had defeated in battle. The giant Goliath had been a Philistine. David was recognized and had to pretend to be a mad man to escape.

The words of this psalm record the thoughts that comforted David during this time. They also provide comfort for us when we are overwhelmed by life's circumstances.

Scripture to read: Psalms 56:1-13

Question to ponder: *What does verse 8 reveal about God's omniscient watch over our lives?*

Day 205   Date: _____

The LORD's Anointed

"And he said unto his men, The LORD forbid that I should do this thing unto my master, the LORD's anointed, to stretch forth mine hand against him, seeing he is the anointed of the LORD."
(I Samuel 24:6)

On two separate occasions while David was fleeing from Saul, he was given opportunities to avenge himself. Each time he was close enough to touch Saul, to kill him if he desired, and each time he refused. The first time Saul entered a cave in which David was hiding (*I Samuel 24:1-22*). The second occasion is found in today's scripture reading.

David recognized an important principle. Certain people have been placed in their positions by God, and though they may be scoundrels, they deserve our respect because of the position they hold. Saul had been anointed as king of Israel by the prophet Samuel, at God's direction. David did not have the right to intervene to remove Saul from office unless God had specifically directed him to do so.

Scripture to read: I Samuel 26:1-25

Question to ponder: *According to I Samuel 26:9, how would God view one who hurt His anointed?*

Day 206   Date: _____

Pray for the King

"For kings, and for all that are in authority; that we may lead a quiet and peaceable life in all godliness and honesty." (I Timothy 2:2)

Because all authority comes from God, and all "powers" are ordained of God (see Lessons 192 & 193), we therefore have a responsibility to remember them in prayer before God. Verse 3 from today's scripture reading says, *"this is good and acceptable in the sight of God and our Saviour".*

Notice from today's scripture reading that four kinds of prayers are mentioned. <u>Supplications</u> are requests for personal needs. <u>Prayers</u> are requests, as a child would ask his father. <u>Intercessions</u> (see Lesson 138) are requests made on behalf of another. We are also to <u>give thanks</u> for our leaders. Also notice that these prayers are not conditional upon the quality of the men in leadership. In fact, our prayers may be used of God to influence poor leaders towards good, that we may lead quiet and peaceable lives.

Scripture to read: I Timothy 2:1-4

Question to ponder: *From reading verse 4, to what purpose do you suppose we should use the quiet and peaceable lives?*

Day 207   Date: _____

Saul's Death

"So Saul died, and his three sons, and his armourbearer, and all his men, that same day together." (I Samuel 31:6)

The Philistines continued to battle the Israelites. David meanwhile had been living amongst the Philistines. He and his men appeared to be loyal to the Philistine king, but were only seeking a place to be free from Saul's pursuit. When the Philistines gathered themselves to go to battle against Israel, God providentially intervened to keep David from being required to go with them.

In the battle Saul and his sons, including Jonathan, were killed. David had been given two opportunities to kill Saul himself, but had refused (see Lesson 205). Now, God used the Philistines to remove Saul from the throne of Israel. David was now free to become king, yet he mourned for Saul, his enemy, with a great sorrow.

Scripture to read: II Samuel 1:17-27

Question to ponder: *How could David heap such praise as we read in today's scripture reading on one who had hunted him for his life?*

Day 208   Date: _____

The Three Heavens

"And God called the firmament Heaven. And the evening and the morning were the second day." (Genesis 1:8)

On the second day of creation God divided the waters on earth from the waters in the atmosphere. The firmament that He created was called Heaven. In our scripture reading for today, reference is made to the "third heaven". In Genesis 2:1 we read, *"Thus the heavens and the earth were finished, and all the host of them."* Notice that "heavens" is plural.

God created three heavens. The <u>first</u>, referred to in our text verse for today, is the earth's atmosphere. The <u>second</u> heaven is what we call "outer space". The <u>third</u> heaven, from today's scripture reading, is the dwelling place of God.

Scripture reading: II Corinthians 12:1-5

Question to ponder: *Why do you suppose the man referred to in today's scripture reading was not allowed to speak of what he heard?*

Day 209   Date: _____

The Heavens Shall Perish

"Of old hast thou laid the foundation of the earth: and the heavens are the work of thy hands. They shall perish, but thou shalt endure: yea, all of them shall wax old like a garment; as a vesture shalt thou change them, and they shall be changed." (Psalms 102:25-26)

The Bible teaches that some day God is going to destroy the present heavens (and earth) and make new heavens. God will replace the present heavens and earth much like we would change from old to new clothes. Since the fall of man the present creation has been under the curse of sin and death. Notice the reference above to the most basic law of science: everything in creation grows old and wears out. By contrast, God Himself never changes or passes away (*"But thou art the same, and thy years shall have no end."* Psalms 102:27).

Today's scripture reading is a passage in the New Testament (*Hebrews*) that quotes the above verses from the Old Testament.

Scripture to read: Hebrews 1:10-12

Question to ponder: *What kind of things should we be living for if the above things are true?*

Day 210   Date: _____

New Heavens and Earth

"For, behold, I create new heavens and a new earth: and the former shall not be remembered, nor come into mind." (Isaiah 65:17)

Today's text verse instructs us that in the new heavens and earth there will be no remembrance of the present heaven and earth so familiar to us today. This certainly will require an act of God, but will probably also be, in part, a natural reaction to the glory and splendor of the new.

Of course, only those people who have trusted in Jesus Christ for their salvation will be allowed to enjoy the new creation. Those who have rejected Him will not only miss the new creation, and suffer in eternal torment, but will probably also be haunted forever by the memory of former things.

Scripture to read: Revelation 21:1-2

Question to ponder: *Why do you think it will it be necessary for God to remove the memory of this present age from our minds?*

Day 211   Date: _____

No More Death

"And God shall wipe away all tears from their eyes; and there shall be no more death, neither sorrow, nor crying, neither shall there be any more pain: for the former things are passed away." (Revelation 21:4)

For the believer, the former things will pass away and no longer be remembered. Those things that are such a part of our everyday lives: tears, death, sorrow, crying, pain: will be forever gone! The above verse has provided great comfort to many through the ages who have suffered grief and pain.

Notice from today's scripture reading that God Himself will dwell among His people! When the children of Israel were wandering in the wilderness, they would pitch their tents around the tabernacle (see Lesson 131) when they set up camp. That tabernacle represented God's presence in their midst. In the new heavens and earth, God will "tabernacle" with His believers. Certainly this is the most glorious aspect of Heaven!

Scripture to read: Revelation 21:3-5

Question to ponder: *Why do you think there might be tears in our eyes to be wiped away at the time we prepare to enter Heaven?*

Day 212   Date: _____

The Holy City

"And I John saw the holy city, new Jerusalem, coming down from God out of heaven, prepared as a bride adorned for her husband."
(Revelation 21:2)

Today's scripture reading describes the holy city, new Jerusalem, which people most commonly refer to when they talk about Heaven. In today's reading, you will find the "pearly gates" and the "streets of gold". This city is also referred to as a bride, the Lamb's (Jesus Christ) wife. When Jesus was about to leave His disciples and return to Heaven He said, *"I go to prepare a place for you"* (*John 14:2*). No doubt He was referring to this city which is *"prepared as a bride adorned for her husband"*.

When today's scripture is compared to the Bible's teaching concerning the church (future lesson), it would appear that this holy city is to be the special dwelling place of the believers living between the time of Christ's departure from the earth and His return for His church (future lesson). This city, approximately 1,300 miles long, wide, and tall, will sit on, or just above, the new earth.

Scripture to read: Revelation 21:9-27

Question to ponder: *Who provides the light for the city?*

Day 213   Date: _____

Heaven on Earth

"Nevertheless we, according to his promise, look for new heavens and a new earth, wherein dwelleth righteousness." (II Peter 3:13)

In addition to new heavens and the new Jerusalem, there will also be a new earth. Exactly what role this new earth plays in eternity is not given in scripture, but *Revelation 21:24-26* seems to indicate that there will be people in those days who do not dwell inside the holy city. The reference to *"the nations"* may refer to non-Jewish believers who were born before Christ came to earth, or even born in a future age.

Regardless, our scripture for today briefly describes a pure river of water of life, and the tree of life, which will be found there. Verse three of today's scripture promises that there will be no curse in the new earth. The curse placed upon the earth when Adam and Eve sinned (*Genesis 3:17-19*) will be removed forever!

Scripture to read: Revelation 22:1-7

Question to ponder: *According to Genesis 3:22, what benefit did the original tree of life provide?*

Unit Seven Review
Lessons 184 to 213

List the key historical people found in these lessons:

Lesson 188: Samuel's mother _____

Lesson 188: prophet _____

Lesson 189: priest _____

Lesson 194: first king _____

Lesson 200: new king _____

Lesson 202: David's friend _____

From the lessons noted in parenthesis, list some contrasting aspects of Hell and Heaven:

Hell		*Heaven*	
(184)	_____	(211)	_____
(184)	_____	(211)	_____
(184)	_____	(211)	_____
(185)	_____	(211)	_____
(210)	_____	(210)	_____
(186)	_____	(208)	_____
(187)	_____	(211)	_____
		(213)	_____

Unit Eight

Lessons 214 to 244

Bible History

David
Solomon

<u>Bible Truths</u>

Home
Principles from Proverbs

Day 214 Date: _____

Abner and Joab

"And Abner sent messengers to David on his behalf, saying, Whose is the land? saying also, Make thy league with me, and, behold, my hand shall be with thee, to bring about all Israel unto thee."
(II Samuel 3:12)

After the death of King Saul, there followed a civil war in Israel between the family of Saul and David's followers. The captain of Saul's army, Abner, led the fight, seeking to make one of Saul's sons king. David's army was led by one of his nephews, Joab. In today's scripture reading the account is given of Abner's desertion to David's side after being accused of immorality with one of Saul's concubines (a sort of supplementary, or lesser, wife).

Joab was a very rough man. His story weaves together incidents of godly counsel to David and many occasions of murder and deceit. Today's scripture includes the story of Joab's murder of Abner. For some unexplained reason, David never made Joab accountable for this action, except to pronounce a curse on his family.

Scripture to read: II Samuel 3:7-39

Question to ponder: *How did David view Abner?*

Day 215   Date: _____

Jerusalem

"And David gathered all Israel together to Jerusalem, to bring up the ark of the LORD unto his place, which he had prepared for it."
(I Chronicles 15:3)

After the murder of Abner, the revolt of Saul's son was defeated and David, at the age of 30, became king over a united Israel. One of David's early acts as king was to take the city of Jerusalem from its inhabitants and make it his capital. Jerusalem, also known as Zion, has become known as the "city of David".

Today's scripture tells the story of David's efforts to have the Ark of the Covenant (see Lessons 157 & 190) brought to Jerusalem. The first time it was not handled the way God had prescribed (*Numbers 4:1-15*) and two men died. The second time it was done the right way (*I Chronicles 15:2*) and the mission was successful.

The book of I Chronicles covers much of the same history as *II Samuel*. It focuses more on the religious endeavors of David and less on the natural history. It also includes many family genealogies.

Scripture to read: II Samuel 6:1-23

Question to ponder: *Is it right to do a right thing in a wrong way ("the end justifies the means")?*

Day 216   Date: _____

The Davidic Covenant

"And it shall come to pass, when thy days be expired that thou must go to be with thy fathers, that I will raise up thy seed after thee, which shall be of thy sons; and I will establish his kingdom. He shall build me an house, and I will stablish his throne for ever." (I Chronicles 17:11-12)

David built himself a great house in Jerusalem, but felt guilty that the Ark of the Covenant dwelt in the old tabernacle made of curtains. His great heart's desire was to build a beautiful temple for the Ark to reside in. Today's scripture reading is the story of God's reply to David and David's response to God. This story is also given in *I Chronicles 17*. David, a man of much bloodshed, would not be allowed to build the new temple.

God's promise that David's son would build the temple went beyond the next generation to a future Son who would be born into the lineage of David and rule from Jerusalem forever! This promise given to David is known as the Davidic Covenant.

Scripture to read: II Samuel 7:1-29

Question to ponder: *Did David have to do anything in order for this promise to be fulfilled?*

Day 217   Date: _____

Mephibosheth

"And David said, Is there yet any that is left of the house of Saul, that I may shew him kindness for Jonathan's sake?" (II Samuel 9:1)

Under King David, the nation Israel enjoyed great prosperity and military success. One by one Israel's enemies were subdued and David's kingdom expanded. After some years passed, David had a desire to show (same as "shew") kindness to the household of Saul. Normally, a new king would exterminate all members of a rival's family to secure his kingdom and remove all threats. David wanted to demonstrate a better way.

Today's scripture tells the story of David's kindness to Saul's grandson, the remaining son of Jonathan. In it we have a wonderful illustration of God's tender care over we who were once his enemies because of sin.

Scripture to read: II Samuel 9:1-13

Question to ponder: *What kind of treatment was Mephibosheth expecting to receive from David?*

Day 218   Date: _____

Bathsheba

"And it came to pass in an eveningtide, that David arose from off his bed, and walked upon the roof of the king's house: and from the roof he saw a woman washing herself; and the woman was very beautiful to look upon." (II Samuel 11:2)

This incident is the great turning point in David's life. At a time when he should have been on the battlefield with his men, he tarried behind. David lusted after the woman he saw washing, and soon had committed adultery.

As is so often the case, one sin requires another sin, and then another, to cover its tracks. The downward path of David's sins led to murder. This story is a vivid illustration of the process that sin follows, as taught in *James 1:14-15* (see Lesson 19).

Scripture to read: II Samuel 11:1-27

Question to ponder: *How do you suppose David felt during the time in his life that he was attempting to hide his sin?*

Day 219   Date: _____

The Home's Foundation

"Except the LORD build the house, they labor in vain that build it: except the LORD keep the city, the watchman waketh but in vain." (Psalms 127:1)

The <u>home</u> is the most important institution ordained by God. It is the most basic unit of society. It is in the home that we find our primary source of identification (family name). The Bible records the mistakes and failures of many of its greatest characters, including David. God doesn't hide their blemishes, but records them so we can learn from them. The act of adultery committed by David would wreak havoc in his home.

Today's scripture reading is a psalm that sings the praises of a home properly established on a foundation of God's Word. Children are seen as a <u>blessing</u> from God, not a curse or mistake. They are seen as arrows sent out from the parent's quiver. A home with many children is not frowned upon, but encouraged and "rewarded".

Scripture to read: Psalms 127:1-5

Question to ponder: *If children come from God, who then are we accountable to for how we raise them?*

Day 220　Date: _____

The Wife of Thy Youth

"Let thy fountain be blessed: and rejoice with the wife of thy youth."
(Proverbs 5:18)

God's original (and only) pattern for marriage is one man and one woman joined together "till death do us part". The Bible portrays the marriage relationship as a joyful one that is satisfying to both partners. Moses allowed divorce in limited circumstances, but Jesus pointed his critics to the original creation of Adam and Eve: one woman and one man (Matthew 19:3-8).

Today's scripture reading is taken from a love song written by David's son, King Solomon. The book, *Song of Solomon*, is a vivid account of the special love shared between Solomon and his bride. Tender words of love flow freely between them as they *"rejoice with the wife* (and husband) *of their youth"*.

Scripture to read: Song of Solomon 4:1-16

Question to ponder: *How can a husband and wife keep this kind of love flowing?*

Day 221   Date: _____

Submit One to Another

"Submitting yourselves one to another in the fear of God." *(Ephesians 5:21)*

The fifth chapter of *Ephesians* is the definitive Bible passage on husband and wife relationships. Chapter six goes on to cover parent and child relationships. This section begins with the above verse. The core underlying principle in family relationships is <u>submission to each other</u>. This, of course, runs in direct opposition to the world's philosophy.

The wife is to submit to her husband as a matter of rank within the home. God has assigned the husband the headship of the home. A godly wife submits to her husband, recognizing that in so doing she is submitting to the One who gave him his position. The husband is to submit to his wife by loving her more than himself. His pattern is Christ. Therefore there is no limit to how much he should be willing to sacrifice for his wife. Children are to submit to their parents by obeying them. Parents are to raise their children lovingly and tenderly.

Scripture to read: Ephesians 5:21 – 6:4

Question to ponder: *If all family members are submitting to God, will any of these things be hard?*

Day 222   Date: _____

A Virtuous Woman

"Who can find a virtuous woman? for her price is far above rubies." (Proverbs 31:10)

Our scripture reading for today is a favorite passage on Mother's Day. It begins with the question posed above and proceeds to detail the qualities of a virtuous woman. It closes with a reminder similar to the well-known saying; "beauty is only skin deep". True beauty, the writer reminds us, is found in a life lived trusting God.

Notice that the woman praised in this passage finds her fulfillment at home. She is busy, and out in the marketplace, but her activity revolves around her family and home. Her reward also comes from her own family. She has no need of the plaudits of the commercial world, for her husband and children bestow upon her all the praise that she needs.

Scripture to read: Proverbs 31:10-31

Question to ponder: *Where do you suppose the modern day feminist philosophy finds its source?*

Day 223   Date: _____

Thou Art the Man

"And David said unto Nathan, I have sinned against the LORD. And Nathan said unto David, The LORD also hath put away thy sin; thou shalt not die." (II Samuel 12:13)

God sent a prophet by the name of Nathan to confront David. Nathan told a story of a rich man who took advantage of a poor man and his family. David, in a fit of self-righteous anger, declared that the rich man must be brought to justice. Then he heard the words he had been dreading, *"Thou art the man!"* As Nathan pronounced the judgment that would fall on him for his sin, David repented immediately.

The events that unfolded in David's life from this point illustrate that forgiveness of sin does not guarantee escape from the natural consequences of sinful deeds. David was forgiven by God, but suffered horrible consequences in his family for the remainder of his life. The reference to his dead child in verse 23 provides comfort that God receives such children into Heaven upon their death.

Scripture to read: II Samuel 12:1-25

Question to ponder: *Do I take full responsibility for my sin as readily as David did?*

Day 224   Date: _____

Restore Unto Me the Joy

"Restore unto me the joy of thy salvation; and uphold me with thy free spirit." (Psalms 51:12)

Today's scripture is a psalm written by David expressing his sorrow and regret over his sin with <u>Bathsheba</u>. The psalm reveals the heart of a man who is truly repentant concerning his sin. David properly identifies sin as an offence against God, taking full responsibility for his actions. The psalm also gives a beautiful description of the forgiveness that God promises to those who confess their sin to Him.

Today's verse declares the motive a believer should have for seeking forgiveness. A saved person does not seek forgiveness to restore his salvation, because it is secure. Rather, forgiveness for the believer is a matter of restoring the <u>joy</u> of salvation. In other words, the issue is <u>fellowship</u>, not <u>relationship</u>.

Scripture to read: Psalms 51:1-19

Question to ponder: *According to verse 17, what is more important to God than our outward actions?*

Day 225   Date: _____

Amnon and Absalom

"And Absalom spake unto his brother Amnon neither good nor bad: for Absalom hated Amnon, because he had forced his sister Tamar."
(II Samuel 13:22)

Following his sin with Bathsheba, David experienced nothing but tragedy in his family. The child that was conceived out of his adulterous act died. Today's scripture tells the story of another terrible tragedy. David's oldest son, Amnon, raped his half-sister, Tamar. Tamar's brother, Absalom, responded by having Amnon murdered. Absalom fled from his father and was gone three years. Joab intervened to attempt to reconcile father and son, but even after Absalom returned to Jerusalem David refused to see him for two more years (chapter 14).

No doubt David was prevented from acting in this situation because of his own sin. Many fathers have watched idly and helplessly as their children have wandered deep into sin. Oftentimes it is because they have no credibility with their children because of sin in their own life.

Scripture to read: II Samuel 13:1-39

Question to ponder: *Where did David's children learn to act immorally?*

Day 226   Date: _____

Absalom's Rebellion

"And the king was much moved, and went up to the chamber over the gate, and wept: and as he went, thus he said, O my son Absalom, my son, my son Absalom! would God I had died for thee, O Absalom, my son, my son!"
(II Samuel 18:33)

Chapters fifteen through seventeen tell the story of a son, shunned by his own father, who lives a life of bitter rebellion in an effort to gain his father's attention. Absalom was a very handsome and charming young man, and easily won the hearts of many of the people. He led an effort to overthrow his father from the throne, but was no match for the seasoned veterans of David's band when it came time for battle.

Today's scripture reading tells the story of the battle and of Absalom's death. Today's text verse is the touching cry of a father grieving for his lost son.

Scripture reading: II Samuel 18:1-33

Question to ponder: *If David could have foreseen the death of Absalom, would he have committed his terrible sin with Bathsheba?*

Day 227   Date: _____

Train Up a Child

"Train up a child in the way he should go: and when he is old, he will not depart from it." (Proverbs 22:6)

Any parent looking for help in raising children should look to the book of *Proverbs* for help. It is a treasury of wisdom, much of it relating to the raising of children. Today's verse teaches that children do not turn out right by accident. Parents have a responsibility to train their children. Today's scripture reading repeats the reading of Lesson 153. This passage teaches that children are to be taught (trained) as an everyday way of life in the home.

Correction is a vital part of training children. *Proverbs* teaches, contrary to popular contemporary opinion, that corporal punishment (spanking) is an essential part of correcting children. See verses *19:18, 22:15, 23:13-14*, and *29:15*. When done properly, spanking a child for doing wrong is very effective. This involves explanation of the wrong, administering the discipline, and restoration of fellowship after the spanking is finished (hugs, etc.).

Scripture to read: Deuteronomy 6:4-12

Question to ponder: *Should a parent administer a spanking when his emotions are not under control?*

Day 228   Date: _____

Numbering the People

"And the king said unto Araunah, Nay; but I will surely buy it of thee at a price: neither will I offer burnt-offerings unto the LORD my God of that which doth cost me nothing. So David bought the threshingfloor and the oxen for fifty shekels of silver." (II Samuel 24:24)

Today's scripture reading tells the story of the second great sin of David's life. His sin wasn't in the act of having the people numbered, but in the selfish motive behind it. Notice the choice of punishments given to David and notice his choice and the reasoning behind it. David's trust in his God was complete, even when caught in sin. He understood that *"whom the LORD loveth he correcteth"* (Proverbs 3:11-12).

The spot where the plague was stayed (stopped) is very significant. The location of the threshingfloor that David purchased from the man called Ornan in *I Chronicles*, and Araunah in *II Samuel 24*, became the site of the temple, which would soon be built.

Scripture to read: I Chronicles 21:1-30

Question to ponder: *Why did David insist on paying for the threshingfloor (II Samuel 24) and the land around it (I Chronicles 21)?*

Day 229   Date: _____

Preparing to Build the Temple

"But who am I, and what is my people, that we should be able to offer so willingly after this sort? For all things come of thee, and of thine own have we given thee." (I Chronicles 29:14)

David knew he couldn't build the temple (see Lesson 216), but that didn't stop him from making the preparations. In his latter days, he made his son Solomon king in his place and gave him instructions for the building of the temple. David prepared the "blueprints" and created an organizational structure for the priests, Levites (see Lesson 163), and musicians who would serve in the temple. He also led the people in gathering the necessary materials.

The people gave generously and David gathered them together to praise their God. Today's text verse is part of David's heartfelt prayer to God. Notice that when we give to God, we can only give out of what He has already given to us. We are dependent upon Him, even for what we give back to Him. By contrast, God is totally self-sufficient. He has no need and is not dependent on any other being for anything. He has all He needs within Himself.

Scripture to read: I Chronicles 29:1-22

Question to ponder: *Can we ever outgive God?*

Day 230   Date: _____

The Wisdom of Solomon

"And God said to Solomon, Because this was in thine heart, and thou hast not asked riches, wealth, or honour, nor the life of thine enemies, neither yet hast asked long life; but hast asked wisdom and knowledge for thyself, that thou mayest judge my people, over whom I have made thee king: Wisdom and knowledge is granted unto thee; and I will give thee riches, and wealth, and honour, such as none of the kings have had that have been before thee, neither shall there any after thee have the like."
(II Chronicles 1:11-12)

Shortly after the death of David, God appeared to Solomon and offered him anything he desired. Solomon could have asked for anything that people normally long for, but he asked instead for wisdom. Today's text verse gives God's favorable answer to his request. Today's scripture reading records an example of the wisdom of Solomon.

The books of *I Kings* and *II Chronicles* are historical books, which cover much of the same history.

Scripture to read: I Kings 3:4-28

Question to ponder: *What would I have asked for if I had been in Solomon's place?*

Day 231   Date: _____

The Fear of the LORD

"The fear of the LORD is the beginning of wisdom: and the knowledge of the holy is understanding." (Proverbs 9:10)

God granted Solomon the wisdom he requested, above all the wise men of his day. People came from all over the earth to hear him speak on subjects ranging from practical wisdom to science. Indeed, Solomon is the wisest man who ever lived, excepting the Lord Jesus Christ. *I Kings 4:32* says, *"And he spake three thousand proverbs: and his songs were a thousand and five."* Today's verse instructs us in how we can find wisdom. True wisdom begins with the fear of the LORD, or <u>faith</u>, as we know it.

By now you may have noticed that the title "LORD" often appears in all capital letters. Wherever this is found in the Bible, it is referring to God's special relationship to Israel as "Jehovah" (see Lesson 113).

Scripture to read: Proverbs 1:1-33

Question to ponder: *According to verse 5, how can we use the book of Proverbs to become wise?*

Day 232   Date: _____

Trust in the LORD

"Trust in the LORD with all thine heart; and lean not unto thine own understanding. In all thy ways acknowledge him, and he shall direct thy paths." (Proverbs 3:5-6)

Today's text verses have been a blessing to many people through the ages. They form a perfect guide for a happy life. The problem is that we are so prone to "*leaning unto our own understanding*". We tend to turn to God for direction only <u>after</u> we have exhausted all other alternatives. If we truly acknowledge Him <u>first</u>, in <u>all</u> our ways, we eliminate many troubles.

From today's scripture reading, find some other building blocks for a happy life. God intends for us to lead happy, fulfilled lives. His Word gives us all we need. In it we find true wisdom.

Scripture to read: Proverbs 3:1-24

Question to ponder: *What benefits are promised as a result of applying wisdom, as found in verses 13 through 16?*

Day 233   Date: _____

The Liberal Soul

"There is that scattereth, and yet increaseth; and there is that withholdeth more than is meet, but it tendeth to poverty." (Proverbs 11:24)

The book of *Proverbs* gives practical wisdom that finds its application "where the rubber meets the road". Its pages speak of human nature, relationships, politics, business, and many other subjects. Today's text verse speaks of the benefits of <u>generosity</u> as contrasted with the detriments of stinginess. It could be rephrased this way: sometimes you will gain more by giving than by hoarding. The word "meet" means "appropriate".

The same principle is found in *II Corinthians 9:6*. *"But this I say, He which soweth sparingly shall reap also sparingly; and he which soweth bountifully shall reap also bountifully."*

Today's scripture reading is a selection of verses from Proverbs that speak on the subject of the blessings of giving.

Scripture to read: Proverbs 3:9-10, 13:7, 22:9, 28:27

Question to ponder: *What example does God set for us in this area?*

Day 234   Date: _____

Sluggards

"Go to the ant, thou sluggard; consider her ways, and be wise."
(Proverbs 6:6)

In today's scripture, Solomon addresses the issue of <u>laziness</u>. It is quite obvious that he had no time for slothful people. In the above verse, he advises the "sluggard" to consider the industriousness of the common ant. Solomon points out that ants appear to have more wisdom than many people do. They plan ahead and make provision while the opportunity presents itself.

He vividly portrays the person who has difficulty getting out of bed in the morning, and predicts the poverty that surely awaits him. For an additional passage on sluggards, read *Proverbs 26:13-16*.

Scripture to read: Proverbs 6:6-11

Question to ponder: *How would the person in verse six respond to the sound of an alarm clock?*

Day 235   Date: _____

The Temple Completed

"Now when Solomon had made an end of praying, the fire came down from heaven, and consumed the burnt-offering and the sacrifices; and the glory of the LORD filled the house." (II Chronicles 7:1)

King Solomon led the people in building the temple that David, his father, had desired to build. The location of the temple was Mount Moriah, on the land David had purchased from Araunah (see Lesson 228). It was upon this same mountain, approximately 850 years earlier, that Abraham had prepared to offer his only son, Isaac, to God (see Lessons 58 & 59).

The temple took seven years to build. Chapters 2 through 4 of *II Chronicles* tell the story of its construction. Today's scripture reading tells of its completion and the assembling of the people for the dedication service.

Scripture to read: II Chronicles 5:1-14

Question to ponder: *How did the people know that God approved of the new temple?*

Day 236   Date: _____

If My People

"If my people, which are called by my name, shall humble themselves, and pray, and seek my face, and turn from their wicked ways; then will I hear from heaven, and will forgive their sin, and will heal their land."
(II Chronicles 7:14)

In the dedication service for the new temple, Solomon prayed a beautiful prayer enumerating several *"if"* situations followed by a *"then hear"* plea to God. <u>If</u> we commit this sin, or fall into this distress, <u>then hear</u> from heaven and answer our prayer. In each instance, Solomon conditioned God's answer upon a prayer offered from, or prayed toward, the new temple.

After the people returned to their homes, God appeared to Solomon and assured him that He would indeed answer such prayers. The above verse is from God's answer to Solomon. It has been claimed by God's people through the years as a prescription for healing any land that has turned its back upon God.

Scripture to read: II Chronicles 7:1-22

Question to ponder: *According to today's text verse, the healing of any land is dependent upon which people?*

Day 237   Date: _____

A Soft Answer

"A soft answer turneth away wrath: but grievous words stir up anger." (Proverbs 15:1)

Today's verse is typical of the practical wisdom found in *Proverbs*. When facing a person who is filled with anger, harsh words will only serve to fan the flame of their wrath. Words spoken quietly and calmly, on the other hand, will serve to quiet the person and calm their anger.

Today's scripture, a selection of various proverbs, has several selections regarding the tongue. The proper use of the tongue brings great blessing. Foolish use of the tongue wreaks much destruction. Many of the proverbs in today's reading use a contrasting style. An act or attitude of goodness is contrasted with an act or attitude of evil. Meditate upon each verse to find the wisdom contained therein.

Scripture to read: Proverbs 15:1-33

Question to ponder: *According to verse 28, what difference is found between the answer of a righteous man and that of a wicked man?*

Day 238   Date: _____

Friends

"A man that hath friends must shew himself friendly: and there is a friend that sticketh closer than a brother." (Proverbs 18:24)

Friends can be the strength of a person, or the undoing. Wise parents will monitor the friends of their children very closely, and exercise control over the kinds of friends chosen by them. Peers often exert more influence over children than their parents do, so friends should be chosen who will encourage submission to parents and devotion to God.

Today's text verse can be interpreted several ways. A person who is friendly themselves will never lack for friends. On the other hand, a person whose highest goal is to be popular is obligated to be friendly in order to gain popularity. Today's scripture reading reminds us that it is not necessary to be friends with everyone.

Scripture to read: Proverbs 22:24-27

Question to ponder: *Do we need to have a lot of friends, or is it better to find a few friends who "stick closer than a brother"?*

Day 239   Date: _____

Business Dealings

"Divers weights, and divers measures, both of them are alike abomination to the LORD." (Proverbs 20:10)

The Bible has much to say about the business world. In today's text verse, the businessman who cheats his customers is called an abomination to God. Weights and measures were used as scales in the market place. Charging a customer for more than they purchased by adjusting the scales is stealing, and God is angered by such dishonesty.

Verse 14 from today's scripture reading speaks to sales pressure. The salesman complains of being shorted ("I'm giving this away!") when in front of the buyer, then brags how much he made as soon as they are gone.

Scripture reading: Proverbs 20:4-23

Question to ponder: *Is God concerned about how we act in the "secular" world?*

Day 240   Date: _____

Wine Is A Mocker

"Wine is a mocker, strong drink is raging: and whosoever is deceived thereby is not wise." (Proverbs 20:1)

In the languages in which the Bible was written, the words translated "wine" in English are generic words that speak of "the fruit of the vine". To determine whether the Bible is referring to intoxicating drink, one must look at the context that the word is being used in. The word "wine" refers to non-intoxicating grape juice in most passages.

In the text verse above, and in today's scripture reading, the context clearly indicates intoxicating beverage. In every case where this use of "wine" is found, it is denounced and the reader is warned to abstain from its use. The reason is given in *Ephesians 5:18*. *"Be not drunk with wine, wherein is excess; but be filled with the Spirit"*. We are to be controlled by God's Spirit, and nothing else. Strong drink is a controlling substance and incompatible with the Holy Spirit, and the believer.

Scripture to read: Proverbs 23: 29-35

Question to ponder: *How much alcohol does it take to affect (control) the mind of the consumer?*

Day 241   Date: _____

Solomon's Wealth

"And the king made silver to be in Jerusalem as stones, and cedars made he to be as the sycamore trees that are in the vale, for abundance."
(I Kings 10:27)

When God offered Solomon anything he desired, the new king chose wisdom over any of the other things he could have asked for (see Lesson 230). Because he chose wisely, God granted him the things he could have asked for, but didn't. News of Solomon's splendor spread through all the earth. Today's scripture reading tells the story of the queen of Sheba (in southern Arabia) who came to Jerusalem to satisfy her curiosity and prove Solomon with hard questions. What she saw completely removed any doubt in her mind.

The scripture reading also tells of the wealth of Solomon. He had so much wealth continually coming in that he scarcely knew what to do with it all.

Scripture to read: I Kings 10:1-29

Question to ponder: *When God decides to bless us, is there any limit to what He can do?*

Day 242   Date: _____

Solomon's Wives

"For it came to pass, when Solomon was old, that his wives turned away his heart after other gods: and his heart was not perfect with the LORD his God, as was the heart of David his father."
(I Kings 11:4)

Sons often follow in their father's footsteps, and Solomon was no different. David had fallen in the area of morality, and Solomon's downfall was related. Verse 3 from today's scripture reveals that Solomon had 700 wives and 300 concubines (see lesson 214). This was a clear violation of God's principle for marriage, and led to Solomon forsaking the God who had blessed him with his great wealth and power.

Because of Solomon's sin, God informed him that the kingdom of Israel would soon be split. His family, the descendants of David, would retain a small portion. Most of the tribes of Israel would be taken from them.

Scripture to read: I Kings 11:1-14

Question to ponder: *How important is it to marry someone who shares your faith in God?*

Day 243   Date: _____

All is Vanity

"And I gave my heart to seek and search out by wisdom concerning all things that are done under heaven: this sore travail hath God given to the sons of man to be exercised therewith."
(Ecclesiastes 1:13)

The book of *Ecclesiastes* (meaning, "the preacher") is a very unusual book. It contains the thoughts of Solomon during the time of his life when he had forsaken God. One of the key phrases of the book is *"under the sun"*. The wisdom contained in most of this book reaches no higher than the sun. As a result, the conclusion Solomon reaches again and again is *"all is vanity"*. Without God, all of life is meaningless and devoid of purpose.

Solomon describes all the pursuits he followed in his effort to find meaning to life, i.e. knowledge, pleasure, industry, riches, and concludes that all these things are "vanity".

Scripture to read: Ecclesiastes 1:1-18

Question to ponder: *Do people who try to find fulfillment in similar pursuits today reach any different conclusion?*

Day 244   Date: _____

The Conclusion of the Whole Matter

"Let us hear the conclusion of the whole matter: Fear God, and keep his commandments: for this is the whole duty of man." (Ecclesiastes 12:13)

After Solomon devoted his whole heart to seek and search out by human reasoning all the things a man could give his life to, he reached the conclusion he had begun his kingly reign with – but had forgotten. The whole duty of man is to obey his Creator. The entire message of the Bible can be summarized in one word – OBEDIENCE! Or, in other words, *"keep His commandments"*.

The reason is found in *Ecclesiastes 11:9*. *"Rejoice, O young man, in thy youth; and let thy heart cheer thee in the days of thy youth, and walk in the ways of thine heart, and in the sight of thine eyes: but know thou, that for all these things God will bring thee into judgment"*. God has made us creatures with a <u>free will</u>. We can do what we want. But, God will have the last word!

Scripture to read: Ecclesiastes 12:1-14

Question to ponder: *What is at the heart of the atheist's denial of God's existence?*

Unit Eight Review
Lessons 214 to 244

Identify people from these lessons that played a key role in David's life:

Lesson 214: _____ _____

Lesson 217: _____

Lesson 218: _____

Lesson 223: _____

Lesson 225: _____ _____

Lesson 228: _____

Lesson 230: _____

Briefly summarize the Biblical principles learned in these lessons:

Lesson 219: _____

Lesson 220: _____

Lesson 221: _____

Lesson 227: _____

Lesson 233: _____

Lesson 234: _____

Lesson 237: _____

Lesson 240: _____

Lesson 244: _____

SUMMARY OF THE STORY OF THE BIBLE

- ✓ Creation
- ✓ The Fall of Man
- ✓ The Flood
- ✓ The Tower of Babel
- ✓ The promise to Abraham
- ✓ The promise passed on to Isaac and Jacob
- ✓ The Captivity in Egypt
- ✓ The Exodus, Wilderness Wanderings, and the Law
- ✓ The conquest of the Promised Land under Joshua
- ✓ The Judges
- ✓ The Prophet Samuel, The reign of King Saul
- ✓ The reign of King David and King Solomon
- ✓ The kingdom divided: Judah and Israel
- ✓ The Babylonian Captivity
- ✓ The return to Jerusalem and rebuilding of the Temple
- ✓ Silent years between the Old & New Testament
- ✓ The birth of Jesus Christ
- ✓ The earthly ministry of Jesus Christ
- ✓ The death, burial, and resurrection of Jesus Christ
- ✓ The ministry of the Apostles

Unit Nine

Lessons 245 to 274

Bible History

Judah & Israel
The Kings
The Prophets

<u>Bible Truths</u>

The Judgments
Rewards

Day 245   Date: _____

The Kingdom Divided

"And when all Israel saw that the king would not hearken unto them, the people answered the king, saying, What portion have we in David? and we have none inheritance in the son of Jesse: every man to your tents, O Israel: and now, David, see to your own house. So all Israel went to their tents." (II Chronicles 10:16)

All the building done under Solomon's reign came at a price, the labors of the people. After his death, the people approached Rehoboam his son, requesting that their burden be made lighter. Rehoboam promised an answer in three days and consulted with two groups of advisors. The men who had been his father's counselors advised him to lighten the load. His own peers, those of his own age, advised him to get even tougher.

As seen in today's text verse, the people reacted strongly to his decision to follow the advice of his peers. Ten tribes left Rehoboam and made a man by the name of Jeroboam their king. The family of Israel was now split; the kingdom was divided.

Scripture to read: I Kings 12:1-24

Question to ponder: *What danger is there in seeking advice from your own peers?*

Day 246   Date: _____

He Made Israel to Sin

"And he shall give Israel up because of the sins of Jeroboam, who did sin, and who made Israel to sin." (I Kings 14:16)

Jeroboam, the son of Nebat, was made king of the 10 tribes that refused to follow Rehoboam. These 10 tribes were the northern tribes and became known as **Israel**. The southern 2 tribes that stayed with the family line of David became known as **Judah**.

Jeroboam, though an industrious man (*I Kings 11:28*), was a wicked man. He feared that if the people of Israel continued to go to Jerusalem to observe the feasts and sacrifices, their hearts would be drawn back to Rehoboam and to the house of David. To prevent this, he set up a pagan religion with new places to worship and new feasts and sacrifices. The northern kingdom of Israel would never again have a godly king to lead them.

Scripture to read: I Kings 12:25-33

Question to ponder: *Where do you think Jeroboam got the idea for worshipping calves made of gold (see I Kings 11:40)?*

Day 247   Date: _____

Asa and Baasha

"For the eyes of the LORD run to and fro throughout the whole earth, to shew himself strong in the behalf of them whose heart is perfect toward him. Herein thou hast done foolishly: therefore from henceforth thou shalt have wars." (II Chronicles 16:9)

The kings of the southern kingdom, Judah, were all direct descendants of King David. Many, like Rehoboam, were ungodly kings. Several, however, were good kings. Asa, the grandson of Rehoboam, reigned for 41 years and was mostly good. His father, King Abijah, warred against Jeroboam and permanently weakened him, but was a sinful king.

During the reign of Asa, Baasha, king of Israel, engaged Judah in battle. Asa formed a league with the king of Syria for protection, and sealed it with the silver and gold that had been dedicated to the temple. God sent the prophet Hanani to rebuke the king, reminding Asa that he had trusted in God alone in an earlier situation against the Ethiopians.

Scripture to read: II Chronicles 16:1-14

Question to ponder: *Does one spiritual victory guarantee immunity from falling in the future?*

Day 248   Date: _____

Elijah the Tishbite

"And Elijah the Tishbite, who was of the inhabitants of Gilead, said unto Ahab, As the LORD God of Israel liveth, before whom I stand, there shall not be dew nor rain these years, but according to my word." (I Kings 17:1)

Several kings after Baasha, Ahab the son of King Omri became king of Israel. Ahab was a wicked king. Adding to his sins, he married a woman named Jezebel, a worshipper of the pagan god, Baal. Jezebel was even more wicked than Ahab was. The extent of her wickedness has made her name synonymous with womanly treachery even today.

The very first mention of the prophet Elijah is found in today's text verse. Imagine a total unknown, in the dress of a rugged outdoorsman, marching into the king's palace and making a pronouncement such as this! God does not wink at sin, and Ahab was about to experience God's judgment. Today's scripture reading details the events in Elijah's life while he was hiding from Ahab.

Scripture to read: I Kings 17:1-24

Question to ponder: *In what ways did God take care of his prophet while Elijah was hiding from Ahab?*

Day 249   Date: _____

Showdown on Mt. Carmel

"And Elijah came unto all the people, and said, How long halt ye between two opinions? if the LORD be God, follow him: but if Baal, then follow him. And the people answered him not a word." (I Kings 18:21)

After three years without rain, Elijah again showed himself to Ahab. Elijah proposed a contest to take place on top of Mount Carmel, which overlooks the Mediterranean Sea. Elijah <u>alone</u> represented the true, living God. On Carmel he faced 450 prophets of Baal, and another 400 false prophets, all personally supported by Jezebel. Elijah began the contest with the words of our text verse. Notice the response of the people. *James 1:8* says, *"A double minded man is unstable in all his ways."*

Today's scripture reading tells the story of the thrilling encounter between God's faithful prophet and the false prophets of Baal. Parts of the account are humorous, but more so they are very sobering.

Scripture to read: I Kings 18:17-46

Question to ponder: *How sincere do you believe the response of the people in verse 39 was?*

Day 250   Date: _____

Accountability

"So then every one of us shall give account of himself to God."
(Romans 14:12)

One of the key principles of scripture is that of <u>accountability</u>. None of us really seek after it, but verse seven of today's scripture reading instructs us, "For *none of us liveth to himself, and no man dieth to himself.*" We are not accountable only to <u>ourselves</u>. We <u>shall</u> face our Creator someday. Every one of us! He will not forget or procrastinate. Neither will He soften the holy standard by which we are to be judged. God's truth is absolute and cannot be rationalized away. We will answer for His <u>absolute</u> truth, not our <u>relative</u> version of it.

There will be, however, differing <u>judgments</u>. Some have taken place already, and some are scheduled at a future time known only to God. All are certain. We can determine which of these judgments will apply to ourselves by our response to the Word of God in our everyday life.

Scripture to read: Romans 14:1-13

Question to ponder: *According to today's scripture reading, who should we be most concerned about facing God's judgment?*

Day 251   Date: _____

Delivered From the Law

"Verily, verily, I say unto you, He that heareth my word, and believeth on him that sent me, hath everlasting life, and shall not come into condemnation; but is passed from death unto life." (John 5:24)

For the believer in Jesus Christ who has truly repented of his sin and been born again, there is one judgment that he will <u>not</u> have to face. That is the judgment of condemnation for sin. The Law demands complete, perfect, obedience (see Lesson 15). For those who fail (all of us) the Law demands the penalty of condemnation – eternal damnation. When He died on the cross, Jesus was made sin for us (see Lesson 29), and our sins were judged in Him. Therefore <u>our sins have already been judged</u>!

Today's scripture reading compares our relationship to the Law with that of a wife to her husband. While her husband is living, she is bound by her marriage vows. Upon his death, she is released from those vows and is free to marry again. We are bound to the penalty of the Law until salvation. Through the substitutionary death of the Savior, we are freed from the claims that the Law has upon us.

Scripture to read: Romans 7:1-6

Question to ponder: *Will I ever have to be judged for my sin?*

Day 252   Date: _____

The Judgment Seat of Christ

"For we must all appear before the judgment seat of Christ; that every one may receive the things done in his body, according to that he hath done, whether it be good or bad." (II Corinthians 5:10)

When we were saved it was by grace, not of <u>works</u>. We then became the <u>work</u>manship of Jesus Christ *"unto good <u>works</u>"* (*Ephesians 2:8-10*). Once saved, we are to <u>work</u> for Jesus Christ (see Lesson 50). Some day we will be judged according to the <u>works</u> we have done for Him. This judgment, the Judgment Seat of Christ, has nothing to do with our <u>salvation</u>, but rather, our <u>service</u> for Him. Our <u>works</u> will be judged as to their worth to the Savior. Today's text verse refers to <u>works</u> that are either good (of value to Him) or bad (worthless).

Today's scripture likens these works to building upon a foundation (Jesus Christ, i.e. salvation). Works of a sort that abide will cause us to receive a reward. Works that are worthless to Him, will be consumed, and cause us to suffer loss of rewards. Yet, our eternal salvation is not in jeopardy.

Scripture to read: I Corinthians 3:10-15

Question to ponder: *How would it be to stand before the Savior and see our works revealed as worthless?*

Day 253   Date: _____

Judging Your Self

"For if we would judge ourselves, we should not be judged."
(I Corinthians 11:31)

Believers in Jesus Christ have the privilege (and responsibility) of judging <u>themselves</u>. This means we must look inward and be honest with ourselves regarding the condition of our heart. We first must judge ourselves to be a sinner and in need of a Savior. If we do this, and accept that Savior, we will not face the judgment of eternal condemnation. We then must judge ourselves concerning the sins we commit <u>after</u> salvation. These affect our <u>fellowship</u> with the Savior (see Lesson 55). We must confess these sins, seeking forgiveness.

To judge <u>self</u> also means to realize and admit that, in ourselves, we can produce nothing of value to Christ. We are totally dependent upon Him to produce the very good works that He will reward.

Scripture to read: I John 1:8-10

Question to ponder: *Will Christ judge us for sins He has already forgiven?*

Day 254   Date: _____

The Believer's Crowns

"If any man's work abide which he hath built thereupon, he shall receive a reward." (I Corinthians 3:14)

Today's scripture reading speaks of the crown given to the winner of a race. This crown was not a kingly crown, but a wreath (garland) of woven branches and leaves. It went to one who had trained diligently, depriving himself of pleasures that would detract from his purpose, in order to cross the finish line ahead of the other runners. His crown, however, would soon fade away.

The Bible speaks of incorruptible crowns that will be given to believers who have "run the race well".

The crown of rejoicing   (*I Thessalonians 2:19-20*)
The crown of righteousness   (*II Timothy 4:8*)
The crown of life   (*James 1:12, Revelation 2:10*)
The crown of glory   (*I Peter 5:4*)

Revelation 4:10 seems to indicate that we will cast our crowns before the Savior's throne, acknowledging that He has caused us to win them.

Scripture to read: I Corinthians 9:24-27

Question to ponder: *Who really deserves the credit for the crowns we may win?*

Day 255   Date: _____

Wicked King Ahab

"But there was none like unto Ahab, which did sell himself to work wickedness in the sight of the LORD, whom Jezebel his wife stirred up."
(I Kings 21:25)

Of all the wicked kings of the northern kingdom, Israel, Ahab was the worst. After Elijah's successful confrontation with the prophets of Baal on top of Mount Carmel, he had to again flee for his life from Ahab and Jezebel. Today's scripture reading tells the story of how Ahab stole the vineyard of a man named Naboth. It reveals how he was "stirred up" by Jezebel.

Again, Elijah was sent to confront the wicked king. Ahab would be held accountable for his murderous act, and judgment would come. Ahab did repent temporarily, and God rewarded his humility with a brief respite.

Scripture to read: I Kings 21:1-29

Question to ponder: *Look at today's text verse. Can we perform any sinful act away from "the sight of the LORD"?*

Day 256   Date: _____

Good King Jehoshaphat

"But Jehoshaphat said, Is there not here a prophet of the LORD besides, that we may enquire of him?" (II Chronicles 18:6)

After the death of King Asa (see Lesson 247), Jehoshaphat succeeded his father to the throne of Judah. Jehoshaphat was a godly king who led Judah in returning to the teachings of the law. Because of his good heart, God blessed him with riches and honor. Jehoshaphat repeated one mistake of his father, however. He made an alliance with wicked Ahab, the king of Israel, in order to do battle against Syria. Today's scripture reading tells the story of the two kings seeking the LORD's direction for battle.

Ahab's prophets were "yes men", unwilling to confront a wicked king with the truth. God sent Micaiah, a faithful prophet, to deliver His message. Verse 38 records the fulfillment of the prophecy given by Elijah *in I Kings 21:19. II Chronicles 19 and 20* give more details of Jehoshaphat's life.

Scripture to read: I Kings 22:1-50

Question to ponder: *According to II Chronicles 19:2, how did God view Jehoshaphat's alliance with Ahab?*

Day 257   Date: _____

The Chariot of Fire

"And it came to pass, as they still went on, and talked, that, behold, there appeared a chariot of fire, and horses of fire, and parted them both asunder; and Elijah went up by a whirlwind into heaven." (II Kings 2:11)

Shortly after his confrontation with the prophets of Baal upon Mount Carmel, God instructed Elijah to anoint the man who would replace him in his ministry. *I Kings 19:19-21* records the call of Elisha. Today's scripture reading tells the remarkable story of the conclusion of Elijah's ministry. God would take him home to heaven without having to experience death! The Bible tells of only one other man who was spared from the experience of death – Enoch (*Genesis 5:24*).

Before he left this earth, Elijah gave Elisha the opportunity to make a request of him. Elisha asked for a double portion of Elijah's spirit to be upon him. Elijah granted the request, providing Elisha see him when he was taken away. The next chapters of *II Kings* record the ministry of Elisha.

Scripture to read: II Kings 2:1-15

Question to ponder*: If you could escape death like Enoch and Elijah would you prefer that?*

Day 258   Date: _____

Naaman the Leper

"And Elisha sent a messenger unto him, saying, Go and wash in Jordan seven times, and thy flesh shall come again to thee, and thou shalt be clean." (II Kings 5:10)

After the departure of Elijah, Elisha was used of God to perform many miracles. These miracles demonstrated that his request for a double portion of Elijah's spirit had been granted. He also was used of God to reprove King Jehoshaphat for yet another ill-advised alliance, this time with Ahab's son, King Jehoram.

Today's scripture reading tells the story of Naaman, the captain of the army of Syria. Naaman had been stricken with the dreaded disease, leprosy. Although Syria was a mortal enemy of Israel and Judah, Elisha ministered to Naaman's need. Notice, at the end of the story, the consequences of the greed of Elisha's servant.

Scripture to read: II Kings 5:1-27

Question to ponder: *After observing the miraculous healing of Naaman at the hand of God, how could Gehazi have sought for riches from a man?*

Day 259   Date: _____

Jehu

"But Jehu took no heed to walk in the law of the LORD God of Israel with all his heart: for he departed not from the sins of Jeroboam, which made Israel to sin." (II Kings 10:31)

The story of Jehu illustrates two interesting things about how God works in the affairs of this world. God had pronounced judgment upon the household of Ahab through the prophet Elijah (*I Kings 21:21-22*), yet the judgment did not come for 14 years, after two of Ahab's sons had reigned over Israel. God's judgment is certain, but His timetable is His own. He is not confined to the restraints of time as we are. Second, He used a man, Jehu, who was almost as wicked as Ahab to accomplish the judgment. Jehu became king of Israel, exterminated the family of Ahab, and yet did not follow God. God is sovereign in the affairs of men, and will use both good and bad men to accomplish His purposes.

Today's scripture reading tells how Jehu was used to fulfill the prophecy given by Elijah (*I Kings 21:23*) concerning Jezebel.

Scripture to read: II Kings 9:30-37

Question to ponder: *Does God have to answer to anyone for how He chooses to do things?*

Day 260   Date: _____

Joash, Seven Year Old King

"And Joash did that which was right in the sight of the LORD all the days of Jehoiada the priest." (II Chronicles 24:2)

In the course of killing off the family of Ahab, Jehu also killed Ahaziah, king of Judah, the grandson of Jehoshaphat. Upon Ahaziah's death, Athaliah his mother assumed the throne and killed all members of the royal family of Judah. However, one of the sons of Ahaziah was saved alive by Ahaziah's sister and hid for six years. While wicked Athaliah reigned, the young boy Joash was kept by the woman and her husband, Jehoiada the priest. Today's scripture reading tells the story of Joash's ascension to the throne of Judah, and the spiritual revival that followed.

As today's text verse indicates, Joash was very dependent upon Jehoiada for spiritual guidance. Upon the death of Jehoiada, Joash forsook God and led Judah into idol worship.

Scripture to read: II Chronicles 23:1-21

Question to ponder: *Am I strong enough to stand for God alone, if necessary?*

Day 261   Date: _____

Jonah and the Great Fish

"Now the LORD had prepared a great fish to swallow up Jonah. And Jonah was in the belly of the fish three days and three nights." (Jonah 1:17)

The story of the prophet <u>Jonah</u> is one of the most controversial in the Bible. That a grown man could be swallowed whole by a fish, live inside the fish for three entire days, and live to tell about it, is more than skeptics will believe. Yet, none other than Jesus Christ Himself referred to this event as an historical <u>fact</u> (*Matthew 12:38-41*).

Jonah lived in the days of <u>Jeroboam II</u>, the great-grandson of Jehu. II Kings 14:25 records the fulfillment of a prophecy given by Jonah regarding Jeroboam II. God directed Jonah to go to Ninevah, the capitol city of Assyria, and warn them of God's impending judgment. The Assyrian people were extremely cruel and Jonah did not want to risk the possibility that they might repent and that God would then withhold judgment. Today's scripture reading, the entire book of *Jonah* (48 verses), gives the Biblical account of what happened.

Scripture to read: Jonah 1-4

Question to ponder: *Should we be reluctant to see extremely wicked people repent?*

Day 262   Date: _____

The LORD's Controversy

"Hear the word of the LORD, ye children of Israel: for the LORD hath a controversy with the inhabitants of the land, because there is no truth, nor mercy, nor knowledge of God in the land." (Hosea 4:1)

Israel, the northern kingdom, had failed to produce even one godly king. Ahab had been the worst. During the reign of Jehu, God began to cut Israel's power short (*II Kings 10:32*). Judgment was now certain, yet God began to send prophets to warn the people. Elijah, Micaiah, Elisha, and Jonah were among the first.

Hosea was another faithful prophet of God commissioned to deliver a hard message. God directed Hosea to marry a woman who would prove unfaithful to him. This would illustrate Israel's unfaithfulness to Jehovah God. After leaving him, Hosea was to take her back, demonstrating the forgiveness that God would grant Israel when she would one day return to worship the LORD.

Scripture to read: Hosea 4:1-19

Question to ponder: *Does God judge anyone who has not had proper warning beforehand?*

Day 263   Date: _____

Can Two Walk Together?

"Can two walk together, except they be agreed?" (Amos 3:3)

God often uses the most common of men to perform His work. <u>Amos</u>, a common shepherd, was such a man. Yet, when God called him to warn the people of Israel, Amos answered the call. Like Jonah and Hosea, Amos ministered during the reign of Jeroboam II. His message was primarily to the northern kingdom, yet he also sounded warnings to Judah and several surrounding heathen kingdoms.

Today's scripture reading is a selection from the book of *Amos*. Today's text verse asks an important question that is as relevant for us today as it was in the days of Amos. God was asking Israel how He could walk with them when they were living in disagreement with His holy standards.

Scripture to read: Amos 3:1-15

Question to ponder: *Am I walking in agreement with God in my life?*

Day 264   Date: _____

King Uzziah's Trespass

"And they withstood Uzziah the king, and said unto him, It appertaineth not unto thee, Uzziah, to burn incense unto the LORD, but to the priests the sons of Aaron, that are consecrated to burn incense: go out of the sanctuary; for thou hast trespassed; neither shall it be for thine honour from the LORD God." (II Chronicles 26:18)

Uzziah was a king of Judah who started out doing what was right. God blessed his reign, and he became a very strong king. In his strength, however, he forgot God and became lifted up with pride. Today's scripture reading tells the story of his intrusion into the temple to burn incense upon the altar of incense. This is something that was reserved for the priests alone (see Lesson 135).

God has ordained the institutions of government (the state) and religion (the church today). Each has its God-given responsibility, but there is a separation that exists between them. One ought not to intrude into the arena of the other.

Scripture to read: II Chronicles 26:16-21

Question to ponder: *How severe a penalty did God impose upon Uzziah for his violation of this separation principle?*

Day 265   Date: _____

Here Am I, Send Me

"Also I heard the voice of the Lord, saying, Whom shall I send, and who will go for us? Then said I, Here am I; send me." (Isaiah 6:8)

Even though judgment was certain upon Israel (the northern kingdom) things were not all well in Judah (the southern kingdom), either. <u>Isaiah</u> was a prophet sent more to Judah than to Israel. His ministry spanned the reigns of Uzziah, Jotham, Ahaz, and Hezekiah. Of these, only Ahaz was a wicked king, yet Judah was declining spiritually.

Today's scripture reading records the call of Isaiah as a result of a vision he saw (see Lesson 6). Notice the implicit teaching of the Trinity (see Lesson 72) in God's words *"who will go for <u>us</u>?"* Notice also that Isaiah was told that very few would heed his message. Verse 13 promises that someday there would be a "remnant" that would return after having been removed from the land.

Scripture to read: Isaiah 6:1-13

Question to ponder: *Would I be willing to go for God if I knew beforehand that no one would listen to my message?*

Day 266   Date: _____

Jehovah's Vineyard

"What could have been done more to my vineyard, that I have not done in it? wherefore, when I looked that it should bring forth grapes, brought it forth wild grapes?" (Isaiah 5:4)

One of the most common sights in the land of Palestine, then and now, was vineyards. Isaiah drew upon the people's familiarity with vineyards to illustrate their unfaithfulness to Jehovah God. He tells the story of a man who plants a vineyard and takes every measure possible to make sure it is fruitful. Yet, in spite of his efforts, it produces nothing.

The story quickly switches to a plea from God to Judah. Where did the fault lie, that Judah was not producing spiritual fruit for God? The unproductivity of the "vineyard" would only bring one end – judgment! Verse 7 is the key to interpreting this message sent through Isaiah.

Scripture to read: Isaiah 5:1-30

Question to ponder: *Do we have any more excuse today than the people of Judah had?*

Day 267   Date: _____

A Sign for King Ahaz

"Therefore the Lord himself shall give you a sign; Behold, a virgin shall conceive, and bear a son, and shall call his name Immanuel." (Isaiah 7:14)

In the days of Ahaz, king of Judah, the kings of Syria and Israel (King Pekah) made a league together and attacked Jerusalem. Ahaz was successfully defending Jerusalem, but was looking for help. God sent Isaiah to him to encourage him, telling him that they would not prevail against him. God offered Ahaz to request a specific sign from Him to confirm the truth of the message. With pious sounding words, Ahaz refused.

Although Ahaz refused, God insisted on giving a sign. As is often the case in the writings of the prophets, the sign given looked beyond the immediate circumstance to a future day. This sign became a reality when Jesus Christ was born of the virgin, Mary (see lesson 105). We can find the reason for Ahaz's refusal when we look at what he did after this meeting; he sent to Assyria for help. The story is given in *II Chronicles 28* (see verse 16).

Scripture to read: Isaiah 7:1-16

Question to ponder: *Was Ahaz really concerned with tempting the LORD?*

Day 268   Date: _____

What Does the LORD Require?

"He hath shewed thee, O man, what is good; and what doth the LORD require of thee, but to do justly, and to love mercy, and to walk humbly with thy God?" (Micah 6:8)

Micah was another prophet, sent by God to warn Israel, who lived during the same time period as Hosea and Isaiah. The book that bears his name and message is typical of most of the other books of the prophets. It reveals in very graphic language how God views the sins of His people (see *Micah 2:1-2*).

In the middle of a message of warning and judgment, Micah includes a prophetic picture of a day when the LORD's promise to David will be fulfilled (see Lesson 216). *Micah 5:2* speaks of the One who will rule over Israel in that day: *"But thou, Beth-lehem Ephratah, though thou be little among the thousands of Judah, yet out of thee shall he come forth unto me that is to be ruler in Israel; whose goings forth have been from of old, from everlasting."*

Scripture to read: Micah 6:1-16

Question to ponder: *What attribute of the coming ruler is revealed in Micah 5:2 (see Lesson 73)?*

Day 269   Date: _____

Israel Taken Captive

"For the children of Israel walked in all the sins of Jeroboam which he did; they departed not from them; Until the LORD removed Israel out of his sight, as he had said by all his servants the prophets. So was Israel carried away out of their own land to Assyria unto this day."
(II Kings 17:22-23)

After years of warnings from many of God's prophets, judgment day finally came to the northern kingdom. In the year 721 B.C., Israel was carried away captive by Assyria. The Assyrian's practice was to deport conquered peoples away from their homeland to make them more easily subject.

Today's scripture reading summarizes the sins for which Israel was judged. They had 19 kings, all of whom walked in idolatry and rebellion against God.

Scripture to read: II Kings 17:1-23

Question to ponder: *After reviewing the sins identified in today's scripture reading, do you think that God showed sufficient patience in dealing with Israel?*

Day 270   Date: _____

Hezekiah's Prayer

"And Hezekiah received the letter of the hand of the messengers, and read it: and Hezekiah went up into the house of the LORD, and spread it before the LORD." (II Kings 19:14)

Hezekiah, the son of Ahaz, was a godly king. He led the people in great spiritual revival. According to *II Kings 18:5*, he was the best of all the kings of Judah. He destroyed idols, restored temple worship, celebrated the Passover (see Lesson 121), which had not been done since Solomon, and reordered the priests.

However, the Assyrians were not content to conquer the northern kingdom only. Today's scripture reading tells the story of Hezekiah's reaction to the threats of the Assyrians. God used the prophet Isaiah to deliver a message of comfort to Hezekiah.

Scripture to read: II Kings 19:1-37

Question to ponder: *Sennacherib, king of Assyria, had boasted that his gods were stronger than the God of Judah. How did God get "the last laugh"?*

Day 271   Date: _____

Judah's Worst King

"Moreover Manasseh shed innocent blood very much, till he had filled Jerusalem from one end to another; beside his sin wherewith he made Judah to sin, in doing that which was evil in the sight of the LORD."
(II Kings 21:16)

After the death of Hezekiah, Manasseh his son reigned over Judah. He restored the idol worship, which his father had driven from the land. He *"seduced them (the people) to do more evil than did the nations whom the LORD destroyed before the children of Israel"* (*II Kings 21:9*). Because of his wickedness, God determined to judge Judah also.

In his latter years, God humbled him by causing him to be carried away captive to Babylon. Manasseh responded by repenting of his wicked ways and God restored him to his kingdom, but he was only able to effect a minor spiritual revival among the people. See II Chronicles 33:11-20 for this story.

Scripture to read: II Kings 21:1-18

Question to ponder: *In verse 7, what is the "house" that is referred to?*

Day 272   Date: _____

Judgment Upon Ninevah

"Woe to the bloody city! it is all full of lies and robbery; the prey departeth not" (Nahum 3:1)

Ninevah, the capitol city of Assyria, had been visited 150 years earlier by the prophet Jonah (see Lesson 261). They had responded to his message by repenting completely, and God granted them mercy, sparing them from judgment. But they returned to their wicked ways, and now, God sent another prophet to warn them of judgment. Nahum's message is entirely to Ninevah. He most likely lived during the reign of Hezekiah.

In today's scripture reading, we read of some attributes ascribed to God, which we normally view as negative: jealousy, revenge, wrath, anger, and fury. Could these possibly describe the same God identified as "good" in verse seven? It is important to understand that God's anger is always directed at evil, and is never out of control as ours most often is. When God executes revenge, justice is always served. And, God has a legitimate right to be jealous.

Scripture to read: Nahum 1:1-7

Question to ponder: *Is my anger always directed at evil?*

Day 273   Date: _____

Judah's Other Best King

"And like unto him was there no king before him, that turned to the LORD with all his heart, and with all his soul, and with all his might, according to all the law of Moses; neither after him arose there any like him."
(II Kings 23:25)

Hezekiah had been a great king, leading the people of Judah in spiritual revival. After him, however, his son Manasseh reigned for 55 years and the people soon forgot about the God of their fathers. After Manasseh, Amon his son reigned for two years. He also was wicked. His own servants conspired against him and killed him. His son, Josiah, became king at the age of eight, and when he was sixteen, he began to seek after God.

Today's scripture reading tells the story of the spiritual revival under Josiah's leadership. In the process of repairing the temple, they discovered a book of the law of Moses. The reading of the law revealed the sin of their nation, and Josiah led the people in repentance. God blessed during Josiah's reign, but Judah's fate was already sealed because of the wickedness of Manasseh.

Scripture to read: II Chronicles 34:1-33

Question to ponder: *Can the law do any more for us beyond revealing our sin to us?*

Day 274   Date: _____

The Message of Zephaniah

"The great day of the LORD is near, it is near, and hasteth greatly, even the voice of the day of the LORD: the mighty man shall cry there bitterly." (Zephaniah 1:14)

In spite of the great revival under King Josiah, the wickedness of Manasseh had been so great that God's determination to judge Judah was unchanged. During the reign of Josiah, God sent another prophet to warn the people of impending judgment. Zephaniah's message is one of warning to the people of Judah.

The warning contained in today's text verse speaks of the day when judgment would fall upon Judah. It is described as the "*day of the LORD*". Similar to many signs given through the prophets, this warning has a future as well as an immediate application. In addition to the people of Zephaniah's generation, it also speaks to those of a future generation when God will again bring judgment, this time over all the nations of the world.

Scripture to read: Zephaniah 1:1-18

Question to ponder: *According to verse 12, did the people of Jerusalem believe judgment would actually come?*

Unit Nine Review
Lessons 245 to 274

List the kings of Judah and Israel that we have discussed in the lessons noted in parenthesis:

Judah	Israel
(245) _____	(246) _____
(247) _____	(247) _____
(247) _____	(248) _____
(256) _____	(258) _____
(260) _____	(259) _____
(260) _____	(261) _____
(264) _____	(267) _____
(265) _____	
(265) _____	
(265) _____	
(271) _____	
(273) _____	
(273) _____	

List some of the prophets you have read about:

_____ _____ _____ _____
_____ _____ _____ _____
_____ _____ _____

List the four crowns that believers can receive, from Lesson 254:

_____   _____
_____   _____

THE KINGS OF ISRAEL

Saul
David*
Solomon*

<u>Judah</u>   <u>Israel</u>

Judah	Israel
Rehoboam	Jeroboam
Abijah	Nadab
Asa*	Baasha
Jehoshaphat*	Elah
Jehoram	Zimri
Ahaziah	Omri
Athaliah (queen)	*Ahab*
Joash*	Ahaziah
Amaziah*	Joram
Uzziah*	Jehu
Jotham*	Jehoahaz
Ahaz	Joash
Hezekiah*	Jeroboam II
Manasseh	Zechariah
Amon	Shallum
Josiah*	Menahem
Jehoahaz*	Pekahiah
Jehoiakim	Pekah
Jehoiachin	Hoshea
Zedekiah	

* kings that were primarily good
* **bold** – the best kings
   italics – the worst kings

Unit Ten

Lessons 275 to 305

Bible History

The Captivity
Daniel
Ezra & Nehemiah

<u>Bible Truths</u>

Future Things

Day 275   Date: _____

The Weeping Prophet

"Before I formed thee in the belly I knew thee; and before thou camest forth out of the womb I sanctified thee, and I ordained thee a prophet unto the nations." (Jeremiah 1:5)

Jeremiah began his ministry in the thirteenth year of King Josiah. Today's text verse is from the call of God to Jeremiah. Notice here when God considers life to begin! Jeremiah resisted his call because of his youth, but God promised to go with him. Notice also, from today's scripture reading, the claim of divine inspiration for the words of Jeremiah.

Jeremiah's message was a hard one, and the people's resistance made life very difficult for him. Once, after suffering derision on a daily basis, he vowed to quit, but found he couldn't (see *Jeremiah 20:7-9*). He delivered the unpopular message that the people of Judah would be slaves to Babylon for 70 years (*Jeremiah 25:11*) and lived to see it happen. Because of the many tears he shed while warning his people, and while mourning for their captivity, he has been called "the weeping prophet".

Scripture to read: Jeremiah 1:1-19

Question to ponder: *Do I weep for the sins of my nation?*

Day 276   Date: _____

I Raise Up the Chaldeans

"For, lo, I raise up the Chaldeans, that bitter and hasty nation, which shall march through the breadth of the land, to possess the dwellingplaces that are not their's." (Habakkuk 1:6)

The book of *Habakkuk* is an interesting "conversation" between the prophet and God. While other prophets were concerned for the impending judgments upon Israel and Judah, Habakkuk's concern was for the holiness of God to be vindicated. He begins by crying out to God, asking how God could allow such wickedness to go unpunished. Today's text verse is part of the response of God; He would judge Judah by the Chaldeans (Babylonians).

Habakkuk then wonders how God could use a nation that was more wicked than Judah to judge them. He pleads to understand and waits for God to answer. The answer: Babylon would itself be destroyed at a later date.

Scripture to read: Habakkuk 1:1-17

Question to ponder: *Am I more interested in God receiving glory than myself?*

Day 277   Date: _____

Judgment Upon Jacob's Brother

"For the day of the LORD is near upon all the heathen: as thou hast done, it shall be done unto thee: thy reward shall return upon thine own head." (Obadiah 1:15)

It is not known exactly when the prophet Obadiah lived and delivered his message. His message was not for Israel or Judah, but for the land of Edom. Edom was a rugged, rocky land to the south of Judah. It was inhabited by the descendants of Esau, Jacob's brother (see Lesson 67).

When the children of Israel were moving through the wilderness on their way from Egypt to the Promised Land, they sent word ahead to the king of Edom, asking for safe passage through his land (read *Numbers 20:14-22*). Edom refused their request, and now Obadiah was warning them that they were to be judged for their pride.

Scripture to read: Obadiah 1:1-16

Question to ponder: *According to verses 10 to 14, in what ways did Edom go beyond mere refusal to allow the children of Israel passage through their land?*

Day 278   Date: _____
Judah Taken Captive

"In the third year of the reign of Jehoiakim king of Judah came Nebuchadnezzar king of Babylon unto Jerusalem, and besieged it."
(Daniel 1:1)

After Josiah, a succession of kings reigned over Judah including three of his sons, and one grandson. During the reign of one son, Jehoiakim, Judah was overthrown by Nebuchadnezzar, the powerful king of Babylon. Babylon had defeated the Assyrians in 625 B.C., and now (604 B.C.) 117 years after Israel had been taken captive by Assyria (see Lesson 269), captives from Judah were taken away to Babylon. Among them was a young boy named Daniel.

Today's scripture reading is the inspiring story of a young Jewish boy, taken from his homeland and family, who courageously lives for his God in the face of a wicked king. The practice of the Babylonians was to take young boys from the royal families of their captives, raise them and educate them, and hope to use them to gain the loyalty of all the captives.

Scripture to read: Daniel 1:1-21

Question to ponder: *According to verse 8, why did Daniel refuse to eat or drink the king's food?*

Day 279   Date: _____

Jeremiah's Lamentation

"They have heard that I sigh: there is none to comfort me: all mine enemies have heard of my trouble; they are glad that thou hast done it: thou wilt bring the day that thou hast called, and they shall be like unto me." (Lamentations 1:21)

Jeremiah had worked long and hard to try to turn the people back to God, but they would not listen. After the first of the captives were led away to Babylon in 604 B.C. (including Daniel), a second deportation occurred in 597 B.C. The city of Jerusalem was burned to the ground, and its walls broken down, in 586 B.C. At this time, Zedekiah, the son of Josiah and last king of Judah, had his eyes put out and was taken in chains to Babylon. Only a small remnant of the people was allowed to remain in the land of Judah. Jeremiah remained as well and ministered to them.

After all these events, Jeremiah wept bitter tears over the city he loved so much. The book of *Lamentations* records his words of grief.

Scripture to read: Lamentations 1:1-22

Question to ponder: *According to the last phrase of our text verse, did Jeremiah believe his enemies would triumph forever?*

Day 280   Date: _____

Nebuchadnezzar's Dream

"But there is a God in heaven that revealeth secrets, and maketh known to the king Nebuchadnezzar what shall be in the latter days. Thy dream, and the visions of thy head upon the bed, are these;"
(Daniel 2:28)

King Nebuchadnezzar had a dream that troubled him, but he couldn't remember it. When his own counselors couldn't help him, Daniel learned of the situation and promised an answer. Giving God the credit, Daniel repeated the dream and its interpretation to the king. This dream lays out an outline for the rest of Israel's history, and the world powers (kingdoms) that would rule over it, from Daniel's day to the time when Jesus Christ rules the earth forever (*Daniel 2:44*). Nebuchadnezzar was impressed with Daniel's God, and promoted Daniel over his governors and wise men.

Babylon was the first kingdom, to be followed by the Media-Persian empire. The third kingdom foretold the empire of Greece. The fourth, and final kingdom, is the Roman empire. It was in power in the days of Jesus Christ, and will be again someday.

Scripture to read: Daniel 2:1-49

Question to ponder: *According to verse 37, how did Nebuchadnezzar become king?*

Day 281   Date: _____

God's Watchman

"Son of man, I have made thee a watchman unto the house of Israel: therefore hear the word at my mouth, and give them warning from me." (Ezekiel 3:17)

The prophet Ezekiel was among those carried away captive in the deportation of 597 B.C. He ministered to the captives while living among them. God did not promise Ezekiel that the people would heed his message, but wanted them to at least *"know that there hath been a prophet among them" (Ezekiel 2:5).*

Today's scripture reading is the commission given to Ezekiel by God. He was to warn the people of God's judgment, without regard to their response. Whether they listened, or not, he was responsible only for sounding a warning. In this way he was like the watchman of a city, responsible to sound a warning if the enemy was observed approaching.

Scripture to read: Ezekiel 3:10-21

Question to ponder: *Do we have a responsibility to warn the people of our day of impending judgment for sin?*

Day 282   Date: _____

Nebuchadnezzar's Humbling

"Now I Nebuchadnezzar praise and extol and honour the King of heaven, all whose works are truth, and his ways judgment: and those that walk in pride he is able to abase." (Daniel 4:37)

When interpreting his dream, Daniel informed King Nebuchadnezzar that the head of gold in the image of his dream represented his kingdom. Years later the king made an image of gold and commanded everyone to bow down to it. Daniel's three friends refused to comply. Chapter three tells the thrilling story of their faith and God's miraculous protection from a fiery furnace. Again, Nebuchadnezzar was impressed, but unconverted.

Today's scripture reading, written by the king himself, tells how he learned once and for all Who is really in power over the earth. God humbled him by causing him to go insane for seven years. When he was restored to sanity, and his throne, he was a changed man.

Scripture to read: Daniel 4:1-37

Question to ponder: *According to this story, Who rules "in the kingdom of men"?*

Day 283   Date: _____

The Handwriting on the Wall

"In the same hour came forth fingers of a man's hand, and wrote over against the candlestick upon the plaister of the wall of the king's palace: and the king saw the part of the hand that wrote." (Daniel 5:5)

Several Babylonian kings after Nebuchadnezzar, the Babylonian people would again see the power of God over their kingdom. Belshazzar, a descendant of Nebuchadnezzar, shared the throne of Babylon with his father. Today's scripture reading tells the story of the last night of their kingdom. While the Medes camped outside the walls of Babylon, the king partied defiantly within the "invincible" city with a thousand of his lords. Cyrus, king of Persia, had the Euphrates River diverted into a new channel, and Darius the Median, his general, marched by the dry river bed into the city and took it without a fight in the year 539 B.C.

Notice in verse 29, Belshazzar's response to the message of judgment. He acted as if nothing would change!

Scripture to read: Daniel 5:1-31

Question to ponder: *According to verse 22, what should Belshazzar have known?*

Day 284   Date: _____

Daniel's Seventy Weeks

"Seventy weeks are determined upon thy people and upon thy holy city, to finish the transgression, and to make an end of sins, and to make reconciliation for iniquity, and to bring in everlasting righteousness, and to seal up the vision and prophecy, and to anoint the most Holy."
(Daniel 9:24)

Today's scripture reading is perhaps the key passage in all of scripture in unlocking the doctrines of prophecy (future things). Its proper understanding paves the way for understanding all other passages on the subject. The most important thing to note in this passage is that it relates to *"thy people"*, the people of Israel. It cannot be applied to any other.

It speaks of seventy weeks of years (70 x 7) that begin with a proclamation to rebuild Jerusalem. There would be 483 years (seven and sixty-two weeks, 69, x 7) from this proclamation to the Messiah. The Messiah would then be "cut off" and the city (Jerusalem) would be destroyed by the *"people of the prince that shall come"*. This future prince will confirm a covenant (peace treaty) for seven years (one week), but break it after 3 ½ years.

Scripture to read: Daniel 9:20-27

Question: *Who is the Messiah?*

Day 285   Date: _____

The Fulness of the Gentiles

"For I would not, brethren, that ye should be ignorant of this mystery, lest ye should be wise in your own conceits; that blindness in part is happened to Israel, until the fulness of the Gentiles be come in." (Romans 11:25)

The Jewish Messiah did indeed come, as foretold by Daniel and many other Old Testament prophets. Instead of accepting Him, however, the Jewish leaders rejected him (they were "blinded"). They delivered Him to the Romans to be crucified. After His resurrection and return to Heaven, Jesus Christ began to work through a new agency – the local church. The message of salvation began to reach directly to the Gentile (non-Jewish) world.

But what about Israel? Have they been cast away forever? The apostle Paul addresses this question in today's scripture reading. Israel has been <u>temporarily</u> set aside, and Daniel's seventieth week has been postponed (see Lesson 284). When the time is right, and God's program with the Gentiles is completed, Israel will again move to the forefront.

Scripture to read: Romans 11:1-25

Question to ponder: *Should Gentiles boast against the Jewish people?*

Day 286   Date: _____

The Rapture

"For the Lord himself shall descend from heaven with a shout, with the voice of the archangel, and with the trump of God: and the dead in Christ shall rise first" (I Thessalonians 4:16)

The apostle Paul wrote this letter to the believers of the local church at Thessalonica (see Lesson 186) to help them grow in their faith. They apparently had questions about friends and family who had died. Paul wrote the words of today's scripture reading to comfort them. Here, he teaches them about a future event called "the rapture". The word "rapture" comes from the words *"caught up"* in verse 17.

The rapture is the event that will remove the believers of the local church from this world in *"the twinkling of an eye"* (see I Corinthians 15:51-52). It will be the event that marks the *"fulness of the Gentiles"*. Believers who have died since the time of Christ will be resurrected, and those alive will be "raptured" without experiencing death. This event can happen at <u>any time</u> (including today!) since there are <u>no prerequisite signs</u> that precede it. The Judgment Seat of Christ for believers follows this (see Lesson 252) while history continues on earth.

Scripture to read: I Thessalonians 4:13-18

Question to ponder: *How would this teaching comfort the Thessalonian believers, and us?*

Day 287   Date: _____

The Man of Sin

"Let no man deceive you by any means: for that day shall not come, except there come a falling away first, and that man of sin be revealed, the son of perdition" (II Thessalonians 2:3)

In Paul's first letter to the Thessalonian church, he followed his teaching on the "rapture" with teaching about a time of destruction (chapter 5). Apparently the believers became concerned that they would go through this terrible time. In his second letter, he explained further that the time of destruction would not begin until *"there come a falling away first, and that man of sin be revealed."*

Soon after the rapture, "that" man will rise to prominence on the world scene. This *"man of sin"* is none other than *"the prince that shall come"* of Daniel's vision (see Lesson 284). He cannot be revealed until the One who is restraining ("letting", verse 7) him is *"taken out of the way"* – the Holy Spirit residing within believers. This happens at the rapture. Notice in verses 10-12, it appears that those who have rejected Christ at the time of the rapture will have their eternal fate sealed.

Scripture to read: II Thessalonians 2:1-12

Question to ponder: *Can you see in verse 4 why this "man of sin" is called the "Anti-Christ"?*

Day 288   Date: _____

Dry Bones

"Then he said unto me, Son of man, these bones are the whole house of Israel: behold, they say, Our bones are dried, and our hope is lost: we are cut off for our parts." (Ezekiel 37:11)

One of the themes of Ezekiel's ministry among the captives was encouragement that God had not forgotten His promise to David of a descendant of his Who would rule from Jerusalem forever (see Lesson 216). The captivity would not last forever; Israel would return someday to the Promised Land!

In today's scripture reading we see one such message, taken from a vision God gave Ezekiel. Judah and Israel would be reunited, they would dwell in their homeland, and David's descendant would rule over them. Although this has been fulfilled in part, the complete regathering of Israel will take place <u>after</u> the rapture of the church. Chapters 37 and 38 speak of an invasion of Israel by a confederacy of nations from the north. It is believed this will take place shortly after the rapture.

Scripture to read: Ezekiel 37:1-28

Question to ponder: *According to verse 14, Who will be responsible for reviving Israel?*

Day 289 Date: _____

Daniel's Seventieth Week

"And said to the mountains and rocks, Fall on us, and hide us from the face of him that sitteth on the throne, and from the wrath of the Lamb: For the great day of his wrath is come; and who shall be able to stand?" (Revelation 6:16-17)

After the church is removed in the rapture, Israel again moves to the forefront and the seventieth week of Daniel's vision (see Lesson 284) can be completed. This "week" (seven-year period) is called the <u>Tribulation</u>. The man of sin (Anti-Christ) is revealed and confirms a covenant. Israel is regathered to the Promised Land and is invaded by a confederacy of nations led by Russia (Magog).

The book of *Revelation* describes horrible events on earth during the Tribulation. These are unleashed in a series of judgments labeled as "<u>seal</u>" judgments (chapter 6), "<u>trumpet</u>" judgments (chapters 8 & 9), and "<u>vial</u>" judgments (chapter 16).

Scripture to read: Revelation 6:1-17

Question to ponder: *Does the reaction of the earth's leaders as recorded in verses 15 to 17 indicate repentance on their part?*

Day 290   Date: _____

The Great Tribulation

"When ye therefore shall see the abomination of desolation, spoken of by Daniel the prophet, stand in the holy place, (whoso readeth, let him understand:) Then let them which be in Judea flee into the mountains" (Matthew 24:15-16)

When He was on earth, Jesus was asked by his disciples for the signs of His return, and the end of the world. He answered by giving them a general outline for the Tribulation period. Verses 4 to 14 correspond to the judgments given in *Revelation*. Today's text verse refers to *Daniel 9:27*, which foretells that the *"prince that shall come"* will break the peace treaty in the *"midst of the week"* by performing an abominable act in the Jewish temple.

Verses 15 to 26 refer to the second half of the Tribulation. This period of extreme persecution for Israel is called the Great Tribulation. The prophet Jeremiah referred to it as *"the time of Jacob's trouble"* (*Jeremiah 30:7*). For 3 ½ years Satan will make an all-out effort to destroy Israel. Jesus warns the Jewish people alive at that time to "flee into the mountains" and not delay their flight for anything.

Scripture to read: Matthew 24:1-26

Question to ponder: *According to verse 22, how severe will the persecution be?*

Day 291   Date: _____

The Saved of the Tribulation Period

"And I heard the number of them which were sealed: and there were sealed an hundred and forty and four thousand of all the tribes of the children of Israel." (Revelation 7:4)

As the Tribulation begins, the entire population of believers has just been removed, raptured, out of the world. Those left on earth, who have already heard the gospel, will *"believe a lie"* and never accept Christ (see Lesson 287). At this time God will raise up 144,000 single men in Israel who will spread the gospel and lead Israel in finally turning to accept Jesus Christ as their Messiah and Savior. Notice in today's scripture reading that a great multitude of people of all nations (Gentiles) will respond to their message. Many of these people will lose their lives for their faith before the seven years is complete.

Chapter 11 includes the story of two very unique witnesses who minister for half of the Tribulation. Many have speculated about the identity of these two men, but their identities have been kept from us. Notice the incredible end to their ministry.

Scripture to read: Revelation 7:1-17; 11:3-12

Question to ponder: *Will it be easy to live for Christ during the Tribulation?*

Day 292   Date: _____

KING OF KINGS, AND LORD OF LORDS

"And I saw heaven opened, and behold a white horse; and he that sat upon him was called Faithful and True, and in righteousness he doth judge and make war." (Revelation 19:11)

Chapters 13 and 14 of *Revelation* reveal Satan's plan to copy the Divine Trinity (see Lesson 72). In addition to the man of sin, or <u>Anti-Christ</u>, there will arise a man (beast) who will mimic the Holy Spirit. This "<u>false prophet</u>" will cause all men to worship the first beast, or Anti-Christ. The power behind all this is the first person of this evil trinity – the Dragon, the Serpent, <u>Satan</u> himself! Chapters 17 and 18 describe the sudden and complete collapse of the false religion (the *"great whore"*) and world economic system.

Today's scripture reading tells the story of the return of Christ to the earth. (At the rapture, He returns only as far as the clouds.) This return is also spoken of in *Matthew 24:27-31*. Unlike the first time He came to earth (see Lesson 100), this time He is coming to *"judge and make war"* as KING OF KINGS, AND LORD OF LORDS!

Scripture to read: Revelation 19:1-16

Question to ponder: *According to verse 10, what is the whole point of Bible prophecy?*

Day 293   Date: _____

Armageddon

"I will also gather all nations, and will bring them down into the valley of Jehoshaphat, and will plead with them there for my people and for my heritage Israel, whom they have scattered among the nations, and parted my land." (Joel 3:2)

In preparation for the return of Jesus Christ to earth as King, God will cause all the nations of the earth to descend on Israel in a combined attempt to defy His power. The beast (Anti-Christ) will have gathered the armies of the earth together and will seek to make war against God. It is at this point that Jesus Christ will appear in the skies, in power and great glory, and will defeat all the armies of the earth in an instant by merely speaking (*Revelation 19:11-21*), and cast the beast and false prophet into "*a lake of fire burning with brimstone*".

A prophet by the name of Joel had spoken of this battle in the days of Joash, king of Judah (see Lesson 260). He spoke of the captivity of Judah long before it actually happened. In today's scripture reading, notice how concerned God is to defend His people Israel.

Scripture to read: Joel 3:1-16

Question to ponder: *Does the beast have any chance at all of defeating God?*

Day 294   Date: _____

The Judgment of the Nations

"And before him shall be gathered all nations: and he shall separate them one from another, as a shepherd divideth his sheep from the goats" (Matthew 25:32)

Today's scripture reading is one of the most misunderstood and misinterpreted passages in the entire Bible. Verse 31 sets the time and the scene. Jesus Christ has just returned in glory, so this judgment happens immediately after the Battle of Armageddon. He is seated upon a throne, with His angels around Him. Verse 32 identifies the <u>nations</u> as the objects of judgment. The "nations" are made up of Gentiles. Verses 40 and 45 provide the basis upon which the judgment is rendered: "How have you treated these, my (Jewish) brethren?"

During the <u>Great Tribulation</u> (see Lesson 290) some Gentiles will provide refuge to persecuted Jews (verses 35 & 36; see Lesson 291), and some will seek to exterminate them (verses 42 & 43). The Gentiles will be separated as sheep or goats based upon which treatment they rendered to the Jews.

Scripture to read: Matthew 25:31-46

Question to ponder: *What nationality was Jesus when on earth?*

Day 295   Date: _____

The Millennial Kingdom

"Then shall the King say unto them on his right hand, Come, ye blessed of my Father, inherit the kingdom prepared for you from the foundation of the world" (Matthew 25:34)

Those found to be righteous at the Judgment of the Nations will be granted entrance into a new kingdom. Believers who have died, or been killed, during the Tribulation will be resurrected and enter this kingdom. Believers who have participated in the Rapture (see Lesson 286) will enjoy the kingdom as well. It is in this kingdom that God will fulfill his promise to David (see Lesson 216) that a descendent of his would rule the entire earth from Jerusalem forever, beginning with this one thousand year kingdom.

Today's scripture reading is from a prophecy by Isaiah in which he foretells the general character of this kingdom. Satan will be bound for one thousand years (a millennium) and the King will enforce peace over the entire earth, including the animal kingdom.

Scripture to read: Isaiah 11:1-16

Question to ponder: *Under these ideal conditions do you think everyone born will accept salvation?*

Day 296   Date: _____

The Great White Throne Judgment

"And I saw a great white throne, and him that sat on it, from whose face the earth and the heaven fled away; and there was found no place for them." (Revelation 20:11)

At the end of 1,000 years Satan will be loosed and allowed one final chance to deceive people and defeat God. Unbelievably, he will succeed in gathering an army of people that will march against Jerusalem and seek to overthrow it. He will be defeated and cast into the lake of fire and brimstone (see Lesson 181). Immediately following his defeat the judgment mentioned above takes place.

Notice that there is no reference in today's scripture reading to saved people. All the people at this judgment are <u>unbelievers</u>, all are judged according to their own <u>works</u>, and all receive the same fate (see Lesson 26). Believers will have already been judged (see Lesson 252) immediately following the rapture. After the Great White Throne Judgment is complete, God will create a new heavens and new earth (see Lessons 209-213), and rule forever!

Scripture to read: Revelation 20:7-15

Question to ponder: *Do I want my family, friends, and acquaintances to appear at this judgment?*

Day 297   Date: _____

The Decree of Cyrus

"Thus saith Cyrus king of Persia, The LORD God of heaven hath given me all the kingdoms of the earth; and he hath charged me to build him an house at Jerusalem, which is in Judah." (Ezra 1:2)

Cyrus, king of Persia, was a man who held the Jewish people in high regard. Perhaps he was influenced by the presence of Daniel within his court. In the same year in which the Medes and Persians overthrew the Babylonian empire (see Lesson 283), he issued the decree recorded in today's scripture reading. This decree authorized the rebuilding of the temple (Solomon's, see Lesson 235) that had been destroyed by the Babylonians.

Ezra was a priest who ministered to the people during this time. It is believed that he is also the author of *I and II Chronicles*. Upon this decree by Cyrus, approximately 42,000 Jews were allowed to return to their homeland. It had been 70 years since Nebuchadnezzar had carried captives to Babylon.

Scripture to read: Ezra 1:1-11

Question to ponder: *Who had prophesied many years earlier that the captivity would last 70 years (see Lesson 275)?*

Day 298   Date: _____

Daniel and the Lions' Den

"Then said Daniel unto the king, O king, live for ever. My God hath sent his angel, and hath shut the lions' mouths, that they have not hurt me: forasmuch as before him innocency was found in me; and also before thee, O king, have I done no hurt." (Daniel 6:21-22)

After the overthrow of Babylon, Darius (co-king with Cyrus) organized his government and gave Daniel a position of prominence. Daniel, of course, was a captive. His promotion created enemies among his peers in leadership. Daniel's character was so impeccable that it was impossible to find fault in him, except in the observance of his devotion to God. Today's scripture reading is the remarkable story of the entrapment of Daniel, and of his deliverance from a horrible death.

Although this is a favorite story of children, Daniel was most likely above 90 years of age when this happened!

Scripture to read: Daniel 6:1-28

Question to ponder: *Was Daniel truly delivered, or were the lions simply not hungry?*

Day 299   Date: _____

What Time Is It?

"Then came the word of the LORD by Haggai the prophet, saying, Is it time for you, O ye, to dwell in your cieled houses, and this house lie waste?" (Haggai 1:3-4)

The decree issued by Cyrus had authorized the rebuilding of the temple. The returning remnant of Jews began the work, laid the foundation, and praised God for His goodness and mercy. The older people, who had seen the splendor of Solomon's temple, wept instead. After the foundation was laid the work drew opposition, and a new king, Artaxerxes, commanded the work to cease.

No work was done on the temple for fifteen years. At that time, God raised up a prophet by the name of Haggai to stir the people to action. He scolded the people for building houses for themselves and leaving God's house lying in waste. He pointed out that their lack of action on the temple was the cause of their economic problems. God raised up a man named Zerubbabel to lead in resuming the work. The Darius mentioned here is a different one from the one Daniel knew.

Scripture to read: Haggai 1:1-15

Question to ponder: *Have I put my personal convenience ahead of serving God?*

Day 300   Date: _____

The New Temple Completed

"And this house was finished on the third day of the month Adar, which was in the sixth year of the reign of Darius the king." (Ezra 6:15)

In response to the messages by the prophet Haggai, and another prophet named Zechariah, the people resumed work on the new temple. Zerubbabel lead the people in the work. Soon after the work resumed the people were asked by what authority they were building. They replied by referring back to the decree of Cyrus made many years before (see Lesson 297). A complaint was sent to Darius the king along with a request to search the records to verify if such a decree existed.

Today's scripture reading tells the story of the search for the decree of Cyrus. Darius added to it a decree of his own, and the temple work was allowed to continue until its completion.

Scripture to read: Ezra 6:1-18

Question to ponder: Can *God use unsaved people to further His cause?*

Day 301 Date: _____

Personal Separation

"For they have taken of their daughters for themselves, and for their sons: so that the holy seed have mingled themselves with the people of those lands: yea, the hand of the princes and rulers hath been chief in this trespass." (Ezra 9:2)

After the completion of the new temple, Ezra made a trip to Jerusalem. Soon after his arrival a delegation of Jewish leaders came to him with distressing news. The people who had returned from captivity to the homeland had intermarried with the heathen people of the land. Ezra was horrified and led the people in confessing this sin, and making things right with God again.

Notice in verse one of today's scripture reading, where Ezra was told that the people had not "*separated themselves*". God had instructed His people to be "set apart" from all others (see Lesson 130). This was to maintain a distinct testimony of His working in their life. This principle of <u>separation</u> is basic to Christian life (see Lesson 53).

Scripture to read: Ezra 9:1-15

Question to ponder: *How did Ezra feel about the seriousness of this sin according to verse 6?*

Day 302   Date: _____

Esther the Jewish Queen

"For if thou altogether holdest thy peace at this time, then shall there enlargement and deliverance arise to the Jews from another place; but thou and thy father's house shall be destroyed: and who knoweth whether thou art come to the kingdom for such a time as this?" (Esther 4:14)

The next Persian king after Darius was <u>Ahasuerus</u> (or Xerxes). One day his queen, Vashti, embarrassed him in front of all his nobles and princes. Ahasuerus removed her from being queen, and sought a replacement. Today's scripture reading is the story of how a young Jewish girl became queen of the powerful Persian Empire.

Chapter three tells of wicked <u>Haman</u>, second in power only to the king, and how he convinced the king to issue a decree that all Jews be destroyed. Chapter four tells how <u>Esther</u> was informed of this decree by her cousin, <u>Mordecai</u>. Today's text verse is Mordecai's plea for Esther to risk her life for her people.

Scripture to read: Esther 2:1-20

Question to ponder: *According to our text verse, did Mordecai believe Esther was the Jew's only hope?*

Day 303   Date: _____

The Feast of Purim

"Therefore the Jews of the villages, that dwelt in the unwalled towns, made the fourteenth day of the month Adar a day of gladness and feasting, and a good day, and of sending portions one to another." (Esther 9:19)

Haman, a very wicked man, had deceived the king into issuing a decree that at a certain day all Jews, both young and old, were to be totally destroyed. Esther, the Jewish queen of Persia, was the only person with access to the king - the only person with a chance to save her people. Esther devised a bold plan to reveal to the king her nationality and expose Haman. Chapter five tells of the first part of Esther's plan. Chapter six tells of the beginning of Haman's end. Chapter seven, today's scripture reading, records the just reward of Haman's deeds.

The remainder of the book of *Esther* tells of the deliverance God gave to the Jews. A day scheduled for disaster and destruction was turned into a day of great victory. The Jews established the Feast of Purim to remember this day of deliverance.

Scripture to read: Esther 7:1-10

Question to ponder: *Although God is never mentioned in Esther, can you see Him at work here?*

Day 304   Date: _____

Nehemiah

"And it came to pass in the month Nisan, in the twentieth year of Artaxerxes the king, that wine was before him: and I took up the wine, and gave it unto the king. Now I had not been beforetime sad in his presence."
(Nehemiah 2:1)

One of the finest examples of leadership in the Bible is the story of <u>Nehemiah</u>. He served in the king's court as cupbearer. He was anxious to hear news of the Jews who had been allowed to return to Jerusalem. The news was not good, however. Although the temple had been rebuilt, the city itself still lay in ruins. Today's scripture reading tells of Nehemiah's request to lead the rebuilding effort. It is important to realize that he could have been put to death for exhibiting sadness in the king's presence.

The king granted Nehemiah's request and gave letters securing all that he needed. The year was 445 B.C. This proclamation to rebuild Jerusalem marks the beginning of Daniel's seventy prophetic weeks (see Lesson 284).

Scripture to read: Nehemiah 2:1-20

Question to ponder: *What was Nehemiah's first response when the king offered to grant his request?*

Day 305   Date: _____

The Walls Rebuilt

"So the wall was finished in the twenty and fifth day of the month Elul, in fifty and two days. And it came to pass, that when all our enemies heard thereof, and all the heathen that were about us saw these things, they were much cast down in their own eyes: for they perceived that this work was wrought of our God." (Nehemiah 6:15-16)

Nehemiah overcame much opposition in leading the people in the rebuilding effort. He retained a single focus that kept him from falling short of his goal. No obstacle caused him to lose faith! He always found his strength in the Lord. After the city walls were rebuilt, Nehemiah gathered the people together and Ezra read the Law of Moses to them. The remainder of the book of Nehemiah records corrections in the lives of the people as they responded to a renewed understanding of the law.

Although the book of Nehemiah is found in the middle of the Old Testament, its story closes out the historical events of the Old Testament.

Scripture to read: Nehemiah 8:1-18

Question to ponder: *According to verse 8, did Ezra believe it important that the average person be helped to understand the Bible?*

Unit Ten Review
Lessons 275 to 305

List the kings that held the Jews captive, and the prophets that ministered to them:

Kings	Prophets
(278) _____	(275) _____
(283) _____	(276) _____
(297) _____	(277) _____
(298) _____	(280) _____
(302) _____	(281) _____
	(299) _____
	(300) _____

List the key future events of prophecy, as given in the lessons noted in parenthesis:

(286): _____

(287): _____

(288): _____

(289): _____

(290): _____

(292): _____

(293): _____

(294): _____

(295): _____

(296): _____

Unit Eleven

Lessons 306 to 336

Bible History

The Life of Christ

Bible Truths

Christian Living
Prayer

Day 306   Date: _____

Thou Shalt Call His Name JESUS

"And she shall bring forth a son, and thou shalt call his name JESUS: for he shall save his people from their sins." (Matthew 1:21)

The Old Testament's history closes with the Jewish people under Persian dominion. This continued for about 100 years until Greece came to power. By the time of Christ, the Roman Empire was in control of the land of Palestine (see Lesson 280). There are approximately 400 years between the end of Old Testament history and the birth of Christ.

The birth of Jesus Christ, foretold by Old Testament prophets, was announced separately by an angel to Mary (today's scripture reading) and to Joseph. Both were told that his name should be **JESUS**. This name means "Savior". It is the name, given by his parents, which refers to his humanity. The name "Christ" is a title, meaning, "anointed". It means He is the Anointed One, the Messiah: the Promised One of Israel. This title refers to His deity. (See Lessons 98 and 100).

Scripture to read: Luke 1:26-38

Question to ponder: *What then is the full meaning of the name "Jesus Christ"?*

Day 307   Date: _____

The Christmas Story

"And she brought forth her firstborn son, and wrapped him in swaddling clothes, and laid him in a manger; because there was no room for them in the inn." (Luke 2:7)

Almost everyone is familiar with the beautiful Christmas story. Joseph and Mary were required to travel to Bethlehem, and there Jesus was born in fulfillment of Micah's prophecy (see Lesson 268). Angels announced the birth to shepherds, who came and worshipped the newborn child. Jesus was presented to the Lord, because He was a first-born son. There, in the temple at Jerusalem, Simeon and Anna adored Him and spoke prophetically of Him.

Joseph and Mary lived for a time in Bethlehem, and wise men came from the east to worship him and present gifts. Herod became jealous, and Joseph took his family to Egypt to avoid Herod's attempt to destroy the child. After Herod's death, Joseph moved his family back to Nazareth, where Jesus lived a quiet childhood as a carpenter's son.

Scripture to read: Luke 2:1-40

Question to ponder: *Who do you think was behind Herod's evil plot to kill the Christ child (see Lesson 177)?*

Day 308   Date: _____

The Baptism of Jesus

"And it came to pass in those days, that Jesus came from Nazareth of Galilee, and was baptized of John in Jordan." (Mark 1:9)

The public ministry of Jesus Christ began when He was about 30 years of age, with His baptism (see Lesson 72). The prophet Isaiah had prophesied that God would send a "forerunner" to prepare the way for the coming Messiah (*Isaiah 40:3-5*). This forerunner was a prophet by the name of <u>John the Baptist</u> (see Lesson 121). Today's scripture reading tells of his ministry. John called upon the people to confess their sins and be baptized as a public token of their repentance.

John's message was that *"the kingdom of heaven is at hand" (Matthew 3:2)*. His purpose was to announce that the promised King was about to appear on the scene. Once Jesus began his ministry, John faded into the background and about two years later was executed while in prison.

Scripture to read: John 1:15-34

Question to ponder: *Who did John the Baptist understand Jesus to be?*

Day 309   Date: _____

The Temptation of Christ

"Thy word have I hid in mine heart, that I might not sin against thee." (Psalms 119:11)

Immediately after his baptism, Jesus was subjected to temptation by the devil in the wilderness. Today's scripture reading gives one account of this forty-day trial. Satan's intent was to destroy the Son of God. The Savior, of course, was not capable of committing sin (see Lesson 106). He resisted each attempt of Satan by quoting scripture (see verses 4, 8, and 12). Today's text verse reminds us that one of the benefits of the Bible is to keep us from sinning. The best way to be prepared to fight temptation is to have the Word of God "hid" in your heart. In other words, memorize it! In particular, find verses that will give strength in the areas that you are the weakest – and commit them to memory!

Accounts of the temptation of Christ are also recorded in the gospels of *Matthew* (see Lesson 5) and *Mark*. Along with the gospels of *Luke* and *John*, they provide us with four accounts of the life of Jesus Christ, each written by a different man.

Scripture to read: Luke 4:1-13

Question to ponder: *If the Son of God used memorized scripture to defeat Satan, how should I fight against him?*

Day 310   Date: _____

Common Temptations

"There hath no temptation taken you but such as is common to man: but God is faithful, who will not suffer you to be tempted above that ye are able; but will with the temptation also make a way to escape, that ye may be able to bear it." (I Corinthians 10:13)

The Bible teaches us that Jesus was tempted *"in all points like as we are, yet without sin"* (see Lesson 107). Our text verse reminds us that any temptations we face will never be something new and different, but will always be common forms of temptation that all men face. When Jesus was tempted by the devil, He was tested in three different categories that all sins are classified by. Today's scripture reading gives us those three kinds of sin.

The *"lust of the flesh"* is a sin that would satisfy a sensual desire. The *"lust of the eyes"* includes those sins that begin by wanting something we can see, especially that someone else has. The *"pride of life"* is the desire to exalt ourselves in some way.

Scripture to read: I John 2:15-17

Question to ponder: *What wonderful promise of deliverance is given to us in today's text verse?*

Day 311   Date: _____

The First Miracle of Christ

"This beginning of miracles did Jesus in Cana of Galilee, and manifested forth his glory; and his disciples believed on him." (John 2:11)

Each of the four men who wrote the "gospel" accounts of the life of Jesus Christ wrote from a different perspective and with a different purpose in mind. The word "gospel" means simply, "good news". John (not John the Baptist) wrote his gospel to present Jesus Christ to the world as the Son of God (*John 20:30-31*). Therefore he includes in his writing many proofs of the <u>deity</u> of Jesus Christ.

Today's scripture reading tells the story of the very first miracle performed by Jesus. It was done at a wedding, and Jesus turned water into wine (see Lesson 240). The miracles of Jesus include healings of many sorts, demonstrations of authority over nature, and power over demons (see Lesson 173). Today's text verse gives the purpose for these miracles. They manifested (made visible) the glory of God in Jesus Christ, and strengthened the faith of His disciples.

Scripture to read: John 2:1-12

Question to ponder: *According to John 21:25 do we have a record of all of the miracles of Jesus?*

Day 312   Date: _____

True Worship

"But the hour cometh, and now is, when the true worshippers shall worship the Father in spirit and in truth: for the Father seeketh such to worship him." (John 4:23)

Today's scripture reading tells of an encounter Jesus had with a Samaritan woman (see Lesson 122) when travelling from the province of Judea to Galilee. In an attempt to distract Jesus from the sin in her life the woman changed the subject to that of where the proper place was to worship God. Jesus replied by teaching her that true worship is not found in external requirements, but within the heart.

God has the right to define how He is to be worshipped. Here we are told that He must be worshipped according to the truth (God's Word). He must also be worshipped "in spirit", because He is a Spirit. This means that true worship is not found in ritualistic, formalistic, ceremonies. It comes from the heart. To "worship" means to ascribe worth ("worth-ship") to God.

Scripture to read: John 4:1-39

Question to ponder: *If a person attempts to worship God in a manner that contradicts the truths contained in God's Word, is that true worship?*

Day 313   Date: _____

Opposition in His First Year

"And it came to pass on a certain day, as he was teaching, that there were Pharisees and doctors of the law sitting by, which were come out of every town of Galilee, and Judea, and Jerusalem: and the power of the Lord was present to heal them." (Luke 5:17)

Shortly after performing his first miracle, Jesus went to Jerusalem to attend the Passover feast. The miracles He did there caused many people to believe in him. He stayed in the surrounding area for approximately eight months, during which time His disciples baptized those who became His followers. Mounting opposition from the Jewish religious leaders caused Jesus to return to Galilee. He was rejected in his native Nazareth (*Luke 4:16-30*) and moved His headquarters to the city of Capernaum. His miracles attracted large crowds of common people and His fame grew throughout the area.

During this time, one year into His public ministry, religious leaders and teachers of the Law of Moses began to follow Him everywhere He went. Their motive, however, was to find fault with Him.

Scripture to read: Luke 5:1-26

Question to ponder: *What does verse 21 reveal about the intent of the Pharisees?*

Day 314   Date: _____

Twelve Apostles Chosen

"And when it was day, he called unto him his disciples: and of them he chose twelve, whom also he named apostles" (Luke 6:13)

In His first year of ministry, Jesus attracted many who became His <u>disciples</u>. The word disciple simply means, "learner". Many of these disciples had been disciples of John the Baptist, and left him to follow Jesus. Jesus became their teacher and they followed Him wherever he went.

Early in the second year of his public ministry Jesus chose twelve men out of the greater number of disciples for a special calling. These men He named <u>apostles</u>. The word apostle means, "one sent forth". These men were given a special ministry and received specialized training from the Lord. They came from many walks of life (see Lesson 37). Several of them were used to write the New Testament. One of them betrayed Him. Excepting that one, and the Apostle John, they all ultimately gave their lives for the sake of the gospel.

Scripture to read: Luke 6:12-19

Question to ponder: *According to verse 12, how did Jesus prepare to select the twelve apostles?*

Day 315   Date: _____

The Lord's Prayer

"After this manner therefore pray ye: Our Father which art in heaven, Hallowed be thy name." (Matthew 6:9)

Shortly after choosing the twelve apostles, Jesus gave the famous "Sermon on the Mount". The gospel of *Matthew*, written to present Jesus Christ as the Jewish King, contains the most complete record of this sermon (chapters 5 through 7). See Lessons 14 and 90 for excerpts from this sermon.

Today's scripture reading includes what is commonly referred to as "the Lord's Prayer". People mistakenly repeat it believing that the Lord intended for us to do so. Notice that Jesus said, "*after this manner therefore pray ye*". This prayer, more properly called "the disciple's prayer", is a pattern for us to follow. Prayer is to be addressed to the Father. It should include praise ("*Hallowed be thy name*") and an acknowledgment of submission to His will. Our requests to the Father may include personal needs, forgiveness of sins, and divine assistance in overcoming evil.

Scripture to read: Matthew 6:1-15

Question to ponder: *According to verse 7, how does God view repeating the same prayer over and over?*

Day 316   Date: _____

Men Ought Always to Pray

"And he spake a parable unto them to this end, that men ought always to pray, and not to faint" (Luke 18:1)

Jesus taught His disciples that prayer is vitally important. In fact, He demonstrated it by his life. Over and over again, the gospels record Jesus spending time in prayer. Today's scripture reading is one of the parables of Jesus; this one about prayer. Jesus told the story of a judge who was not moved by any man. Yet, a widow motivated him to act on her behalf, simply because <u>she refused to give up</u>! How much more would our Heavenly Father reward us if we exhibited such persistence in our requests to Him?

The Bible encourages us to *"Pray without ceasing" (I Thessalonians 5:17)*. This means to make talking with God a consistent, regular habit of life. He has made it easy for us to have access to Him (see Lessons 107, 137 and 138). Consistent prayer is one of the key building blocks of a strong Christian life. Be sure not to neglect it!

Scripture to read: Luke 18:1-8

Question to ponder: *How often do I pray?*

Day 317   Date: _____

Hindrances to Prayer

"If I regard iniquity in my heart, the Lord will not hear me" (Psalms 66:18)

The Bible speaks of several things that can hinder our prayers. Today's text verse reminds us that we cannot hide our thoughts from God. He cannot be deceived. If we dwell upon sin inwardly He knows it and will not respond to our prayers until we have asked for forgiveness. Other hindrances include unbelief (*James 1:6-7*) and a poor relationship between husband and wife (*I Peter 3:1-7*).

Notice the promise found in today's scripture reading. Notice also the condition attached to it. We are responsible to search out God's will and pray that it be done *("Thy will be done..." Matthew 6:10)*. If we do, God promises to answer our prayer. The only prayer of an unbeliever that God has promised to answer is the prayer calling out to God for salvation (see Lesson 34).

Scripture to read: I John 5:14-15

Question to ponder: *According to today's scripture reading, what condition does God attach to answering our prayers (see also James 4:3)?*

Day 318 Date: _____

Parables

"And the disciples came, and said unto him, Why speakest thou unto them in parables?" (Matthew 13:10)

Jesus did not use <u>parables</u> as a teaching method until halfway through His public ministry. On the occasion when He first began to use parables, His disciples immediately questioned Him about this change. His answer was, *"Because it is given unto you to know the mysteries of the kingdom of heaven, but to them it is not given"*. To understand His answer, you must review what had just happened.

In *Matthew, chapter 12*, the story is told of Jesus healing a man possessed with a devil, blind and dumb. The Pharisees accused Jesus of performing the miracle by Satan's power. These Jewish religious leaders had gone too far! The nation of Israel is, from this point, viewed as having rejected their promised King and Messiah. Jesus would have no further word for these leaders who had spurned Him and persisted in unbelief. Teaching by parables would be a means of concealing truth from these men, while still presenting it to believers.

Scripture to read: Matthew 12:22-37

Question to ponder: *Had Jesus demonstrated sufficient proof of His claims?*

Day 319   Date: _____

Five Thousand Fed

"And Jesus took the loaves; and when he had given thanks, he distributed to the disciples, and the disciples to them that were set down; and likewise of the fishes as much as they would." (John 6:11)

Jesus spent almost the entire second year of His public ministry in the region of Galilee. The Jewish religious leaders in Jerusalem sought to kill Him, so he avoided the region of Judea. Today's scripture reading tells of a miracle he performed at the end of his second year. With only five barley loaves and two small fishes He fed a multitude of five thousand men, besides women and children. This great miracle caused many people to follow Him, but Jesus gently rebuked them, saying they were following Him for the wrong reason.

He followed this with his great teaching proclaiming himself to be the "Bread of Life" (see Lesson 128). As He spoke of "eating my flesh" and "drinking my blood" many of His followers were offended and left Him. Jesus Himself taught that many people would reject Him and that few would follow Him (*Matthew 7:13-14*). It is the same today.

Scripture to read: John 6:1-71

Question to ponder: *According to verse 63, was Jesus speaking of His literal flesh and blood?*

Day 320   Date: _____

I Will Build My Church

"And I say also unto thee, That thou art Peter, and upon this rock I will build my church; and the gates of hell shall not prevail against it."
(Matthew 16:18)

Everywhere Jesus went He was the topic of discussion and debate. Who was He? The religious leaders called Him an imposter and a blasphemer. The common people were divided. Jesus asked His disciples what people were saying about Him. Then he asked, *"But whom say ye that I am?"* Peter answered, *"Thou art the Christ, the Son of the living God."* Jesus blessed Peter for his correct answer.

Jesus then proclaimed that upon the faith demonstrated in that answer (but not upon Peter himself), He would build his "church". He was here announcing a new program necessary because of His rejection by the Jewish leadership. God's program for Israel would be temporarily suspended (see Lessons 285 and 289), and He would work through his church. Jesus would spend the remainder of His earthly ministry preparing His disciples for this work – the work of the local church.

Scripture to read: Matthew 16:13-27

Question to ponder: *Who do I say that Jesus is?*

Day 321   Date: _____

The Transfiguration

"And after six days Jesus taketh with him Peter, and James, and John, and leadeth them up into an high mountain apart by themselves: and he was transfigured before them." (Mark 9:2)

Today's scripture reading tells the story of Jesus revealing His heavenly glory to His three closest disciples. On top of a high mountain, Jesus was transfigured before <u>Peter</u>, and <u>James</u>, and <u>John</u>. His face and His clothing became exceedingly shiny and white. Moses and Elijah appeared and talked with Jesus. God the Father spoke audibly from Heaven.

Peter later wrote about this tremendous experience. In *II Peter 1:15-21* (see Lesson 61) he writes to argue that the things he and the other apostles write about in the Holy Scriptures are not fables. They were <u>eyewitnesses</u> of the glory of the Savior. Yet, as incredible as that experience was, Peter calls the written Word of God a <u>more sure testimony</u> than his experience. Our experiences are not more reliable than God's Word!

Scripture to read: Mark 9:1-13

Question to ponder: Is *my faith based solely upon the written Word of God?*

Day 322   Date: _____

The Parable of the Prodigal Son

"It was meet that we should make merry, and be glad: for this thy brother was dead, and is alive again; and was lost, and is found." (Luke 15:32)

Shortly after his transfiguration, Jesus left Galilee and began to make His way to Jerusalem. There were now less than six months left before He would be crucified. The events of Lessons 106 and 113 took place after He arrived in Jerusalem, at the Feast of Tabernacles (see Lesson 146).

Today's scripture reading includes the beautiful parable of the prodigal son. The parable teaches us how God rejoices over each sinner that repents and confesses Jesus Christ as Savior. *II Peter 3:9* says, *"The Lord is not slack concerning his promise, as some men count slackness; but is longsuffering to us-ward, not willing that any should perish, but that all should come to repentance."* Like the father in the parable, God longs to see people repent, and gladly receives all who come to ask for forgiveness. He is a God of infinite <u>longsuffering</u>, or patience.

Scripture to read: Luke 15:1-32

Question to ponder: *Did the father in the parable rebuke his son in any way when he returned?*

Day 323   Date: _____

The Good Shepherd

"I am the good shepherd: the good shepherd giveth his life for the sheep." (John 10:11)

About four months before His crucifixion, Jesus attended the feast of the Dedication at Jerusalem. There He proclaimed Himself to be the Good Shepherd. Jesus often used object lessons from everyday life. The illustrations He used regarding shepherds and sheep drew upon subjects familiar to the people. Sheep are extremely vulnerable animals and are totally dependent upon the care given by their shepherd. They become very attached, and will not follow another shepherd. Jesus explained that His sheep could be identified by the fact that they follow Him. Notice also, in today's verse, that He was foretelling His death on our behalf.

At the end of this teaching, Jesus exclaimed, *"I and my Father are one."* Though some today may say that Jesus never claimed to be God, His enemies had no difficulty understanding what He was claiming. They accused Him of blasphemy, saying, *"thou, being a man, makest thyself God."*

Scripture to read: John 10:1-39

Question to ponder: *Read the 23rd Psalm. How does today's lesson make this psalm more meaningful?*

Day 324   Date: _____

The Raising of Lazarus

"Jesus said unto her, I am the resurrection, and the life: he that believeth in me, though he were dead, yet shall he live" (John 11:25)

When in the Jerusalem area, Jesus had come to enjoy the hospitality of two sisters and their brother. One day the sisters, <u>Mary</u> and <u>Martha</u>, sent for Jesus with the message that <u>Lazarus</u>, their brother, was sick. Jesus waited where He was, and did not arrive at their home until Lazarus had been dead four days. This is significant because the Jews taught (incorrectly) that the soul remained with the body until three days after death. Martha went to meet Jesus as He came, and expressed her faith that Jesus could have healed her brother had He arrived earlier. Jesus replied that He had power over death. After meeting Mary, and being taken to the gravesite, Jesus called Lazarus back to life from the grave!

This miracle caused many to believe in Him. The chief priests and Pharisees, however, responded by increasing their determination to eliminate Him.

Scripture to read: John 11:1-57

Question to ponder: *According to verse 48, what was the primary concern of the religious leaders?*

Day 325   Date: _____

The Rich Young Ruler

"Not every one that saith unto me, Lord, Lord, shall enter into the kingdom of heaven; but he that doeth the will of my Father which is in heaven." (Matthew 7:21)

Today's text verse is taken from the Sermon on the Mount. Today's scripture reading is an account that illustrates the truth of this verse. Jesus was approached by *"a certain ruler" (Luke 18:18)* who asked him, *"Good Master, what shall I do that I may inherit eternal life?"* In the exchange that followed, Jesus brought the man to the very issue that was keeping him from true repentance. He was carefully observing the law as best he could, but was unwilling to give up his riches and comfortable life in exchange for *"treasure in heaven"*.

"Enter ye in at the strait gate: for wide is the gate, and broad is the way, that leadeth to destruction, and many there be which go in thereat: Because strait is the gate, and narrow is the way, which leadeth unto life, and few there be that find it." (Matthew 7:13-14)

Scripture to read: Mark 10:17-31

Question to ponder: *In our text verse, what is Jesus implying about Himself ("saith unto me")?*

Day 326   Date: _____

Occupy Till I Come

"And he called his ten servants, and delivered them ten pounds, and said unto them, Occupy till I come." (Luke 19:13)

Jesus spent the last few months of His life on earth near Jerusalem. His disciples anticipated that He was about to make himself king and establish His kingdom in fulfillment of the promise to King David (see Lesson 216). Although He plainly told them that He must die, they did not understand. Today's scripture is a parable told to instruct His disciples that the kingdom's appearance would be delayed, and to instruct them in Christian service.

The ten pounds given to each servant represent the talents and opportunities we have to serve Christ. We are expected to be fruitful and use our "pounds" for His gain, not our own. One of the keys to enjoying the Christian life and to full assurance of salvation (see Lesson 42) is active Christian service (see Lesson 50). We are "saved to serve". A Christian not actively serving God will be an unhappy and insecure Christian.

Scripture to read: Luke 19:11-27

Question to ponder: *Which of the three servants mentioned would I prefer to be?*

Day 327   Date: _____

Behold, Thy King Cometh

"Rejoice greatly, O daughter of Zion; shout, O daughter of Jerusalem: behold, thy King cometh unto thee: he is just, and having salvation; lowly, and riding upon an ass, and upon a colt the foal of an ass." (Zechariah 9:9)

<u>Zechariah</u>, like Haggai (see Lesson 299), was a prophet to the returning remnant of Jews after the captivity. Today's text verse is a remarkable prophecy of Zechariah's that Jesus fulfilled <u>exactly</u> 483 years <u>to the day</u> from the proclamation to rebuild Jerusalem (see lessons 284 and 304).

Today's scripture reading records the fulfillment of Zechariah's prophecy. It was one week before the Passover and the crucifixion. Jesus was publicly offering Himself to the Jewish people as their King. The people received Jesus gladly, acknowledging Him as King by saying, "*Hosanna to the son of David*". However, when He didn't act as they expected their King to act, they began to waver and instead acknowledged Him only as a prophet. Only a few days later, many of these same people would call for His death.

Scripture to read: Matthew 21:1-17

Question to ponder: *According to verse 15, how did the religious leaders respond?*

Day 328   Date: _____

The Last Passover

"Jesus saith to him, He that is washed needeth not save to wash his feet, but is clean every whit: and ye are clean, but not all." (John 13:10)

Jesus observed the Passover in an upper room with His twelve apostles. It was at this time that He dismissed the traitor, Judas Iscariot, to perform his dastardly deed. After dismissing the betrayer, Jesus took the Passover elements, bread and the cup (the "fruit of the vine"), and gave them new meaning. He explained that the <u>bread</u> represents His <u>body</u>, given for us. The <u>cup</u> represents His <u>blood</u>, shed for us. In so doing, He implemented what we today call the <u>Lord's Supper</u>, or <u>Communion</u>.

Today's scripture reading tells of an unusual act by Jesus. In washing the feet of His apostles He demonstrated true servant leadership. In those days people bathed in a public bath. Upon arriving at a home their feet would need washing. Jesus likened this to our salvation. We do not need to get saved (bathe) again and again, but we do need to cleanse our feet that get soiled by our daily walk (see Lesson 55). He was teaching about <u>forgiveness</u>.

Scripture to read: John 13:1-20

Question to ponder: *What does this teach about the security of our salvation?*

Day 329   Date: _____

Put that On Mine Account

"If he hath wronged thee, or oweth thee ought, put that on mine account" (Philemon 1:18)

The small book called *Philemon* is actually a letter written by the apostle Paul to a friend of his named Philemon. Onesimus, a slave, had robbed Philemon and fled to Rome. There, Paul led him to salvation and was now returning him to his master. He appealed to Philemon to receive Onesimus, even as he would Paul himself. He wrote the words of our text verse, and promised to repay anything Onesimus owed out of his own pocket. This is a beautiful picture of what Jesus did on the cross for us. Our sins were "placed on His account" (see Lesson 29) and He paid our sin debt in full! This is called imputation (to reckon, put on the account of).

The trials of Jesus Christ (there were several) broke almost every rule of fair play, then and now. In addition to violating many other Jewish and Roman laws, they took place at night and no credible witnesses were ever produced against him. Yet he was pronounced guilty and sentenced to death.

Scripture to read: Matthew 26:47-68

Question to ponder: *Whose testimony was ultimately used to condemn Jesus?*

Day 330   Date: _____

It Is Finished!

"When Jesus therefore had received the vinegar, he said, It is finished: and he bowed his head, and gave up the ghost." (John 19:30)

The Romans had designed crucifixion to be a very cruel and slow death. It was reserved for the worst of criminals. Jesus was crucified between two thieves on a hill outside of the city of Jerusalem, called Golgotha, or Calvary (meaning, "the place of a skull"). Many aspects of His death directly fulfilled prophecy. For three hours, beginning at noon, there was darkness over the whole land. The veil of the temple, that separated the Holy Place from the Most Holy Place, was rent in two from the top to the bottom. This signified that the time of Temple worship was ended and that God was about to introduce a new way to approach Him.

Today's scripture reading is a beautiful prophecy of Isaiah's speaking of the suffering of the Savior. In verse 11 we read that God the Father's wrath against sin was satisfied in full by the Son's sacrifice. The cry given in today's text verse was the victory cry given when returning victorious from battle.

Scripture to read: Isaiah 53:1-12

Question to ponder: *What victory did Jesus win on the cross?*

Day 331   Date: _____

He Is Risen!

"He is not here: for he is risen, as he said. Come, see the place where the Lord lay." (Matthew 28:6)

Jesus had said, speaking of His life, *"I have power to lay it down, and I have power to take it again" (John 10:18)*. On the cross He dismissed His spirit with the words, *"Father, into thy hands I commend my spirit" (Luke 23:46)*. On the third day, He took up His life again and rose from the dead! Although He had repeatedly forewarned His followers of His coming death and subsequent resurrection, they failed to understand either when they happened. It took repeated appearances to His disciples after His resurrection for them to fully believe.

The resurrection of Jesus Christ is the most well documented fact in all of history. Because His enemies remembered His predictions of rising again they took extra precautions to secure the tomb, thereby providing us proof positive that He was actually dead. After He rose again He appeared to many people, including over 500 at once. His fearful disciples became fearless preachers of truth.

Scripture to read: John 20:1-31

Question to ponder: *How important to our faith is the truth of the resurrection?*

Day 332   Date: _____

The Gospel

"For I delivered unto you first of all that which I also received, how that Christ died for our sins according to the scriptures; And that he was buried, and that he rose gain the third day according to the scriptures."
(I Corinthians 15:3-4)

Our text verse today is the most concise and complete definition of the gospel ("good news") that exists. This is the message of salvation for all mankind! The fact of Christ's resurrection from the dead is the cornerstone upon which our faith rests. Without it our faith is without meaning, and we have no remedy for our sin (see verse 17). It is also the basis for all that God has promised us for the future. It secures Christ's exalted position and gives us a living hope for eternity.

Christ's resurrection gives us confidence that we shall someday be resurrected from the dead. Today's scripture reading instructs us that Christ's resurrection came <u>first</u>, and afterward His believers will be raised at His coming. The passage goes on to explain that we will receive new, spiritual bodies.

Scripture to read: I Corinthians 15:1-58

Question to ponder: *According to verses 25 and 26, what enemy of ours has Christ defeated?*

Day 333   Date: _____

Justified By Faith

"Therefore being justified by faith, we have peace with God through our Lord Jesus Christ." (Romans 5:1)

The death, burial, and resurrection of Jesus Christ make possible for all people a great and wonderful salvation. When a person, by faith, receives Jesus Christ as Savior the Bible teaches that we are justified. This means that we are made right with God. God looks upon a converted person and, instead of seeing their sinfulness, sees the perfect righteousness of His Son *(II Corinthians 5:21),* which has been "imputed" to that person (placed on their account, see Lesson 329). God, the Righteous Judge, declares that person to be righteous on the basis of the completed work of Christ on the cross.

Because we have been declared just before God, we have peace with Him because we are no longer in rebellion through sin. We have been reconciled to God. The demands of the law regarding our sin have been satisfied, and we are legally justified!

Scripture to read: Romans 5:1-11

Question to ponder: *If Christ's work on the cross is complete and final, and God has declared us right with Him based upon it, can we ever lose that?*

Day 334   Date: _____

Joint-Heirs With Christ

"And if children, then heirs; heirs of God, and joint-heirs with Christ; if so be that we suffer with him, that we may be also glorified together."
(Romans 8:17)

The Bible teaches that all who accept Jesus Christ as Savior become children of God (see Lesson 38). In fact, the Bible says, *"God the Father...hath begotten us...to an inheritance incorruptible, and undefiled, and that fadeth not away, reserved in heaven for you"(I Peter 1:3-4).* As believers, we can look forward to an <u>inheritance</u>! We are <u>heirs</u> of God, sharing an inheritance with His Son! Part of that inheritance is a new, glorified body that will not experience the pains of this life (see Lesson 211).

Today's scripture reading asks several very important questions before closing with one of the most definite statements concerning the eternal security of the believer found in the Bible. Read it and rejoice in the wonderful salvation that the resurrection of Jesus Christ from the dead has provided for you!

Scripture to read: Romans 8:28-39

Question to ponder: *If God be for us, who can be against us?*

Day 335   Date: _____

The Ascension

"So then after the Lord had spoken unto them, he was received up into heaven, and sat on the right hand of God." (Mark 16:19)

The Lord appeared to His disciples for forty days after His resurrection, providing them many *"infallible proofs" (Acts 1:3)* that He was indeed alive. After this He led them outside of Jerusalem, gave them some final instructions, blessed them, and ascended out of their sight into heaven. Today's text verse tells us where Jesus Christ is today. He is seated at the right hand of the Heavenly Father. The right hand is the position of favor and prominence. He is <u>seated</u> because his work is <u>complete</u> (see Lesson 144).

An exciting truth regarding our salvation is that God sees us as being <u>positionally</u> *"in Christ"*. From today's scripture reading, notice verse six. When God saved us, He gave us spiritual life (quickened us) and raised us up with Christ and (positionally) placed us with Christ Jesus in "heavenly places".

Scripture to read: Ephesians 2:1-10

Question to ponder: *In the mind of God is this future reality as good as done now?*

Day 336   Date: _____

The Great Commission

"And Jesus came and spake unto them, saying, All power is given unto me in heaven and in earth. Go ye therefore, and teach all nations, baptizing them in the name of the Father, and of the Son, and of the Holy Ghost: Teaching them to observe all things whatsoever I have commanded you: and, lo, I am with you alway, even unto the end of the world. Amen."
(Matthew 28:18-20)

The above text verse is the final instruction given by the Lord before His ascension. It is called "The Great Commission". It was given to the eleven apostles directly, but is just as applicable to us today. It is instructive and significant to read how the apostles understood it and how they set about to obey it.

The Great Commission contains three directives. The first, to *"teach all nations"*, means to tell the unsaved peoples of the world the good news that Jesus saves. This is to be followed by <u>baptizing</u> those who respond by accepting Christ. Finally, the new converts are to be <u>trained to observe</u> all the teachings of the Lord.

Scripture to read: Acts 1:1-14

Question to ponder: *In whose authority (power) are we to do these things?*

Unit Eleven Review
Lessons 306 to 336

List a few of the key events of the life of Jesus Christ from these lessons:

Lesson 307: _____

Lesson 308: _____

Lesson 309: _____

Lesson 311: _____

Lesson 314: _____

Lesson 319: _____

Lesson 321: _____

Lesson 324: _____

Lesson 328: _____

Lesson 330: _____

Lesson 331: _____

From the lessons noted below, list some of the blessings and benefits of salvation:

Lesson 310: _____

Lesson 329: _____

Lesson 332: _____

Lesson 333: _____

_____

Lesson 334: _____

SOME OLD TESTAMENT PROPHECIES FULFILLED BY JESUS CHRIST

born of a woman (*Genesis 3:15*)
from the line of Abraham (*Genesis 12:3*)
from the tribe of Judah (*Genesis 49:10*)
from the house of David (*II Samuel 7:12-13*)
born of a virgin (*Isaiah 7:14*)
would have a forerunner (*Isaiah 40:3-5*)
born in Bethlehem (*Micah 5:2*)
worshipped by wise men (*Isaiah 60:3,6,9*)
live in Egypt for a short time (*Hosea 11:1*)
called a Nazarene (*Isaiah 11:1*)
would heal many (*Isaiah 53:4*)
speak in parables (*Isaiah 6:9-10*)
rejected by His own (*Psalm 69:8*)
make a triumphal entry into Jerusalem (*Zechariah 9:9*)
praised by little children (*Psalm 8:2*)
miracles would not be believed (*Isaiah 53:1*)
a man of sorrows (*Isaiah 53:3*)

regarding his death:

betrayed for 30 pieces of silver (*Zechariah 11:12*)
forsaken by His disciples (*Zechariah 13:7*)
scourged and spat upon (*Isaiah 50:6*)
betrayal money would be used to buy a potter's field (*Zechariah 11:13*)
crucified between two thieves (*Isaiah 53:12*)
given vinegar to drink (*Psalm 69:21*)
hands and feet pierced (*Psalm 22:16*)
garments parted and gambled for (*Psalm 22:18*)
surrounded and ridiculed by His enemies (*Psalm 22:7-8*)
He would thirst (*Psalm 22:15*)
none of his bones broken (*Psalm 34:20*)
buried with the rich (*Isaiah 53:9*)
raised from the dead (*Psalm 16:10*)

Unit Twelve

Lessons 337 to 366

Bible History

The Acts of the Apostles
The Epistles

Bible Truths

Discernment
The Local Church
Christian Living

Day 337   Date: _____

Pentecost

"For with stammering lips and another tongue will he speak to this people. To whom he said, This is the rest wherewith ye may cause the weary to rest; and this is the refreshing: yet they would not hear." (Isaiah 28:11-12)

Jesus had instructed His disciples to wait in Jerusalem until the Holy Spirit was given to them as He had earlier promised (see Lesson 124). Today's scripture reading records the fulfillment of that promise. The Day of Pentecost was a feast day implemented as part of the Law (see Lesson 146). It was to be observed 50 days after the Passover feast. Upon receiving the Holy Spirit the disciples were filled with courage and boldly proclaimed the gospel in public. Miraculously, they spoke with many languages with which they were unfamiliar.

It is important to realize that "speaking in tongues" was a specific sign given to the nation of Israel for that particular time just after the departure of Jesus Christ. In I Corinthians 14:21-22, the apostle Paul referred to our text verses for today in warning believers that *"tongues are for a sign, not to them that believe, but to them that believe not"*.

Scripture to read: Acts 2:1-36

Question to ponder: *Is speaking in tongues for today?*

Day 338   Date: _____

When That Which is Perfect is Come

"But when that which is perfect is come, then that which is in part shall be done away." (I Corinthians 13:10)

The Book of Acts, or *"The Acts of the Apostles"*, records the ministry of the apostles in carrying out the Great Commission (see Lesson 336). It was a special time in that the worship system of the Mosaic Law was being superseded by a new way. The apostles had the responsibility of implementing the new program of the <u>local church</u>. God granted them special powers and signs (including tongues) to validate their position as apostles.

Today we have no need of special signs and powers. They have *been "done away"*. The completed Word of God ("that which is perfect") validates true ministers and exposes *"false prophets"*. Today's scripture reading is called the "love chapter" ("charity" refers to godly love). Notice verses 8 to 12. The apostles did not possess the <u>completed</u> Bible to validate their message, so signs and miracles were a necessary part of their ministry.

Scripture to read: I Corinthians 13:1-13

Question to ponder: *What did Paul say in verse 8 would happen to tongues?*

Day 339   Date: _____

Rightly Dividing the Word

"Study to shew thyself approved unto God, a workman that needeth not to be ashamed, rightly dividing the word of truth." (II Timothy 2:15)

It is important to not only <u>read</u> and <u>memorize</u> the Word of God, but to also <u>study</u> it. Notice that this is a <u>personal</u> responsibility *("to shew <u>thyself</u> approved")*. God has given us pastors and teachers to assist us, but the responsibility is <u>ours</u>. The Bible teaches that every <u>individual</u> has the <u>liberty</u> to interpret scripture for himself *("Let every man be fully persuaded <u>in his own mind</u>", Romans 14:5)*. Of course, with that liberty also comes <u>responsibility</u> to "rightly divide" the scripture. Each one of us will give an account to God for how we interpret and apply His Word *(Romans 14:12)*.

God's Word is <u>complete</u>. In it He has given us <u>all</u> we need to know to live our lives. Because the Bible is <u>complete</u>, God no longer reveals truth through dreams, visions, prophets, or experiences. Beware of anyone who relies on any of these instead of the "Word of Truth". In other words, although the process of "illumination" (see Lesson 65) continues, that of "revelation" has ended.

Scripture to read: II Timothy 2:1-26

Question to ponder: *Am I a workman who studies the Word of Truth faithfully?*

Day 340   Date: _____

Addition in the Church

"Then they that gladly received his word were baptized: and the same day there were added unto them about three thousand souls." (Acts 2:41)

Peter boldly preached the gospel on the Day of Pentecost, declaring that the same Jesus whom the mob had delivered to be crucified was both <u>Lord</u> and <u>Christ</u> (Messiah). Today's scripture reading records the response to his message. When the people asked, *"what shall we do?"* Peter replied, *"Repent, and be baptized every one of you in the name of Jesus Christ for the remission of sins"*. Notice the order given from his response and our text verse above. First comes <u>repentance</u> (gladly receive his word). After repentance (salvation, see Lesson 37) comes <u>baptism</u> for (because of) the remission of sins. This order is very important.

Notice in verse 47 that the new believers were added to the <u>church</u>. These believers at Jerusalem, along with the apostles, formed the very first local church. Pentecost is the "birthday" of the church.

Scripture to read: Acts 2:37-47

Question to ponder: *Have I been added to (become a member of) a local church?*

Day 341   Date: _____

The Bride of Christ

"This is a great mystery: but I speak concerning Christ and the church." (Ephesians 5:32)

In the Bible, a <u>mystery</u> is a truth that has been previously hidden from our understanding. Today's scripture reading reveals the truth that the church is the "Bride of Christ" (see Lesson 212). Our earthly marriage relationships have been created by God to teach us about the special relationship between Christ and the church. Christ's love and sacrifice for the church is the pattern for husbands to follow.

The word "church" in our Bibles is translated from the Greek word "*ekklesia*" (*ek* = "out of", *kaleo* = "to call"). Literally, it means "an assembly of called out ones". In Greek usage it applied to the Greek city-states (i.e. Athens, Sparta). Each city-state was <u>independent</u> of the others and made its own decisions. Decisions were made by the <u>local</u> assembly (city council). Assembly members would be "called out" from their homes to the meetings in which they would deliberate and make decisions for the city. That <u>assembly</u> was called the *ekklesia*.

Scripture to read: Ephesians 5:21-33

Question to ponder: *Did Christ choose this word for His church (Matthew 16:18) by accident?*

Day 342   Date: _____

Cheerful Givers

"Every man according as he purposeth in his heart, so let him give; not grudgingly, or of necessity: for God loveth a cheerful giver."
(II Corinthians 9:7)

As people were added to the church in Jerusalem they began to be persecuted. Those religious leaders who rejected the Savior were now actively seeking to stop the growth of the church. This created financial need for many. Today's scripture reading tells of the generosity of many of the believers. The local church became the center for receiving and distributing these gifts.

The local church is to be underwritten financially by the tithes and offerings of God's people. A church ought not to look elsewhere for funding. State sponsored churches in some countries (and in times past even in our country) are supported by taxing all the people. This is a violation of Biblical teaching. Christ wants to demonstrate to His people that He is able to meet all the needs of the church through His people. The church and government (state) are to remain separate from each other.

Scripture to read: Acts 4:32-37

Question to ponder: *Is Jesus Christ able to meet the needs of His bride without government help?*

Day 343   Date: _____

Prove Me Now Herewith

"Bring ye all the tithes into the storehouse, that there may be meat in mine house, and prove me now herewith, saith the LORD of hosts, if I will not open you the windows of heaven, and pour you out a blessing, that there shall not be room enough to receive it." (Malachi 3:10)

Malachi, the last of the Old Testament prophets, ministered to the people of Nehemiah's time (see Lessons 304 and 305). The above text verse comes immediately after God had accused the people of robbing Him by not giving their tithes and offerings. A tithe literally means a tenth. From the beginning God has required of His people that they give to Him a tenth of all their increase. Abraham gave a tithe to a priest of God long before the Law was given *(Genesis 14:20)*. Jacob vowed to give God a tenth of all God gave to him *(Genesis 28:22)*.

Today, the "storehouse" is the local church. Paul, in *I Corinthians 16:1-2*, spoke of a collection to be taken upon the first day of the week (see Lesson 142) and brought into the Corinthian church.

Scripture to read: Mark 12:41-44

Question to ponder: *According to Leviticus 27:30, who does the tithe belong to?*

Day 344   Date: _____

Organizing the Church

"Wherefore, brethren, look ye out among you seven men of honest report, full of the Holy Ghost and wisdom, whom we may appoint over this business." (Acts 6:3)

The fast growth of that first local church in Jerusalem caused some organizational problems. The apostles soon found themselves burdened with administrative duties and unable to keep up with the work. God directed them to lead the church to select seven men to relieve them of certain duties so they could devote themselves *"continually to prayer and to the ministry of the word" (Acts 6:4)*.

In this episode we find the two Biblical offices of the local church revealed. The apostles served as the pastors of the church. The seven men selected to assist the apostles were the first deacons. Today's scripture reading gives the Biblical qualifications of these two offices. This episode also teaches us how decisions are to be made in the local church. The men were apparently chosen by a democratic vote of the multitude.

Scripture to read: I Timothy 3:1-13

Question to ponder: *Can just anyone serve in either of these two offices?*

Day 345   Date: _____

Persecution

"And Saul was consenting unto his death. And at that time there was a great persecution against the church which was at Jerusalem; and they were all scattered abroad throughout the regions of Judea and Samaria, except the apostles." (Acts 8:1)

<u>Stephen</u>, one of the deacons selected in chapter 6 of Acts, began to be mightily used of God. The religious leaders brought him before their council and accused him of speaking against God. In his defense Stephen preached the powerful message recorded in chapter 7. As a result, he was stoned to death. One of those approving of his death was a young Pharisee by the name of <u>Saul</u>. Saul proceeded to harass the church mercilessly.

In today's scripture reading, the Lord Jesus forewarns his disciples that they would be persecuted. Saul meant to destroy the church at Jerusalem. God, however, used the persecution to force the believers to leave Jerusalem. He had instructed the disciples to take the gospel from Jerusalem to the whole earth (*Acts 1:8*). Until Saul's persecution they had not yet begun to do so.

Scripture to read: John 15:15-25

Question to ponder: *Why do we sometimes need to be pushed into doing what we know is right?*

Day 346   Date: _____

What Doth Hinder Me to be Baptized?

"And as they went on their way, they came unto a certain water: and the eunuch said, See, here is water; what doth hinder me to be baptized?"
(Acts 8:36)

Philip, one of the original seven deacons, began to preach the gospel in Samaria. While there, God directed him to head south. On his way he met a man who held a position of authority in the court of the queen of Ethiopia. After Philip helped him understand the scriptures, the man asked Philip the question found in today's text verse. Philip answered, *"If thou believest with all thine heart, thou mayest."* Baptism is a public profession of faith in Jesus Christ done in obedience to Him. As Philip instructed the Ethiopian eunuch, baptism comes after salvation (see Lesson 340).

Many churches "baptize" infants today. Since the infant is not old enough to make a salvation decision, this practice is not Biblical. Our word "baptize" comes from the Greek word *"baptizo"*, which means "to dip, plunge under, or immerse".

Scripture to read: Romans 6:1-13

Question to ponder: *How does baptism by immersion (submerging totally under the water) fulfill the picture found in Romans 6:3-5?*

Day 347   Date: _____

The Lord's Supper

"For as often as ye eat this bread, and drink this cup, ye do shew the Lord's death till he come." (I Corinthians 11:26)

In today's scripture reading, the apostle Paul was giving instruction to the church at Corinth regarding "the Lord's Supper" (also called Communion). The Lord Jesus implemented this the same evening he was betrayed (see Lesson 328) as a memorial for believers. It is to be *observed "in remembrance of me"*. The communion elements (bread and the cup) are symbolic. They picture the Savior's body and blood, which were given for us. Neither of the elements change in any way to become the actual body and blood of Christ, nor do they become mystically mingled with the body and blood of Christ. If they did, we would be guilty of crucifying the Savior over and over again (see Lesson 144).

The Lord's Supper is to be observed in a manner worthy of its importance. The Corinthian church was being rebuked for turning it into a party atmosphere. We are not worthy of what Christ did for us, but we can remember in a worthy manner!

Scripture to read: I Corinthians 11:23-34

Question to ponder: *What warning is given to believers in today's scripture reading?*

Day 348 Date: _____

Two Ordinances

"Now I praise you, brethren, that ye remember me in all things, and keep the ordinances, as I delivered them to you." (I Corinthians 11:2)

Baptism and the Lord's Supper were both given to the local church, and are intended to be administered by the officers of the local church. They are the two ordinances of the church, having been decreed (ordered) by the Lord. They are not sacraments. To call either a sacrament would mean that they have a part in saving a person. The Bible does not teach that. Both are done because of salvation, not for (in order to receive) salvation, or to add to salvation.

Because both ordinances are symbolic of salvation they have no significance to an unbeliever. Baptism is a public means of identifying with Christ and with the local church. A church's membership should consist only of persons who are truly saved and have been Biblically baptized. The Lord's Supper should be served only to believers.

Scripture to read: Ephesians 3:14-21

Question to ponder: *According to Ephesians 3:21 where does God receive glory today?*

Day 349   Date: _____
Saul's Conversion

"And he fell to the earth, and heard a voice saying unto him, Saul, Saul, why persecutest thou me?" (Acts 9:4)

Saul, the Pharisee who was trying to single-handedly stop the spread of the gospel, obtained permission to go to Damascus, in Syria, to capture any believers found there. On the way, he was surrounded by a bright light from heaven, and was confronted with the question of our text verse. The voice belonged to the Lord Jesus, and Saul was converted. His name was later changed to Paul, and today we know him as the apostle Paul. To him was given the specific ministry of taking the gospel message to the Gentiles.

Today's scripture reading gives us some insight into the heart of the apostle Paul. He gave up prestige and power to serve the Lord. In his journeys as a minister of the gospel he suffered much. Yet, he never wavered. In these verses he gives us the driving motivation of his life. May it be ours, too!

Scripture to read: Philippians 3:4-14

Question to ponder: *According to verse 10, what was the most important goal of Paul's life?*

Day 350   Date: _____

No Respecter of Persons

"Then Peter opened his mouth, and said, Of a truth I perceive that God is no respecter of persons" (Acts 10:34)

Although God called Paul to be the "apostle of the Gentiles", He used Peter to begin His work to them. While praying one day Peter was given a vision in which he was commanded to eat foods that were not lawful for Jewish people to eat. He refused the food three times, but each time was rebuked by a voice that said, *"What God hath cleansed, that call not thou common."* Immediately after the vision, Peter was summoned to the home of a Roman centurion named Cornelius. Cornelius wanted to learn more about the true God. Peter realized the purpose of the vision, presented the gospel to this Gentile man, and not only saw him converted, but also witnessed him receiving the Holy Spirit. Peter reported this incident to the church at Jerusalem, and the believers there rejoiced and glorified God.

In today's scripture reading we see that it is the cross that has broken down the barrier between Jew and Gentile, and brought them together in Christ.

Scripture to read: Ephesians 2:11-22

Question to ponder: *Is there any difference between Jews and Gentiles in the church?*

Day 351   Date: _____

The First Missionaries

"As they ministered to the Lord, and fasted, the Holy Ghost said, Separate me Barnabas and Saul for the work whereunto I have called them."
(Acts 13:2)

The first Gentile church was established in Antioch, a Syrian city over 300 miles north of Jerusalem. When the church at Jerusalem heard of the believers in Antioch, they sent Barnabas (*Acts 4:36-7*) to help them. He soon recruited Paul (still called Saul) to assist him. As our text verse indicates, God had other plans for these two. They were sent out by the church of Antioch and became missionaries, journeying from city to city, preaching the gospel.

This incident illustrates some important truths. The church at Antioch made this decision independent of the church at Jerusalem. God has intended each local church to be autonomous (self-governing). Barnabas and Paul were sent by the Antioch church. They did not go out on their own. God has intended believers to work under the direction and authority of a local church.

Scripture to read: Acts 13:1-52

Question to ponder: *Was the Antioch church an independent entity, or a branch of the Jerusalem church?*

Day 352   Date: _____

God's Program

"And when they had ordained them elders in every church, and had prayed with fasting, they commended them to the Lord, on whom they believed." (Acts 14:23)

Paul and Barnabas traveled to many cities on their missionary journey, preaching the gospel to the Jews first, then to the Gentiles. Finally, they retraced their steps and returned to Antioch. It is informative to see how the apostle Paul understood his responsibility in spreading the gospel message. Notice that he and Barnabas established <u>churches</u> in each city, then ordained elders (pastors) in <u>every</u> church. Notice also that they reported back to their sending church. Apparently, Paul and Barnabas understood that the Lord Jesus Christ intended that the Great Commission (see Lesson 336) was to be carried out by establishing local churches.

In *I Timothy 3:15* we read that the church *is "the pillar and ground of the truth"*. God has given the local church a sacred <u>preeminence</u> over all other organizations, except the home. The local church is God's only stated program for doing His work.

Scripture to read: Acts 14:1-28

Question to ponder: *If the scriptures give such priority to the local church, how should I regard it?*

Day 353   Date: _____

The Macedonian Vision

"And a vision appeared to Paul in the night; There stood a man of Macedonia, and prayed him, saying, come over into Macedonia, and help us." (Acts 16:9)

On Paul's second missionary journey he took a man by the name of Silas with him. Today's scripture reading tells how Paul and Silas were led into Macedonia (north of Greece), which led to the establishment of the first church in Europe. See Lesson 35 for the story of the founding of the church at Philippi.

After the book of *Acts*, the Bible contains a series of epistles (letters) written by Paul. The first nine are addressed to churches in Rome, Corinth, Galatia, Ephesus, Philippi, Colosse, and Thessalonica. The next three were written to two pastors, Timothy and Titus. Again, we see God's program being advanced by means of local churches. It is important to understand that the Bible speaks of individual churches in the plural, not of one central, "universal" church expanding itself from Jerusalem.

Scripture to read: Acts 15:36-16:11

Question to ponder: *In Galatians 1:2 is Paul referring to one Galatian church, or several?*

Day 354   Date: _____

Search the Scriptures Daily

"These were more noble than those in Thessalonica, in that they received the word with all readiness of mind, and searched the scriptures daily, whether those things were so." (Acts 17:11)

Everywhere Paul went he searched out the Jews first and preached unto them that Jesus was the Christ (Messiah). Invariably the Jews rejected his message, whereupon Paul would turn to the Gentiles. The above text verse, however, is spoken of the Jews of Berea. They exhibited an open and ready mind to receive Paul's preaching.

There are many ways to spread the gospel, but the method that God has ordained is <u>preaching</u>. Preaching is proclaiming the message of Jesus Christ in an authoritative manner, from the Word of God. Today's scripture reading speaks of preaching as being foolishness to the unbeliever, but the power of God to the believer. Preachers may be looked down upon by the world as lacking intellect, but God has ordained it this way that He, alone, may receive the glory.

Scripture to read: I Corinthians 1:18-31

Question to ponder: *Are there methods that would appear to be more "efficient" than preaching?*

Day 355   Date: _____

The Ephesian Elders

"And from Miletus he sent to Ephesus, and called the elders of the church." (Acts 20:17)

Near the end of Paul's second missionary journey he spent a brief time in the city of Ephesus. On his third journey Paul returned to Ephesus and spent over two years there. He left Ephesus for several months to minister in many other churches, but determined to have one last contact before returning to Jerusalem in time for the day of Pentecost. From nearby Miletus he sent for the Ephesian "elders".

Some church groups see in elders a third Biblical office, which they set up as a ruling body over the church and its pastor(s). A careful analysis of today's scripture reading will reveal that the elders mentioned here were the pastors of the Ephesian church. In verse 28 these same elders are called "overseers" and directed to "feed" the church. The word overseers is the same word as bishop found in *I Timothy 3:1-2*. It refers to the responsibility of the pastor to manage the church. The word feed means to shepherd, or pastor, the church (see Lesson 344).

Scripture to read: Acts 20:17-38

Question to ponder: *Can you find the same three words (bishop, elder, pastor) used for the one office in I Peter 5:1-5?*

Day 356   Date: _____

Paul Goes to Rome

"And the night following the Lord stood by him, and said, Be of good cheer, Paul: for as thou hast testified of me in Jerusalem, so must thou bear witness also at Rome." (Acts 23:11)

After leaving the Ephesian elders Paul continued on to Jerusalem. There, unbelieving Jews accused him of turning people from the Law and temple worship, and of other false charges. Roman soldiers took Paul into custody to prevent his being killed by the mob. As our text verse indicates, the Lord encouraged Paul that it was His will that Paul realize his goal of ministering the gospel in Rome.

Today's scripture reading was written by Paul to the Roman believers before he ever made it to Rome. It reveals that, although Paul earnestly desired to go to Rome, God had thus far not allowed him to (verse 13). Paul continually prayed that he may go, but submitted himself to God's will (verse 10). In our lives as believers, it is important that we search out God's will for our lives and submit ourselves to it.

Scripture to read: Romans 1:1-17

Question to ponder: *Why do you suppose that Paul considered himself indebted to preach the gospel?*

Day 357   Date: _____

Almost Thou Persuadest Me

"Then Agrippa said unto Paul, Almost thou persuadest me to be a Christian." (Acts 26:28)

Rather than be tried in Jerusalem for the charges against him, Paul took advantage of his Roman citizenship and appealed to Caesar's judgment seat in Rome. While he was held before leaving for Rome, God gave Paul many opportunities to preach the gospel. Each time Paul related his own testimony. We call this "witnessing". In *Acts 26* Paul witnessed to King Agrippa and asked him if he believed. His answer is today's text verse.

When witnessing to the unsaved, many people have found a series of verses in *Romans* helpful. These verses have come to be called <u>The Romans Road</u>.

Romans 3:10, 23	**All men are sinners.**
Romans 6:23a	**The penalty for sin is death.**
Romans 5:8	**Jesus paid sin's penalty.**
Romans 6:23b	**Salvation is a free gift.**
Romans 10:13	**Call upon Him and accept the gift.**

Scripture to read: II Corinthians 4:3-6

Question to ponder: *Is there someone I can witness to by telling my own salvation testimony and sharing the Romans Road?*

Day 358   Date: _____

By the Church

"To the intent that now unto the principalities and powers in heavenly places might be known by the church the manifold wisdom of God"
(Ephesians 3:10)

The historical story of the New Testament closes in *Acts 28* with Paul, in Rome, awaiting trial. Ultimately, he and all of the twelve apostles except John died martyr's deaths. In spite of great persecution the gospel of Jesus Christ continued to spread throughout the world through <u>independent</u> local churches. In time, people devised a "better" plan than God's and centralized power within "the church", forming denominational hierarchies in which local churches were made subject to higher authorities. This led to many additional erroneous teachings being introduced to Christianity.

God always reserves a remnant of faithful people to Himself, however. Even in times when the gospel light seemed to be totally extinguished there were always faithful believers meeting in small assemblies, apart from the state-run churches, declaring the *"manifold wisdom of God."*

Scripture to read: Ephesians 3:1-12

Question to ponder: *If the denominational heads fall into error, what happens to the entire structure?*

Day 359   Date: _____

Biblical Distinctives

"But speak thou the things which become sound doctrine" (Titus 2:1)

Each church denomination has certain beliefs and practices that become distinctive marks of identification. Here are the distinctives that are most commonly attributed to the people called **"Baptists"**. Some of these may be held in common with other groups, but only Baptists hold all of these distinctives collectively. After each one is the lesson numbers in which each has been discussed.

Biblical Authority   (3,4,5,9,321,338)
Autonomy of the Local Church   (341,351,353,358)
Priesthood of the Believer   (137)
Two Ordinances: Baptism   (340,346) Communion   (328,347,348)
Individual Soul Liberty   (339)
Saved, Baptized Church Membership   (348)
Two Officers: Pastors and Deacons   (344,355)
Separation: Church and State   (196,197,264,342)

Personal   (53,132,240,263,301,364)
Ecclesiastical   (365)

Scripture to read: I Timothy 4:1-16

Question to ponder: *Can each of these distinctives be supported biblically?*

Day 360   Date: _____

Victorious Christian Living

"I am come that they might have life, and that they might have it more abundantly." (John 10:10b)

The Lord Jesus intended that believers enjoy life to the fullest. However, many believers live in a state of defeat, even to the point of doubting the reality of their own salvation. Usually, a believer in this situation is neglecting one or more of the essential ingredients of a victorious Christian life.

To realize the full joy of salvation it is important to regularly <u>confess</u> all known <u>sin</u> in our lives (see Lesson 55). The Bible is our spiritual food, so we need to <u>read</u> it daily (see Lesson 5). <u>Prayer</u> is essential to maintain fellowship with God (see Lesson 316). A believer needs the <u>fellowship</u> of other believers (*Hebrews 10:24-25*). God's place to meet this need is the <u>local church</u> (see Lesson 340). A Christian will also not be content unless actively <u>serving God</u> (see Lesson 326). Again, God's place to serve is in the local church. Do these and you will be on your way to victorious Christian living!

Scripture to read: Ephesians 6:10-18

Question to ponder: *Am I neglecting any of these essential building blocks of a victorious Christian life?*

Day 361   Date: _____

Your Reasonable Service

"I beseech you therefore, brethren, by the mercies of God, that ye present your bodies a living sacrifice, holy, acceptable unto God, which is your reasonable service." (Romans 12:1)

Many church members assume that it is the pastor's job to do the work of the church. They expect that the pastor must meet their needs, and look no further for what their own responsibility may be. A careful look at today's scripture reading reveals that Christ intended His church to function differently.

When the Lord returned (ascended up) to heaven He gave gifts to men. These gifts enable believers to better serve Him. Notice in verse 11 that some of these gifts are the men who began the church (apostles, prophets, and evangelists) and then continue its work (evangelists, pastors, and teachers – or pastor-teachers). In verse 12 we see that their responsibility is the *"perfecting of the saints"*. But, who does the work of the ministry? According to verse 12, the saints who have been prepared by the pastors and evangelists!

Scripture to read: Ephesians 4:1-16

Question to ponder: *Where does this scripture passage assume a believer will serve Christ?*

Day 362   Date: _____

Spiritual Gifts

"Now concerning spiritual gifts, brethren, I would not have you ignorant"
(I Corinthians 12:1)

The Lord gave evangelists and pastor-teachers as gifts <u>to the local church</u> to train and direct its members. Pastors stay in the church and manage it. <u>Evangelists</u> move from church to church in a special ministry of supporting pastors and helping churches reach the lost. The Lord has also given spiritual gifts <u>to each believer</u> through the Holy Spirit. These gifts are given to enable the believer to better serve in the church. They are to be used under the authority of the local church and its pastor.

There are two main scripture passages dealing with spiritual gifts. One is our scripture reading for today. The other one is *Romans 12:1-8*. In each passage we are reminded that every believer is needed in the church. The gifts spoken of are God-given abilities. They enable a believer to excel in a particular area of ministry. Some of the gifts are no longer needed and have ended (see Lesson 338).

Scripture to read: I Corinthians 12:1-31

Question to ponder: *Have I asked my pastor to help me determine my spiritual gifts?*

Day 363   Date: _____

Sanctify Them Through Thy Truth

"Sanctify them through thy truth: thy word is truth" (John 17:17)

Paul addressed his first letter to the church at Corinth *"to them that are sanctified in Christ Jesus, called to be saints" (I Corinthians 1:2)*. The word <u>sanctified</u> simply means "set apart". We are to be set apart <u>unto God</u> and <u>from sin</u>. The Bible teaches that we are sanctified at the moment of our salvation (*I Corinthians 6:11*). This is the <u>past tense</u> of sanctification. All believers can legitimately claim the title of <u>saint</u> ("sanctified one").

We are to be continually resisting the influence and power of sin in our lives. This is the <u>present tense</u> of sanctification. God says, "Be ye holy; for I am holy." (*I Peter 1:16*). This aspect of sanctification is a process, a progressive growth in our Christian life. Some day, in heaven, we will be saved from the very <u>presence</u> of sin. Our daily battle with sin will be over! This is the <u>future tense</u> of sanctification.

Scripture to read: Colossians 3:1-17

Question to ponder: *According to our text verse, what is it that sets us apart (sanctifies us)?*

Day 364   Date: _____

Be Ye Separate

"If there come any unto you, and bring not this doctrine, receive him not into your house, neither bid him God speed" (II John 1:10)

One of the themes running throughout the Bible is that the people who call themselves God's people are to keep themselves <u>separate</u> from the world. Jesus prayed, *"I pray not that thou shouldest take them out of the world, but that thou shouldest keep them from the evil" (John 17:15).* Believers have no choice but to live and conduct business <u>in the world</u> with unbelievers. But, as we read in today's scripture reading, we are not to become *"yoked together"* with unbelievers. The picture is of two animals harnessed together in a single yoke. The application relates to marriage, business, and other close associations.

The apostle John, in his second small letter in the back of the Bible, warns against "deceivers" who seek to gain followers but do not believe the truth. He warns that if we encourage or help them we *are "partakers of their evil deeds"* (verse 11).

Scripture to read: II Corinthians 6:14-18

Question to ponder: *Do unbelievers make decisions on the same basis as we do?*

Day 365   Date: _____

Walk in Truth

"I have no greater joy than to hear that my children walk in truth"
(III John 1:4)

This is the third of John's letters, written when he was an old man. It is addressed to a believer named Gaius. In it, John warns Gaius not to follow a false teacher named Diotrephes. Diotrephes had apparently taken control over a church and was preventing John from communicating with that church. This demonstrates that local churches have a responsibility to separate themselves from false teachers, even as individual believers do.

Gaius had been careful to *"follow ... that which is good"* and John rejoiced in the good reports he was hearing. Gaius was especially known for providing hospitality to travelling brethren. John closes his letter by singling out a man, Demetrius, with a similar testimony. As you close out this Bible study, my prayer for you is that you, too, will maintain a *"good report of all men, and of the truth itself"*. Beloved, walk in truth!

Scripture to read: III John 1:1-14

Question to ponder: *Will I commit myself to continue to follow that which is good?*

Day 366   Date: _____

Even So, Come, Lord Jesus

"He which testifieth these things saith, Surely I come quickly. Amen. Even so, come, Lord Jesus. The grace of our Lord Jesus Christ be with you all. Amen." (Revelation 22:20-21)

We began this study at the very first verse of the Bible. We now end it at the very last two verses. In them we are reminded that the Lord Jesus Christ could come back again at any moment. Today's scripture reading is taken from the Lord's teaching on this subject. We are to be alert and <u>watch</u> for his return. We do not know when it will happen, and do not want to be caught "sleeping". The Lord has given *"to every man his work"* and expects that the work will be done when he returns.

Notice that John refers to the Lord by his full name in the above verses. The disciples never addressed the Savior as "Jesus" when speaking to Him. They always addressed Him as "Lord" or "Master". They only called him "Jesus" when writing about his human life on earth. We would do well to be as careful and respectful ourselves.

Scripture to read: Mark 13:34-37

Question to ponder: *Will the Savior find me watching, or sleeping, when He returns?*

Unit Twelve Review
Lessons 337 to 366

List a few of the men God used to begin the work of the local church as found in these lessons:

Lesson 340: _____

Lesson 345: _____

Lesson 346: _____

Lesson 349: _____

Lesson 351: _____

Lesson 353: _____

_____

_____

Lesson 364: _____

List some of the benefits, from the lessons noted below, that you receive from active membership in a local church:

Lesson 340: _____

Lesson 343: _____

Lesson 348: _____

Lesson 352: _____

Lesson 358: _____

Lesson 360: _____

Lesson 361: _____

Lesson 362: _____

WHERE DO I GO FROM HERE?

Congratulations on completing all 366 devotional lessons! I hope you have learned a lot, and have also formed a consistent habit of spending time in God's Word every day. Now that you have finished the lessons in this book, you may be asking yourself the question at the top of this page. I have a few suggestions.

Please notice that I have included a <u>Subject Index</u> at the back of this book. I compiled it as I was writing the book so it would be as complete as possible. Although the book is mostly arranged by subject there are many lessons in other places which supply additional information about subjects previously covered. The Subject Index will help you find all references to a particular subject. I recommend keeping this book as a personal reference book on basic Bible doctrines. The Subject Index will add to the usability of this book.

I also strongly recommend that you continue a daily practice of reading your Bible. There are many Bible reading schedules available. Your pastor can help you select one that will work for you.

Finally, be sure to get involved in your local church. Your fastest growth will come as you busy yourself serving God faithfully.

May God help you and bless you!

Donald Root

SUBJECT INDEX

Subject	Lesson Number(s)
Angels	
elect	*169, 171, 172*
fallen	*173*
occurrences of	*6*
teaching regarding	*170, 172*
The Angel of the LORD	*59, 112, 138, 167, 168*
Bible	
authority of	*3, 4, 5, 9, 321, 338, 359*
effectiveness of	*9, 64*
eternality of	*63*
infallibility of	*61, 63*
inspiration of	*4, 61, 275*
memorization of	*309*
not to be altered	*66*
power of	*62*
preaching of	*354*
preservation of	*63*
study of	*156, 339*
sufficiency of	*5*
understanding of	*65*
Blood, necessary for remission of sins	*17, 121, 145*
Christian Living	
chastening of the Lord	*228*
Christian service	*326, 361*
fellowship with God	*55*
good works	*50*
holiness, separation	*51, 53, 132, 151, 200, 240, 263 301, 359, 363, 364, 365*
individual soul liberty	*339, 359*
obedience	*159, 199, 244*
priesthood of the believer	*137, 359*
sanctification	*363*
temptation	*5, 19, 94, 174, 175, 309, 310*
the new nature	*51*
tithing	*143, 229, 233, 342, 343*
trials of faith	*48, 58, 59, 154, 201, 204, 345*

Subject	Lesson Number(s)
Christian Living (continued)	
victorious living	360
virtue (making choices)	50, 51, 52, 53, 54, 67
will of God	194, 232, 356
witnessing	357
worship	142, 312
Covenants	
Abrahamic	46, 56
Davidic	216
Creation	
of man	7, 8
of the world	1, 2, 85, 142
Discernment	
completed revelation	338, 339
doctrine	144, 151
Holy Spirit	125
signs	337, 338
tongues	337, 338
Dispensations	
Conscience	47
Government	43, 47
Grace (Church Age)	338
Innocence	47
Kingdom	295
Law	130
Promise	46, 47
Faith	
definition of	2, 3, 49, 231
living by faith	49, 50
necessity of	35
salvation through faith	31, 34, 35, 48
source of	3
Future Things	
Great White Throne Judgement	296
Israel	280, 284, 285, 288, 289, 290

Subject	Lesson Number(s)
Future Things (continued)	
Millennial Kingdom	295
rapture of the church	286
resurrections	286, 295, 332
the new heavens & new earth	296
tribulation	287, 288, 289, 290, 291, 292, 293
Gentiles, salvation of	350
God, Attributes of	
eternity	1, 73, 91
faithfulness	78
goodness	90, 141, 152
grace	31, 81
holiness	6, 22, 276
immutability	77
infinitude	73, 74, 75, 76, 78, 80, 87
justice	79, 272
long-suffering	269, 322
love	28, 30, 86
mercy	36, 80
omnipotence	74
omnipresence	75
omniscience	16, 75
self-existence	113
self-sufficiency	229
sovereignty	104, 118, 193, 259, 282
transcendence	87, 88
wisdom	76
God	
existence of	1
Father	89, 90, 91
nature of	85, 86
only God	71, 119
personality of	116
Trinity	72, 89, 99, 123, 265
Government	
implementation of	43
principles of	192, 193, 195, 196, 197, 198, 205, 206

Subject	Lesson Number(s)
Heaven	
description of	208, 209, 210, 211, 212, 213,
home of God	6, 172
Hell	
description of	184, 185, 186, 187
duration of	185, 186
inhabitants of	26, 181, 187
Holy Spirit	
Creator	123
deity of	123
filling of	240
fruit of	147
gifts of	362
titles of	124, 125
work of	65, 122, 124, 125, 126, 132, 133, 134, 138, 139
Home	
importance of	60, 219
instruction of	153, 227
the model home	82, 164, 219, 220, 221, 222, 242, 341
Israel, God's people	103, 110
Jesus Christ	
advocacy of	108
ascension of	335
central figure of the Bible	109
Creator	96, 97
death, burial of	28, 29, 100, 144, 149, 330
deity of	30, 96, 97, 105, 113, 323
exaltation of	97, 101
glory of	115
High Priesthood of	107, 136, 137
humanity of	98, 100
impeccability of	29, 106, 309
incarnation, virgin birth of	11, 98, 100, 105, 306, 307
Messiah	306, 318, 327

Subject	Lesson Number(s)
Jesus Christ (continued)	
names and titles of	95, 96, 101, 105, 113, 114, 115, 121, 125, 128, 129, 306, 366
pre-existence of	91, 95, 96
prophecies of	11, 46, 57, 59, 95, 105, 155, 216, 267, 268
resurrection of	331, 332
return of	114, 286, 292, 293, 366
Savior	32, 33
sinlessness of	5, 29, 105, 106, 107
Son of God	30, 91, 95
Judgments	
certainty of	21, 22, 25, 44, 54
of believer's self	253
of believer's sins	251
of believer's works	252, 286
of the nations	294
of unbelievers	26, 296
Law	
circumcision	56
priests, ministry of	135, 136
provisions of	131, 135, 142, 144, 145, 146, 168, 183
purpose of	13, 130
the Ten Commandments	13, 14, 152, 153
Local Church	
autonomy of	341, 351, 353, 358, 359
Bride of Christ	341
ecclesiastical separation	365
implementation and growth of	320, 340, 345, 349, 358
members of	348, 359
officers of	344, 355, 359
primacy of	352, 353
purpose of	336
separation of church & state	196, 197, 264, 342, 359
Lord's Day, worship on	142
Man	
creation of	7, 8, 72

Subject	Lesson Number(s)
Man (continued)	
depravity of	12, 16, 21
fall of	10
free will of	10, 194, 244
shortness of life	73
sin nature of	12, 18, 23, 24, 65
Ordinances	
mode of baptism	346
qualifications for baptism	340, 346
qualifications for communion	347
significance of baptism	346, 348, 359
significance of communion	328, 347, 348, 359
Prayer	
commands to pray	206, 316
instructions regarding	107, 138, 206, 236, 315, 316, 317
promises of answers to	34, 55, 317
Principles	
accountability	250
authority	191, 192, 205
identification	192, 219, 358
of wisdom	234, 237, 238, 239, 240, 243
order	89
submission	221
Repentance	
definition of	37, 70
evidence of	69, 70, 224
importance of	224
Rewards (crowns)	254
Salvation	
assurance of	40, 41, 42
eternal life	30, 32, 40
God's free gift	20, 31
God's plan of	11, 12, 18, 20, 28, 34, 357
God's provision	27, 28, 29, 30, 31, 32, 33, 86, 329
offered to all	30, 34

Subject	Lesson Number(s)
Salvation (continued)	
security of	40, 41, 224, 251, 333, 334
the New Birth	38, 39, 126
the Way of	30, 31, 32, 33, 34, 35, 150, 325
Satan	
destiny of	11, 181
fall of	177
origin of	176
work of	10, 85, 179
power of	178
wiles of	178, 180
Sin	
confession of	36, 55, 224, 228
consequences of	11, 17, 18, 19, 20, 23, 25, 26, 218, 223, 225, 226, 228
conviction of	161, 223
definitions of	10, 13, 14, 160, 162, 310
forgiveness of	55, 244, 328
nature of	22
origin of	10
universality of	12, 14, 15

www.ingramcontent.com/pod-product-compliance
Lightning Source LLC
Chambersburg PA
CBHW082033230426
43670CB00016B/2643